MIND'S SECRETS

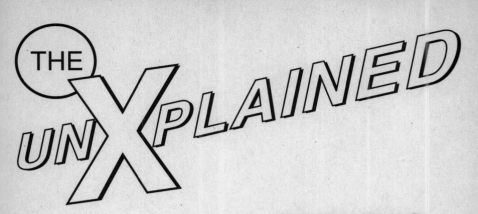

MIND'S
SECRETS

TOM SLEMEN

p

First published in 2000 by Parragon

Parragon
Queen Street House
4 Queen Street
Bath BA1 1HE, UK

Produced by Magpie Books, an imprint of
Constable Robinson Ltd, London

ISBN 0-75253-592-7

Illustrations courtesy of Fortean Picture Library and Popperfoto

Page design by Sandie Boccacci

A copy of the British Library Cataloguing-in-Publication Data
is available from the British Library

Printed and bound in the EC

To the memory of my parents

Contents

••

Contents ■

Introduction

● ●

Within this volume I have culled a fascinating and thought-provoking collection of incidents and accounts from my own extensive files on the powers of the mind and the paranormal. I have researched intriguing and baffling reports of remote viewing, telekinesis, reincarnation, doppelgängers, curses, omens, phone calls from the deceased, banshees, vampires, spine-chilling premonitions, and much more.

The undertaking made me realize how little we know about our own mind, that vaguely defined consciousness which is behind every great invention, every work of art and literature. My researches made me ask myself questions such as: What do we know about reality? What do some freethinkers like the Armenian mystic Gurdjieff mean when they say that we are all in a state of sleep and need to be awakened? Have we lived before or is this the first and only life we have had? Is there such a thing as destiny, or are the courses of our lives already set in stone across the fourth dimension of time? Is there a meaning behind coincidences? Does the mind have hidden powers that only some can access? Does death sometimes give a warning?

The subject matter of a book like this will no doubt

be viewed by some as fantastical and unrealistic, but consider all the things we now take for granted and which were once only someone's wild idea. The computer; space rockets; photography; aeroplanes, and so on. The last century started with the Wright brothers flying at Kitty Hawk in a delicate and dangerous machine which remained airborne for seconds, and ended with space shuttles flying regularly into orbit. Along the way, the human race invented television and changed the face of popular culture forever, developed unprecedented and horrific nuclear weapons of mass destruction, moved faster than sound, put twelve men on the moon and brought them all back safely, created the Internet, cloned mammals, and sent probes to all the planets in the solar system (landing several upon Mars and Venus). What progress will we see in this new century? Without a doubt, the human mind will be one of the new frontiers we make a foray into. From the moment the prominent twentieth-century neurosurgeon Wilder Penfield and his associates at Montreal discovered how to revive long-lost memories by stimulating the brain with electrical currents, the possibilities were realized. Penfield was astounded to discover that his patients relived memories reaching back to childhood when he applied electrodes to parts of their brain cortex. This proved that no memory is ever lost; we only forget because we are unable to retrieve them, rather like a librarian with a short ladder trying to access an out-of-reach book on the top shelf.

Now work is in progress to actually read the mind by scanning the electrical activity and waves it produces as we think. The repercussions of this research are scary and amazing. Imagine in the not-too-distant future being in court when the question is asked, "Where were you on the night of the twenty-fifth?" Should you be in some doubt, the judge sanctions the use of a piece of hardware which is based on Penfield's technique, only much more subtle. A device is placed near your head which not only retrieves your memories of where you were on the aforementioned date, it also shows them to the court on a large television screen.

Not only will it be possible to download information from the brain, it will also one day be possible for you to upload data to your brain as well. Already experiments have been carried out in the United States which have proved that signals carrying speech can be broadcast into the part of the human brain which deals with listening, and volunteers have reported the bizarre experience of hearing the transmitted voices and music in their heads. The next logical development from these experiments will be the transmission of optical information into the visual cortex. Where could this lead? Well, we would not only have a method of high-speed education (by transferring data to the memory cortex, perhaps while the person slept), there would also be the insidious possibility of adverts being broadcast into the mind. Doing this during waking hours would be dangerous. Imagine the vivid distraction of seeing a cola advert in your mind as you are driving along. At the moment, jingles are enough of a nuisance on the car radio, but these mental commercials would also bombard the sense of vision. Perhaps a more likely eventuality would be "dreamverts" – commercials broadcast into the subconscious areas of your brain during the day, where they are stored in the cortex along with the raw material which your mind will utilize in its dreams. Imagine having a wonderful dream which is periodically interrupted with blatant product-placements of certain brands of soft drinks, deodorants and supermarket special offers. This concept seems far-fetched but, believe it or not, something very similar is commonly employed by advertisers even today. I am now referring to the dubious practice of subliminal advertising. In 1958, the *Sunday Times* published an account of "a threat to the integrity of the human mind." They were commenting on the activities of one Jim Vicary, an American market researcher, who arranged for the owner of a New Jersey cinema to install a second special projector which, while the main film was in progress, flashed on the screen such phrases as "Coca Cola" and "Eat Popcorn". These messages were either flashed so quickly or projected with such a weak beam that the conscious mind could not even see them superimposed on the film – even when the individual was told they were going to appear. As a result of these early experiments, Coca Cola sales rocketed and popcorn consumption more than doubled. That was in the 1950s. Britain subsequently banned agencies from using subliminal persuasion on the minds of the public, but detecting subliminal "cuts" as they are known, is extremely difficult. Many governments and political parties in the West, China and the old Soviet Union have therefore employed subliminal commands to sway the people without qualms. It is even a common procedure for supermarkets nowadays to play subliminal audio messages along with the Muzak warning shoplifters of the consequences they will face if they are prosecuted.

Enjoy the private thoughts, memories and opinions

of your mind for now, because later in the century those dearly-held things you take for granted won't always be your psychological private property.

Ghosts feature in several of the accounts covered in this book, but what are they? In most people's minds, ghosts are assumed to be visitors from a supernatural realm. Statisticians say that around one in five people now believe in ghosts and around one in ten people claim to have seen one.

From my own research over the years, I would say that there are several common myths about ghosts. They don't always put in an appearance after dark, and are often encountered in broad daylight, sometimes looking as solid as you and I. One obvious giveaway is their outdated attire, but phantoms of the recently-departed usually wear contemporary clothes. It seems as if the shroud-draped shade is but a corny caricature.

Another myth is that "ghosts can't harm you", yet poltergeists have seriously injured many people by hurling objects at them and lifting them bodily into the air. Many years ago, one man in London was thrown out of a second floor window by a poltergeist and almost broke his neck. Poltergeists have also caused fires, and may be the cause of the occasional blazes which the investigators can't explain.

The sudden appearance of a ghost can cause traumatic shock and may even trigger cardiac arrest in a person who has heart trouble. So ghosts *can* physically harm you, although most spectres are benign entities.

There are roughly six types of ghost:

1. Carnate: a solid-looking entity which you can touch. This type of ghost usually interacts with witnesses.

2. Discarnate: an entity which has no physical body. It usually makes its presence known by a drop in temperature. Poltergeists are always discarnate, and some ghosts of this type have never lived previously in a physical state.

3. Psychological: these "ghosts" are hallucinations which appear to one person for various subjective reasons: hypnagogic (border of sleep) visions, tricks of the light (optical illusions), drugs, alcohol, schizophrenia, etc.

4. Doppelgängers: phantasms of the living which are projected images of a living person who is usually ill or experiencing an emotional crisis.

5. Re-enacting ghost: these are carnate or semi-transparent images of people, animals or inanimate objects which appear to be limited in their actions and merely re-enact a specific scene repeatedly. The cause may be something to do with the nature of time itself (technically called time hysteresis by physicists).

6. Extra-dimensiona: these beings are entities which are thought to originate outside our space-time continuum, and may include visitors from the future.

Belief in ghosts is not confined to one particular culture or class. They have been reported for thousands of years by people of every creed and caste. Even the Royals have reported ghostly encounters. Prince Charles – who has an avid interest in the paranormal – is said to have seen the ghost of Henry VIII at Hampton Court in the 1970s. Her Majesty the Queen, Prince Phillip and the Queen Mother have also allegedly attended many seances over the years to try to communicate with King George VI, the Queen's father, who died in 1952. In May 1997, Prince Edward and a film crew spotted a phantom galleon while filming the second episode of his "Queen and Country" television series on the Isle of Wight. Edward was telling the story of HMS *Eurydice*, a 26-gun frigate which capsized and sank in Sandown Bay in 1878, when one of the film crew shouted: "Look! There's one now!" The ghostly image of a three-masted schooner suddenly started to materialize on the horizon – in broad daylight. What's more, the ghost ship was even filmed, which ruled out a collective hallucination. After five minutes, the mystery ship vanished as eerily as it had appeared but, incredibly, it was all captured on camera. The amazing footage was later shown on television, and video experts who analyzed the tape ruled out camera trickery. Prince Edward later told the press, "I am quite convinced as far as ghosts are concerned that there are too many stories, coincidences, occurrences and strange happenings. There is something definitely out there, but what it is I don't really know."

Ironically, physics has now reached an uneasy point where it has been established that every object in the universe, including me and you, are but "ripples of energy in the quantum field". This means in essence that, in a manner of speaking, we are all ghosts of a sort, as the atoms which make up our very bodies and consciousness are but flickering particles of energy which can never be clearly analyzed. Quantum physics has therefore ascertained that our "personal atoms" are merely as "real" as starlight or a radio wave. The English quantum physicist, Sir James Jeans, once mystically remarked that "the stuff of the universe is mind stuff". Perhaps he was referring in layman's terms to the phantom-like nature of matter at the sub-atomic level. Another renowned physicist, Sir Arthur Eddington, also once commented that "the whole

Universe functions like a great thought." In *The Tempest*, Shakespeare makes a similar conjecture about the ultimately flimsy nature of reality: "These our actors, as I foretold you were all spirits, and are melted into air . . . We are such stuff, as dreams are made on, and our little life is rounded with a sleep."

I am often asked by readers of my books if I believe in an afterlife. I do. I think we go on to a dimension of the mind and end up on some other plane of existence. I suspect that many spirits return to the environment of their old life because of unfinished business; perhaps because they love someone so intensely they decide to wait until that person "comes over" to join them. I can imagine a caring parent returning to oversee his or her children as they grow up. One of the most convincing cases of an afterlife is the so-called "Cross-correspondences" case which took place over a thirty-year period. After the deaths of several founder members of the Society of Psychical Research (SPR), notably that of F.W.H. Myers, fragmentary messages were picked up all over the world by different mediums. When these seemingly nonsensical messages – written in Greek, Latin and complex anagrams – were ultimately compiled over thirty years, they spelt out what amounted to a declaration from the dead SPR founders that they were alive and well and living in the afterlife. As the Edwardian era gave way to twentieth-century scepticism, the messages from Myers and his colleagues stopped. It seems that communications only ceased because mediumship was soon ridiculed and frowned upon in classically educated, upper-middle-class circles. Those with a gift for automatic writing were similarly derided, so perhaps Myers was still transmitting his messages, but there was no one "on his wavelength" to receive and transcribe them. However, in 1972, a gifted English psychic named Matthew Manning received an "automatic script" signed by one "F. Myers". The intriguing message read: "You should not indulge in this unless you know what you are doing. I did a lot of work on automatic writing when I was alive and I could never work it out. No one alive will ever work out the whole secret of life after death. It pivots on so many things – personality – condition of the mental and physical bodies. Carry on trying though because you could soon be close to the secret. If you find it no one else will believe you anyway."

As ever, I leave it to the reader to make up his or her own mind. One thing is certain, however: one day you will find out from first-hand experience what happens at death.

Tom Slemen
tomslemen@hotmail.com

Hidden Powers of the Mind

· ·

> "I teach you the superman. Man is
> something to be surpassed."
> *Nietzsche*

The Mind's Secrets

You have at your disposal the greatest, most complex
personal computer known to science. It is not
burdened with the limitations of RAM capacity, and
Bill Gates and his team would be stumped trying to
replicate its software. You've probably guessed by now
that the personal computer I am referring to is but two
fistfuls of pinkish-grey tissue, wrinkled on the surface
like a walnut, with a liquid interior which has the
consistency of porridge. This computer – your brain –
is not only self-aware, it can hold more data than all
the world's computers and libraries combined, as well
as containing the ego of the person reading these
words. This supercomputer is just "hardware" on its
own, but when it interacts with your conscious and
subconscious thought patterns, the brain becomes the
dynamic organ of the mind.

Neurologists and psychologists investigating the
human brain are certain that it holds potentialities
and powers still largely untapped and unguessed at.

What is sad is that human ability is being wasted regularly in our society because of various factors such as class, tradition, and self-imposed behavioural patterns. How many "bright sparks" slip through our educational institutions because they belong to the wrong class? How many children from lower and middle-class families are playing truant today, but could be encouraged to become astronauts, presidents, conductors of symphony orchestras, painters, writers, secretaries of the United Nations, physicists, or surgeons? And what of those unfortunate people of the middle and upper classes who are also victims of their social ranking? People who are pushed through university by parents who have specific plans for their children. These sorry individuals are pushed through higher education like meat through a processor, despite having ambitions that run at right angles to the vocations chosen for them. Some rebel, but most capitulate in the long run. Then there are people who steer themselves into soul-destroying humdrum work routines which leave them behaving like little more than automatic machines, mere semiconscious simulacrums. Ironically, it isn't until they have retired from their daily grind that they realize that they possess some hidden talent or ability which had never previously had a chance to develop, and by then it's usually too late. Perhaps there is some way to shake ourselves from this kind of stupor. Considerable portions of the human brain are still *terra incognita*; dormant areas that could be the seat of the paranormal powers that have been reported so often down the ages. How do we access these unused parts of our mind?

In the early 1920s there appeared in Paris a charismatic Armenian named George Ivanovich Gurdjieff, who maintained that humankind was hopelessly entangled in self-woven nets of daydreams, sleep and disorganized thinking. Gurdjieff claimed that he had achieved a truly "awakened" state of mind, and that this state was the only way to perceive reality as it is. Gurdjieff preached that there were more than the two basic states of consciousness, waking and sleeping; he asserted that we remain in a sleep-like state even after we have risen from our beds, and continue to go around in this state until the day we die. Gurdjieff devised various exercises which entailed intense periods of concentration to "awaken" his followers. Some tasks required the student to do something simultaneously with each hand and foot. Other exercises designed to instil a heightened state of alertness involved Gurdjieff entering his student's dormitory in the dead of night to snap his fingers. All the students were expected to spring out of bed at this signal to adopt complicated yoga-like positions within seconds.

Another exercise which allowed the student to get a "taste" of the awakened state can be carried out by the reader. Look at a clock and stare at the minute hand, while remaining conscious of the fact that you are actually looking at the hand. Mentally repeat to yourself that "I am (whatever your full name is), and I am here now, at this moment." Try to think of nothing else that will distract you from this mental state of acute self-awareness, and you will soon feel your mind becoming impatient and restless like a spoilt hyperactive child. Other thoughts – usually nonsensical and pointless – will fight to invade your mind to prevent it from becoming focused. Sensations, associations and mental images will attack your mind on all sides. Gurdjieff said that this state is at least useful as the first stepping stone, because it reveals to the student that he is not fully awake; his mind is but a stream of banal thoughts and emotions. Once the student learns to attain the awakened state, he has a clear view of the road ahead and can analyze and remove all the once fuzzy obstacles that impeded the path to his goals. But watching a clock – or any object – and to be simultaneously conscious of yourself looking at it is very difficult. Within seconds you either temporarily forget the clock or forget to be aware that you are watching it. All the same, Gurdjieff held that such exercises were necessary to achieve the awakened state and were to be carried out as regularly as possible. Gurdjieff succinctly summed up his revolutionary notions of man's permanent, lethargic condition:

In order to understand what the difference between states of consciousness is, let us return to the first state of consciousness, which is sleep. This is an entirely subjective state of consciousness. A man is immersed in dreams, whether he remembers them or not does not matter. Even if some real impressions reach him, such as sounds, voices, warmth, cold, the sensation of his own body, they arouse in him only fantastic subjective images. Then a man wakes up. At first glance this is a quite different state of consciousness. He can move, he can talk with other people, he can make calculations ahead, he can see danger and avoid it, and so on. It stands to reason that he is in a better position than when he was asleep. But if we go a little more deeply into things, if we take a look into his inner world, into his thoughts, into the causes of his actions, we shall see that he is in almost the same state as when he is asleep. And it is even worse, because in sleep he is passive, that is, he cannot do anything. In the waking state, however, he can do something all the time and the results of his actions will be reflected upon him or upon those around him. And yet he does not remember himself. He is a machine. He cannot stop the flow of thoughts, he cannot control his imagination, his emotions, his attention. He lives in the subjective world of "I love", "I do not love", "I like", "I do not like", "I want", "I do not want", that is, of what he thinks he likes, of what he thinks he does not like, of what he thinks he wants, of what he thinks he does not want. He does not see the real world. The real world is hidden from him by the wall of imagination. He lives in sleep. He is asleep. What is called "clear consciousness" is sleep and a far more dangerous sleep than sleep at night in bed.

Gurdjieff was initially regarded as a charlatan, but most of those who seriously investigated his teachings discovered that the Armenian was seemingly endowed with psychical powers of healing and telepathy. When he died in October 1949, Gurdjieff's pupils kept a vigil over their master's body for several days while it lay in the chapel of a Parisian hospital. Several journalists present reported that strange electric vibrations buzzed through the people nearest to the open coffin, and there were even visible emanations and radiations from the corpse itself.

Was Gurdjieff deluding himself and his followers, or was he on to something? Since the early 1920s, when Gurdjieff first made his intriguing claims about the mental lethargy of the human race, we have learned much more about the brain's levels of consciousness. Ironically, in 1929, hot on the heels of Gurdjieff's theories of altered states of mind, a German psychiatrist named Hans Berger reported earlier work in which he applied electrodes to various parts of the human head and was able to detect specific waves of electrical activity. Berger gradually established that there were four types of waves, each representative of four different kinds of consciousness. The "beta" waves were fast pulses of 13 to 30 cycles per second, and were associated with alert concentration and sharp attention. Next came the "alpha" wave, which, Berger established, was generated by the brain of a person in a state of poised relaxation. The frequency of the alpha wave was 8 to 13 times per second, no matter whose head the electrodes were adhered to. "Theta" rhythms were of 4 to 8 cycles per second and characteristic of drowsiness, daydreaming, and creative imagination. Lastly, Berger discovered "delta" rhythms, waves of 0.5 to 4 cycles per second, which were generated by a sleeping, dreamless brain. What intrigued Berger was the way in which the consciousness of an average subject moved up and down this electrical spectrum as mood altered from one moment to the next. This revelation only echoed what Gurdjieff had earlier stated about the transience of human consciousness, but now science was catching up with him.

To experience the alpha-wave state, the reader only has to close his or her eyes and stare upwards at a 20-degree angle. For some reason not fully understood, doing this generates alpha waves within the brain, and if you count backwards slowly from 100 at two-second intervals, the alpha-wave state becomes very consistent. This is the state of relaxed attention that the

Indian yogis use for meditation, because it is said to "kick start" the mind and enable it to become uncluttered and positive. Parapsychologists in the United

The Awakened State

Gurdjieff's idea of the mind being blinkered by a sleep-like state has many curious historical parallels with Christianity and Buddhism. Repeatedly, throughout the Gospels, Jesus says, "Awake", "Sleep not", "Watch", and warns his followers to be constantly on guard for the end times, which will "Come like a thief in the night". The most blatant reference to sleep being the enemy of the truth is the Gospel's account of the disciples sleeping in the Garden of Gethsemane on the Mount of Olives, as Jesus remained awake suffering terrible premonitions of his impending crucifixion.

Legend also tells us that Bodhidarma, the founder of Zen Buddhism, once fell asleep while attempting to meditate. Bodhidarma was so appalled by this "relapse" into what he regarded as one of the basest states of consciousness, that he cut off his eyelids. This, presumably allegorical, story goes on to say that the eyelids later sprouted and grew into the first tea plant. Tea, like coffee, contains the central nervous system stimulant caffeine, and was regarded in the Far East as protection against sleep. Even today, Buddhists say that "The taste of tea and the taste of Zen are much alike".

Furthermore, Gurdjieff's exercise to evoke heightened awareness by being mindful of being aware of an object is identical to the mindfulness of the Buddhists. The Buddhist monks say that a monk, breathing in a long breath, knows he is breathing in a long breath and, breathing out a long breath, knows he is breathing out a long breath. This focus of attention on activities is identical to Gurdjieff's exercises.

States have also determined that a brain in the alpha state is apparently conducive to ESP.

The Psychic Detectives

Many critics have asked mediums and psychics why they do not use their extrasensory talents to help the police to solve crimes. Although there undoubtedly are charlatans going about the world claiming to be mediums, there have been many cases where psychics have indeed helped the police with startling results. Here are just a few of these cases.

One of the earliest psychic detectives on record is Jacques Aymar, who was born in Dauphine in southern France in 1662. Aymar was a water diviner of some repute, but one day, as he dug at the spot his divining rod had pointed to, he found no water at all – but the severed head of a woman. Someone recognized the dead woman's face and they decided to take the head in a sack to her husband. However, when Aymar approached the man's house he felt his divining rod vibrating slightly. Aymar lifted it and when the dead woman's husband came near, the rod felt as if it was buzzing in the diviner's hand. Aymar felt they were bad vibrations, and when the widower saw the rod reacting so strangely as it pointed at him, he fled. The man was later arrested and charged with his wife's murder, and Jacques Aymar soon established a reputation for himself as a magical detector of criminals.

Aymar's eerie skills were called upon by the authorities to find the murderers of a wine merchant and his wife in Lyons. Aymar pointed his divining rod to the horizon, then turned slowly until he picked up the vibrations. Aymar's hand shook as he pointed the rod towards the west. He walked along the right bank of the Rhône, trembling and exhibiting feverish symptoms. The diviner's armed escort and a group of intrigued people following closely were shown the various houses the murderers had stayed in along the route they'd taken after killing the couple. Aymar said, "This is a trail of blood." He continued on his pursuit of the killers over land and river until, totally exhausted, he came to a prison over a hundred miles away. There the rod indicated that a man who had just been taken into custody for a petty theft was one of the murderers. The thief denied any knowledge of the double murder at Lyons, but when Aymar described every place and location the thief and his accomplices had travelled through after the heinous killings, the man broke down and sobbed. He confessed that he had been a party to the murders, but swore he did not know where the other two accomplices were. Aymar had a drink and a quick meal, then continued to search for the other two killers, but because he was venturing beyond the French frontier, the search had to be abandoned.

In July 1928, a renowned Austrian medium and alleged mind-reader named Maximilien Langsner, was invited by the Canadian police to put his psychic talents to work on a recent multiple murder case which seemed unsolvable. A woman, her son and two workers had been found dead on a farm at Manville, Alberta. Vernon Booher, the remaining son, claimed that he'd found the bodies after returning home. Police had established that the murder weapon, a rifle, belonged to the Boohers' neighbour, Charles

Stephenson, but the latter had asserted that the weapon had been stolen from his home a week before the murders. Vernon Booher was arrested, but he would not confess to the crime.

During the inquest, Langsner sat outside Vernon Booher's cell and claimed he was reading the boy's thoughts. Langsner told the police that Vernon was definitely the murderer. The boy had sneaked out of church the week before and and stolen the rifle from Mr Stephenson's home. Langsner explained that Vernon had wanted to marry a local girl, but his mother had strongly disapproved and a quarrel had broken out as a result. The quarrel had ended in violence and Vernon had ended up blasting everyone in the household with the rifle as a result. Booher broke down when he was confronted with Langsner's version of events. He confessed to the crimes and was hanged in April 1929.

In the autumn of 1888, the mysterious Victorian serial killer, nicknamed Jack the Ripper, was butchering Whitechapel prostitutes under the noses of scores of policemen and Scotland Yard detectives who had been drafted into the East End of London in a desperate bid to trap the killer. The Ripper terrified the citizens of the capital by the brutal way in which he dispatched his victims, by disembowelling them before disappearing into the night. Some of the more superstitious people of the East End thought Jack was some sort of supernatural demon who spirited himself away after each slaying, because no one ever caught a glimpse of the killer, even though he cut his victims down in the middle of a crowded slum teeming with people. But there was one intriguing account of a man who said he saw the Ripper face-to-face in broad daylight. The man who made this incredible claim was no crackpot; he was Robert James Lees, a celebrated spiritualist who was regularly summoned to Buckingham Palace to give consultations to Queen Victoria. Lees was quietly reading in his study at his London home one night in September 1888 when he had a vivid, harrowing vision of Jack the Ripper carrying out a murder. In the vision, Lees could see the Ripper putting on a long tweed overcoat to hide the heavy bloodstains on his shirt. The medium went to Scotland Yard, but an officer just took down the details of the vision with a grin on his face. As soon as Lees left the building, the policeman crumpled up the statement and hurled it into the wastepaper basket. Later that night, Jack the Ripper struck again.

A couple of weeks afterwards, Robert Lees and his wife boarded a horse-drawn omnibus at Shepherd's Bush. Lees sat down, and suddenly saw Jack the Ripper sitting facing him. Lees turned to his wife and said, "That man is the Ripper." Mrs Lees knew her husband's psychic impressions of people were always reliable, and she trembled as she glanced at the refined-looking man in the top hat sitting opposite. The man in question seemed to hear Lees's incredible claim, and he became very uneasy. He kept turning away, pretending to look out of the window behind him. Lees said he felt an aura of savage evil emanating from the man in the top hat; finally, the medium got to his feet and, pointing an accusing finger at the stranger, he declared: "He is Jack the Ripper!"

The passengers on the bus just smirked and regarded the silver-bearded medium as some kind of eccentric, but the man in the top hat rose from his seat with a blank expression and ran down the aisle to the front of the vehicle. He made repeated requests for the driver to halt and, as soon as the vehicle started to slow down, the suspect leaped from it and ran nonstop down Oxford Street where he hailed a passing hansom cab. The cab then raced off at breakneck speed.

Lees went to Scotland Yard, told them about his encounter with the Ripper, and said he felt as if he was about to strike again. That same night, the Ripper slaughtered two more victims. At the scene of the second murder, Robert Lees focused his psychic powers and told the startled detectives present that he had picked up the murderer's trail. Inspector Fred Abberline and his men followed Lees as he walked along Whitechapel Road in a westerly direction. Police had to fight off a crowd who also trailed along out of curiosity. Almost one hour later, Robert Lees seemed exhausted. He had led the police and detectives along the Thames waterfront, and was now walking down the Strand towards the Mall. By now, police reinforcements were blocking the streets behind the medium to prevent the curious crowds from following. Inspector Abberline and his team were absolutely shocked when Lees walked to the forecourt of Buckingham Palace and gazed through the railings. He said, "You'll find Jack the Ripper in there Inspector."

What happened next was deleted from police files but, curiously, Queen Victoria later summoned Lees and asked him to leave the country for a year, and the monarch apparently paid the medium to stay abroad in Switzerland with his wife. Did this mean the Ripper was a member of the royal family? The Ripper murders later came to an abrupt end and further police investigations were mysteriously hampered by Whitehall officials. Draw your own conclusions from these sinister facts.

A psychic detective also gave accurate details about another serial killer – the Yorkshire Ripper. A clairvoyant named Nella Jones said that she felt the murderer was named "Peter", and that he worked as a long-distance lorry driver. The medium also claimed that the suspect lived in Bradford in an elevated house with the number six on the door. Nella Jones also said that this Peter worked for a company which had its name embossed on the cab door of the lorry, and that the name of the firm began with the letter C. The psychic then foretold that the murderer would strike again on 17 November 1980. All this information later proved to be correct. Lorry driver Peter Sutcliffe worked for a road haulage firm named Clark Holdings, which was indeed printed on the lorry's cab door. And Sutcliffe's address did have a six in it; his address was Number 6 Garden Lane, Bradford. However, despite all the clues, the Yorkshire Ripper was not arrested until a year later in January 1981. Several other mediums on the Ripper case kept saying that Sutcliffe had an accomplice, and that this person had been responsible for making the audio tape which featured the voice of a man who boasted that he was the killer. This alleged accomplice was never brought to justice.

Seven Baffling Accounts of Xenolalia – Speaking in Tongues

1. In the 1630s, there was an outbreak of xenolalia at the Loudun convent in France. Louis XIV sent investigators to the convent to observe the prioress and

several nuns screaming obscenities and babbling in strange-sounding tongues. One language was that of a North American Indian tribe, but most of the languages were never identified. The modern rationalization of the Loudun outbreaks is that the episodes were caused by sexual frustration and religious mania.

2. In 1685, the Camisards, a sect of French Protestants living in the Cevennes Mountains in France, had their freedom to worship revoked by the Roman Catholic authorities. The three thousand Camisards rebelled, but the authorities sent 60,000 troops against them. The Camisards were subjected to appalling atrocities during the subjugation, and it was during this period of violence and intolerance that a strange series of paranormal incidents was reported, namely the phenomenon of the "Little Prophets of Cevennes" – Camisard children aged from fifteen months upwards, who preached lengthy ecstatic sermons in French, a language quite unlike their own dialect. The sight of fifteen-month-old babies preaching before the astounded mobs incited the Roman Catholic authorities to step up their military campaign against the Camisards, and only a small minority of the sect managed to flee the country. Some came to England, where they were allowed to practise their own faith.

3. During the late 1890s, the Swiss medium Helene Smith (1861–1929), claimed she was in telepathic contact with a shy race of Martians she'd become acquainted with through several astral voyages to the red planet. The Martians taught Helene how to speak their language, and although several investigators of the outlandish claims initially thought Miss Smith was

mentally unbalanced, none was able to prove the Martian language was just invented babble. Helene used the language consistently. After weeks had elapsed she would be asked to repeat a Martian phrase, and she would use the same words with the same meanings. When Helene committed the red planet's tongue to paper, sceptical investigators were taken aback by the fully-structured and coherent syntax of the "Martian" language.

4. During World War II, a Norwegian woman was knocked unconscious by shrapnel when the Germans bombed her village. When the woman awoke, she found herself speaking in fluent German, even though she could not normally speak the language and had never been to Germany. In the end she was completely shunned by the other villagers, who despised the Nazis.

5. In 1966, forty-four-year-old Mancunian Freddie Worth was unloading a lorry at the Lybro Uniform Warehouse in Liverpool when a box containing a type-writer fell on his head, knocking him out. When Mr Worth came around, he started to rant in German, and called his colleague a "dumkopf". Mr Worth was taken to a local doctor, but after an hour had elapsed his ability to speak German had vanished and the confused Mancunian was at a complete loss to explain how he had spoken in a language he'd had no previous knowledge of.

6. In December 1992, a sixty-five-year-old Bronx, New York City woman (only identified as Mrs M.), suffered a stroke which initially only slurred her speech, but

then she began to talk in a pronounced Northern Irish brogue. Dr Glenn Seliger, of the Helen Hayes Hospital rehabilitation unit, conjectured that the woman's subconscious language area had somehow picked up on her accent as a pre-school child, which had been Northern Irish. This accent might have been suppressed later on because of peer pressure when the young Mrs M. started school. But how the language resurfaced after sixty years has not been explained.

7. In 1994, forty-nine-year-old London office worker, Lorraine Johnson, was lifting boxes underneath a concrete staircase when she accidentally banged her head. The blow caused slight impairment of Ms Johnson's left brain hemisphere and, as a result, the office worker began to talk in an Italian accent – even though she has no Italian relatives and was born in Harlow, Essex. Ms Johnson spent six weeks in hospital and despite extensive neurological tests, the origins of the Italian accent were never explained.

A Deadly Suggestion

As far as the medical profession is concerned, the nature of hypnotism is still a complete mystery. The word hypnosis is derived from the Greek word hypnos, which means sleep, but hypnotism has nothing at all to do with the state of sleep; it's a state of trance, and psychologists now agree that almost anybody can be hypnotised.

Today, hypnotists can plant powerful suggestions into the mind of a patient to stop them smoking, overeating, or to eliminate various complexes and nervous disorders. Hypnotism is even used on patients so that they can undergo surgery without anaesthetic. Recently, in China, an old man was put into a trance and had his leg amputated without feeling a thing. When hypnosis is used in such a beneficial way it is usually referred to as hypnotherapy, but hypnotism also has a dark history. It is known that in the former Soviet Union, people accused of treason and spying where hypnotized into believing that they were dead. Some of these unfortunate victims were put in cells where hypnotic suggestions were constantly played through hidden loudspeakers in the walls. These suggestions convinced the victims that their hearts were beating faster and faster out of control, or that they would drop down dead on the count of ten, and many of these human guinea pigs actually did die because of the constant amplified bombardment of suggestion.

In 1750 in Copenhagen, one of the most unethical experiments in the abuse of hypnotism took place. A condemned prisoner was taken to a mortuary, where he was stripped naked. He was tied to a chair and a blindfold was fastened tightly around his head. Seven scientists and an experienced hypnotist were seated around the prisoner, and three of those present started to take notes as the obnoxious experiment began. A long needle was inserted into the victim's upper arms and his back, and the prisoner yelled out and jumped. "What are you doing?" he cried.

The hypnotist pretended he had just inserted four rubber tubes into the man's arms and back, and was now connecting them to four taps.

"What for?" asked the prisoner, trembling.

"I'm going to turn on the taps soon and your blood

will flow out of them into the trough. You will of course, bleed to death as a result."

The prisoner started to struggle in the chair and sweat poured from under his blindfold. "No. Please! Please let me go," the prisoner begged.

"Get ready to turn on the taps!" the hypnotist shouted out to an assistant, who placed his hands over two of the taps behind the prisoner.

"Five, four . . . three . . ." the hypnotist shouted out.

"I don't want to die," sobbed the unfortunate prisoner, and his tears stained the blindfold as he struggled to be free.

"Two . . . one!" said the hypnotist. There was an electric pause, then the hypnotist said to his assistant, "Turn on the taps – now!"

The assistant turned on two taps, then another two, and water trickled out of them into a long trough, but

Stage Hypnotism

Three members of the cast of a play about hypnotism went into a real trance when the leading actor, who was playing the part of Svengali, gave a very convincing performance. The curtain had to come down on the production, which was being staged at a theatre in Paris, because three actresses went into a hypnotic trance and became as stiff as a board. Several members of the audience were also affected by the actor Roger Charcoze, who was merely playing the part of a hypnotist. A psychologist explained that the incident was a rare case of extreme suggestibility. Charcoze, the small-time actor who inadvertently mesmerized the women, is now planning a lucrative career as a hypnotherapist.

to the prisoner, it sounded as if his blood was being siphoned out, and he started to scream.

"It's very red isn't it?" joked the hypnotist. The other scientists laughed, and watched the prisoner slump forward. He kept saying over and over, "I don't want to die. I don't want to die," until his voice was but a whisper – and then he seemed lifeless.

The taps were turned off and the prisoner was untied and had his blindfold removed. His eyes were turned up into his forehead and he was quite dead. A subsequent post-mortem established that the victim had died of shock, the sort of shock the body goes into when it loses too much blood. The scientists congratulated the hypnotist and later published the results of their "experiment".

The Ultimate Peeping Tom

The following story was investigated by a paranormal research group based in Los Angeles, and it concerns a creepy Peeping Tom who abuses his unusual psychic talent. What's more, this sinister voyeur is allegedly still active.

For centuries, mystics and occultists have claimed that each of us has a spirit-like counterpart called the astral body, which is stowed away in our physical body. This astral body is said to contain the soul, the consciousness, and the third eye, and it is thought that some people can project their astral body out of their physical body and view things happening miles away. Out-of-body experiences are also thought to take place when a person is in bad health or near death but, according to many yogis and mystics, we can all project ourselves out of our bodies with meditation and regular practice. However, it is thought to be a very dangerous exercise, and there are reports of some people being unable to get back into their bodies after projecting from them, apparently ending up in comas.

If you think all these claims about an astral body are bunkum, think again, because the CIA, FBI and several police forces in the United States and Europe have admitted that they are employing so-called "remote viewers" – experts who know how to project their consciousness out of their bodies – so that they can view events taking place anywhere in the world. The CIA has admitted using remote viewers to spy on nuclear missile installations in the heart of the old Soviet Union, and even NASA has admitted that they have employed remote viewers in experimental trials to see if they can find out data on the planets. Remote viewers have even been used successfully by police to locate bodies of murder victims and missing people.

There is also said to be a remote viewer who lives in the San Fernando Valley area of California, and who is allegedly abusing his strange psychic ability to spy on women in their homes and workplaces. For legal reasons he can't be named, but two paranormal investigators claim to know his identity, and will only state that his first name is Mark.

In August 1997, a woman named Jo, who works as the secretary of a litigator in the Valley area, was enjoying a meal after work at a restaurant, when suddenly a small, middle-aged man wearing yellow-tinted spectacles came over and said, "Hiya Jo."

Jo stopped eating and said, "Who are you?"

"Mark," replied the man, and he sat down opposite her at the table with a sinister sneer on his face.

"I'm sorry I don't know you," said Jo uneasily; she thought the man facing her looked creepy.

"I know you don't know me – but I know you," he said.

"What do you mean?" asked Jo. Her table was in a corner of the restaurant and she felt a bit intimidated by the stranger.

"I saw you painting your toenails on your bed last night," said Mark, "just after you got out of the bath. You shouldn't use your guy's razor to shave your legs, y'know? Very unhygienic."

"Are you some sort of pervert? I'm going to call the police now," said Jo, and she shouted to the waiter.

"Calm down, Jo. I visit you every night and you can't see me. I've even seen your little birthmark." And Mark described the exact location of the birthmark on a very private part of Jo's anatomy.

The waiter came over to see what was going on, and Mark dashed out of the restaurant, giggling. The waiter said Mark had told him that he was Jo's brother. Jo was so upset by the weird encounter she couldn't finish her meal and called for a cab.

Jo didn't know what to think. She wondered if Mark was watching her with binoculars or a telescope from some vantage point. But Jo knew that a Peeping Tom with a telescope wouldn't be able to see into her bathroom or behind the drawn blinds of her bedroom. The secretary mentioned the creepy incident to her friends at work, and they told Jo to phone a group of paranormal investigators in Los Angeles who had recently been featured on a radio show. Jo got the number of the group after enquiring at the radio station. The investigators told Jo that they knew of an eighteen-year-old girl in the Northridge area of the Valley who was also getting strange phone calls and e-mails from a man who said he could visit her in his astral body. The pest had said his name was Mark. The research group said that they couldn't do anything about the psychic Peeping Tom, and advised her to either simply ignore the strange stalker or move to another area.

Jo convinced her boyfriend she wanted to move into a small, newly-built house she'd seen in the Forest Lawn area, and in the end her boyfriend reluctantly agreed, even though the move almost crippled him financially. The couple moved into their new home, and for a while Jo felt at ease – until she encountered the sinister Mark again a fortnight later. Jo was shopping at a supermarket when someone tapped her on the shoulder. It was Mark. Jo was dumbfounded at his presence, and the stalker said, "Your other home was better. The place you're in now is facing north. Very dismal."

Jo swore at Mark and seriously thought about punching him, as she was still under supernatural surveillance.

"Isn't that Mrs Davies an over-inquisitive old neighbour?" Mark asked the infuriated Jo. Then he said, "She stands in the garden at the fence at night and listens to you and your guy when you two make love – which is very rare nowadays."

"That's it, I'm going to the police," said Jo, "There are cameras in this store taping you right now, so they'll know what you look like."

Mark giggled and said, "Hey, your guy isn't very adventurous between the sheets is he?"

Jo lost her temper completely and she picked up a can of soup and viciously hurled it at Mark. The can bounced off his back

"You crazy . . . I'll sue you for that!" Mark seethed, and he ran out of the store.

At work the following day, Jo's friend, Lisa, confronted Jo and said, "You're a real two-faced, gossiping little back-stabber."

"What are you talking about?" asked Jo, looking baffled.

"You know what I'm talking about," Lisa replied, and she went on, "I got a phone call from this guy last night and he said you told your boyfriend that I slept with three different men behind my husband's back."

"Who told you this Lisa?" said Jo, beginning to blush.

"Some guy who said he knows you – Mark," Lisa replied – and took a swipe at Jo. A fight ensued, and both girls ended up dragging each other around the office by the hair until a senior colleague intervened and severely reprimanded them.

When Jo returned home, she burst into tears. She had said those nasty things about Lisa to her boyfriend, but had forgotten about the accursed eavesdropper, Mark. And this story has no pleasant ending either, because Mark is, by all accounts, still roaming about the San Fernando Valley region, spying and eavesdropping on women and causing mayhem.

Remote Viewing Across Time and Space

In recent years, it seems as if remote viewers are not just limited to obtaining information across vast distances; they are also able to explore the realm of time. In a novel experiment in 1999, several ex-military remote viewers were given a sealed envelope containing co-ordinates in space and time of a past event. One envelope contained the date 13 February 1945. The impressions the remote viewer recorded for this date were: "Fast, powerful, movement, red, yellow, cold, dark. Light, fire, energy, vortex, wind." He was later told that on the date he had been given the German city of Dresden had been firebombed. The fires that consumed Dresden were made worse by the high winds that fanned the infernos.

Another remote viewer was given a date in the late 1880s. Within minutes of letting his mind wander off to the date, the viewer saw a Victorian woman standing beneath the flickering yellow flame of a gas lamp. Seconds later, the viewer was almost paralyzed with terror as he saw what he could only describe as a black, vaporous entity which came spiralling down towards the woman. The "thing" enveloped the woman, and immediately she collapsed in a pool of blood. Then several slash marks appeared on her body as if an invisible knife was cutting her up. Only after-wards was the viewer told that the date he had given had been a random one which fell within Jack the Ripper's long reign of terror. The chronological co-ordinates had fallen in November 1888, and the geographical references were for the London district of Whitechapel.

One remote viewer said he visited Elm Street in Dallas on the day President Kennedy was shot, and he distinctly saw three figures behind the famous picket fence with rifles trained on Kennedy's car. One of the riflemen was dressed as a Dallas motorcycle policeman. Before he could take a closer look at the figures behind the fence, however, the remote viewer lost focus and was unable to return to 1963.

The Mystery of Xanadu

> *In Xanadu did Kubla Khan*
> *A stately pleasure-dome decree:*
> *Where Alph, the sacred river, ran*
> *Through caverns measureless to man*
> *Down to a sunless sea.*

So run the first five lines of one of the most controversial and mysterious poems ever written: *Kubla Khan* by the Romantic poet, essayist and critic, Samuel Taylor Coleridge. Coleridge was born in 1772, the son of a Devonshire vicar, and educated at Cambridge and Oxford. He was said to have been a dreamy, precocious young man who was forever in search of a perfect world. In 1794 he caused a furore at Oxford by advocating a communistic master plan which he called "pantisocracy", the blueprint for a utopian society to be set up in the United States. His revolutionary proposal captured the imagination of another rebellious student named Robert Southey. Coleridge and Southey announced their idealistic political aims on the banks of the Susquehanna, but they came to nothing because the two young men had insufficient money to make their dream a reality. In the pantisocratic scheme of things marriage was mandatory, so Coleridge became engaged to Sarah Fricker, the sister of Southey's fiancée. Only after he had taken the plunge did Coleridge discover, to his horror, that a girl he loved named Mary Evans felt the same way about him. There was no turning back for the heartbroken Coleridge, and although he married Miss Fricker he continually yearned for Mary, and his marriage ended in separation after seven years.

For the remainder of his life, Coleridge – who made his living as a poet – was always chasing dreams. In 1796 he optimistically published his first volume of poetry, but ended up in great financial difficulty. The bitter and disillusioned poet-dreamer was about to throw down his quill and join the Unitarian church, when the brothers Josiah and Thomas Wedgwood granted him an annuity of £150 to further his literary career.

By 1797, Coleridge had become a close companion of the poet William Wordsworth, and this relationship stimulated some of Coleridge's finest poetical achievements, including *The Rime of the Ancient Mariner*, *Kubla Khan*, and the first part of *Christabel*. Of these magnificent works, *Kubla Khan* stands out, not solely because of the mystical imagery it evokes, but also because of the strange circumstances of its conception and execution.

Coleridge suffered rheumatic discomfort in the cold, damp climate of England's Lake District, and began to take opium as a remedy, unfortunately developing a full-blown addiction to the drug. During opium-induced trips, the poet reported that he had left his body on several occasions, and described what would now be recognized as out-of-body experiences and several remote-viewing incidents. The drug also apparently "released" Coleridge from his own time and allowed him to voyage into other realms, including a future era of utopian marvels and a long-vanished golden age of man. Those who listened to Coleridge's visions assumed they were the ramblings of a drug addict, and many feared for his sanity and health, including Wordsworth. In 1816, Coleridge's addiction was so severe that he was forced to allow a doctor to take up residence at his home to supervise the amounts of opium being consumed. That same year, Coleridge published his poem *Kubla Khan* because he needed the money desperately, and he explained how the work was but an unfinished fragment depicting a vision he'd experienced twenty years earlier. He had been sitting in his lonely Exmoor farmhouse, recuperating from an illness for which he had consumed two grains of opium. He then felt the peculiar sensation of being lifted out of his physical body and of travelling along a tunnel of light. The green fields of England fell away below him and soon the poet was journeying through space and time to a utopian society somewhere over the Himalayan mountain range. Coleridge felt a strange elation and a feeling of nostalgia upon catching the first sight of an enormous ivory dome, glinting above the clouded mountains. He suddenly found himself uttering the name "Xanadu". He was floating over a mystical land near China, and looking at the fabulous architecture below. Gilded towers and enormous fortified walls, reminiscent of the Great Wall of China, girdled the breathtaking complex. And within and without the walls were shimmering gardens of a myriad of colours, comparable to the fabled Hanging Gardens of Babylon. Cutting through the scenery, beneath bridges and walls, a sparkling blue river coursed from the top of a mountain, flowed through a woodland and vanished into a series of caves. Coleridge "recognized" the river; it was the River Alph, venerated as the sacred, life-giving river of the inhabitants of Xanadu. This river went deep below the mountains through caverns into a subterranean sea where the sun had never shone.

For an indeterminable amount of telescoped time, Coleridge took in the sights, sounds and even the smells (from the exotic incense-bearing trees) of Xanadu, then found himself close to tears as he was torn back to what he called the "earthly plane of the mundane". He awoke in his secluded home, and was so moved by his journey to the magical kingdom that he began to describe it on paper as fast as he could write. He had reached the fifty-fourth line when there was suddenly a hammering at the door.

Coleridge answered. It was an insurance salesman from the nearby town of Porlock. Coleridge said he was busy, but the insurance man was so insistent he ended up detaining the frustrated poet for almost fifty minutes. As soon as the wretched man left, Coleridge tried to continue writing down the rest of the poem, but found that his inspiration had evaporated. The dream of Xanadu had been shattered and, try as he might, Samuel Taylor Coleridge never managed to put the pieces back together to complete one of the most tantalizing and fantastic unfinished poems of all time.

The Phantom Trespasser

When people say they've seen a ghost, it's so easy to respond that they were simply seeing things or had an overactive imagination, but what explanations can we offer when a ghost is actually captured on a closed-circuit television camera? This is precisely what happened at the Butterflies Night Club in Oldham, in the early hours of 27 October 1991.

As it was a Saturday, the nightclub had been full, but

by around 2.30 a.m. the last drinkers and ravers had left. The doormen then made their way home after an exhausting night, and the only two people left on the premises were the manager of the nightclub, Cameron Walsh-Balshaw, and the assistant manager, John Reid. The two men switched on the club's computerized burglar alarms and set them, then turned on the video surveillance cameras. The men then left the club and went to Reid's house, which was situated just around the corner from the nightclub. The two men discussed family and business over a few drinks, then were startled to hear a loud knocking at the front door of the house at 4.30 a.m. It was the police, and they informed the men that the alarms had gone off at the Butterflies Night Club. Walsh-Balshaw and Reid rushed to the club and saw a gaggle of police officers standing outside. The manager unlocked the doors, switched off the alarm and the police stormed the place as other patrol cars arrived at the scene. There wasn't a soul on the premises of the Butterflies Night Club, yet something or someone had activated the expensive and sophisticated alarm system. There were no signs of a forced entry, and everything was in its place. The assistant manager looked at the readout on the alarm console and saw that the alarm had been activated inside the club's cash office.

One of the policemen suggested that the manager should play back the videotape of the office that had been recorded by the security cameras. This was done, and it revealed an astounding mystery that has never been satisfactorily explained. The jaws of the manager and the policemen dropped as they looked at the monitor. It showed scenes of an empty corridor, then suddenly a male figure appeared on the screen, walking down the corridor. The stranger wore a white tee-shirt and dark trousers, but what was extraordinary about the figure was the fact that he looked transparent, almost ghostly. The figure was seen to turn and walk straight through the solid locked door of the cash office. The astonished onlookers looked at each other and the tape was replayed again and again. At the precise moment when the phantom intruder passed through the closed and locked door, the alarm system had been activated.

The video has since been examined by BBC video engineers, and they have discounted all the theories that have tried to explain away the ghost. The image of the man is not a double exposure or a fault in the magnetic videotape, nor is it a deliberate hoax; so what is it? No one will say for sure. One theory suggests tht it was the ghost of a man who was tragically electrocuted while wiring the building years before the club opened, although the premises had no previous history of hauntings. Is it possible – however outlandish the suggestion may seem – that the image captured by the club's security camera was the bi-located "tulpa" or thought image of a living person, possibly a criminal, remotely viewing the club premises to see where the weekly takings were kept?

Doppelgängers

In July 1994, a seventeen-year-old Californian girl, Mercedes Phillips, visited her English penpal, Tanya Owens, in Cuddington, a picture postcard type of village which lies west of Northwich in England.

It was the first time Mercedes had actually met her

friend, although the two girls – who were the same age – had corresponded regularly via e-mail on the Internet on an almost daily basis. However, Tanya felt somewhat inferior to her transatlantic friend. The slim-figured Mercedes was almost six feet tall, with long, natural blonde hair and a genuine golden tan. She had sparkling sky-blue eyes, a little snub nose, and straight, perfect pearly-white teeth. The petite Tanya had shoulder-length fuzzy red hair, a face dotted with freckles, and had to wear a brace on her teeth. Despite their obvious superficial differences, the two penpals got on very well together. A day after Mercedes arrived, Tanya took her jet-lagged friend to Delamere Forest and showed her many of the rural scenes and sights of local historic interest. During their tour of the countryside, a boy on a mountain bike almost ran into Tanya as he came careering down a lane. It was a sixteen-year-old from the nearby village of Weaversham, and his name was Dylan. Tanya's heart somersaulted when she saw him as she'd had her eye on Dylan for almost a year, but he never seemed interested in her. However, Dylan was certainly interested in the ravishing Californian.

"Wow. Who are you?" Dylan asked the American girl, with a look of awe.

"Mercedes," she replied and smiled at the boy.

"Aren't you Dylan? I've seen you around," Tanya said. She was scared to smile at the boy because of her brace.

Dylan was so besotted with the Californian he didn't reply to Tanya, he just gave a mock chuckle and said, "Mercedes? That's a car."

Mercedes giggled and told him, "It's Spanish for mercy, but yeah, my Dad was a car freak."

Tanya's heart was in turmoil. She couldn't endure the boy of her dreams being so spellbound by her friend, so she walked on and pulled Mercedes along by her elbow.

Dylan cycled after the girls until they reached Tanya's home. Before Mercedes went in, Dylan summoned up enough courage to ask her out. Mercedes said she already had a boyfriend back home in San Diego.

"I'll be your new boyfriend then," Dylan cheekily suggested and seriously awaited a reply.

Mercedes just smiled and waved, then entered Tanya's house. Tanya glared back at Dylan before slamming the door behind her.

Over the next couple of days, wherever Tanya and Mercedes went, Dylan would follow like a demented stalker. Then one night in Tanya's home, Mercedes said she thought that Dylan was cute and handsome. She also confessed that she had split with her boyfriend back in San Diego three months ago. Tanya tried to dissuade her friend from getting involved with the boy, but it didn't work, and within a week Mercedes and Dylan were walking about holding hands and gazing into each other's eyes. The more Mercedes got to know the boy from Weaversham, the more she realized how similar he was to her. He was a Libran like her, and he loved poetry. Mercedes was a closet poet. They were both into astronomy and they both believed in reincarnation; in fact, Dylan swore he felt as if he had met Mercedes in a previous life in ancient Greece! Tanya was naturally devastated, but in the end she resigned herself to the fact that Dylan wasn't interested in her. The one hope she clung to was the belief that he would fall in love with her one day; perhaps next summer, when her teeth would be brace-free.

Mercedes had to return to America in the middle of August, and she pleaded for Dylan to visit her soon in California. Dylan had five brothers and sisters, and his parents were barely able to make ends meet, never mind send their son off on holiday to the United States. Dylan was too proud to say that he didn't have the money for the flight, and promised he would visit her soon. In fact, Dylan didn't even have the money to travel to Manchester Airport to see his girlfriend off, and that day he thought his world had ended. He walked around all the places where he had strolled with her, hand in hand, and inwardly cried. At least he had her home and e-mail address. When he searched his untidy bedroom, however, he discovered to his complete horror that he had lost the scrap of paper with the addresses on. He visited Tanya, but she said she'd lost Mercedes's e-mail address too. Tanya was lying, of course, out of jealousy: she didn't want Dylan to have anything to do with the American.

Dylan panicked and searched his bedroom again, but couldn't find the piece of paper. He called at Tanya's house once more, but the girl's mother answered and told him to stop calling for her. As Dylan walked away, he saw the envious Tanya peeping through the blinds from her bedroom window.

Coincidentally, Mercedes had accidentally left Dylan's address on a piece of paper in Tanya's home in England, and when the American realized this, she e-mailed her friend and asked her to send back her boyfriend's address over the Internet. But Tanya lied and said that she didn't have Dylan's address, and she also claimed that Dylan was already dating another girl. Mercedes cried when she read the e-mail from Tanya. She wondered how Dylan could be so cold, when she'd thought they'd had something so special.

The lovelorn Dylan, meanwhile, continued to roam about on his bike, reminiscing about the days he'd spent with Mercedes. She'd been the first proper girlfriend he'd ever had, and now it was all over. One Sunday afternoon at four o'clock, a fortnight after Mercedes's departure, Dylan was cycling along a country lane which was layered in dead autumn leaves. This lane, on the northern peripheries of Cuddington, ran through a quiet wooded area; it was one of his girlfriend's favourite spots and where they had made so many promises to each other. While Dylan was lost in his emotional recollections of Mercedes, he suddenly noticed a figure walking towards him down the lane. His heart missed a beat. It was her – Mercedes.

Dylan braked his bike and, in disbelief, he called out her name and dismounted. Mercedes was only fifty feet away but she didn't react; it was as if she hadn't noticed him yet. As the girl walked with her head bowed, she seemed very pensive, and Dylan suddenly noticed that she was wearing a long, white gown of some sort. The lane was covered with dry, ochrous leaves which crumpled loudly underfoot as Dylan strode eagerly towards Mercedes, yet the girl didn't make a sound as she walked along. Dylan was completely overjoyed and he sighed, "You're back. I knew you'd come back to me."

Suddenly, Mercedes wasn't there any more. She vanished, leaving Dylan rushing towards an empty, cold space. He stood there, trying to fathom out what had just happened. Was he going insane? Was it a ghost? With a mounting sense of dread he wondered if Mercedes had died and returned to him as a vision for one last time. He knew it hadn't been a hallucination or some much-desired image from his despairing mind. The girl had looked so real and solid, yet she had moved silently down the lane.

When Dylan went home, his mother had some good news for him. She said, "Was this what you were looking for?" and held out a piece of paper. It was the paper with Mercedes's home and e-mail addresses. Dylan's mum had found it in the pocket of her son's jeans as she was putting them into the washing machine. The ecstatic Dylan grabbed the paper and kissed it. He hurried to a friend of his older brother who was on the Internet and used his PC to e-mail Mercedes.

Mercedes e-mailed him back shortly afterwards and asked him if he was still dating. Dylan was puzzled by the reply, but he and Mercedes soon realized that Tanya had fabricated the lie to put an end to their relationship. Dylan sent more messages to his American girlfriend, and he told her about the eerie incident in the wood on the outskirts of Cuddington. Mercedes told him a strange tale. At 8 a.m. on the Sunday, when Dylan had seen her wraith, Mercedes had been intensively imagining she was walking through the woods near Cuddington, and feeling rueful and depressed at the thought of losing her English boyfriend. Dylan said he had encountered the phantom Mercedes around 4 p.m., not 8 a.m., but his girlfriend explained that her home in California was eight hours behind the time in England. While it was 8 a.m. in San Diego, it had been 4 p.m. in Cuddington. Dylan remembered the white gown the apparition had worn, so he asked Mercedes to recall what she had been wearing on that Sunday morning. She told him that she'd worn a white bathrobe because she had just showered.

What Dylan encountered in the woods that day is open to speculation, but I suspect that it was what is known in occult circles as a "doppelgänger" or phantasm of the living. These types of apparition are very common and are often mistaken for the ghost of a dead person. Some think that the doppelgänger is an etheric counterpart of the physical body which is reserved for the purpose of carrying the soul after death. Occasionally, in times of illness or great distress, it would seem that this ethereal replica is somehow projected or detached from its physical counterpart through some mysterious process. Many famous people have reported this baffling phenomenon of "bi-location" in which the doppelgänger is projected over considerable distances to materialize in full view of witnesses. In his autobiography, the Irish poet and dramatist W.B. Yeats, writes: "One afternoon I was thinking very intently of a fellow student for whom I had a message. In a couple of days I got a letter from a place some hundreds of miles away where the student was. On the afternoon when I had been thinking so intently, I had suddenly appeared there amid a crowd of people in a hotel and seeming as solid as if in the flesh. My fellow student had seen me, but no one else, and had asked me to come again when the people had gone. I had vanished, but had come again in the middle of the night and had given him the message. I myself had no knowledge of either apparition."

In the 1930s, a similar incident occurred when the

Derbyshire-born novelist, John Cowper Powys, told the American writer, Theodore Dreiser, that he would project himself into the sitting-room of the latter's New York home. Powys then caught the train back to a town on the Hudson where he was staying. Dreiser expected some sort of prank to take place, but two hours later the writer happened to glance up from a book he was reading to see Powys standing in the doorway of the sitting-room with a smug smile. The flabbergasted Dreiser dropped his book and stood up, saying: "Well, you've kept your word – now tell me how you did it." As Dreiser moved towards Powys he vanished in an instant. Dreiser immediately rang Powys at his home to get to the bottom of the mystery. The novelist answered, but despite his staggered friend's repeated requests asking how he had projected himself into the room, Powys remained tantalizingly tight-lipped up until his death in 1964.

A rare – but chilling – experience is to come face to face with your own doppelgänger. The German poet, Goethe, once "met himself" coming towards him in the early nineteenth century. According to European folklore, this should have been an omen of Goethe's imminent death, but the poet lived for many years after the disturbing experience. In Victorian times the doppelgänger was known as a "fetch", and further back in time, in ancient Greece and Egypt, the ghostly double was known as the "ka", which was envisaged as a vaporous mirror-image of the body that was attached to the physical body by an invisible cord. This cord was said to snap when a person died.

A word of caution to those of you who intend to experiment in projecting yourselves; according to the occultists, when the ka leaves the body vacated it is prey to possession by all manner of evil spirits. You have been warned.

The Impostor

The following weird incident happened in London in the 1980s; it was documented in a magazine and several newspapers but it has never been explained.

In October 1987, at 1.30 a.m., a divorced thirty-nine-year-old woman named Rita Carson was awoken by a frantic hammering on the front door of her home in Wimbledon. Rita lived alone with her dog, a podgy old Labrador named Cally, and she was naturally nervous when she heard the knocking at that hour in the morning. She went downstairs, put on a coat, picked up a poker from the fireplace, then peeped through the curtains of the bay window to see who was knocking at the door. It was a man, but because his back was turned, she couldn't see his face. Rita went to the hall and shouted, "Who is it?"

"It's me – Alan," said the stranger on the doorstep.

Cally started barking when she heard the voice. Rita calmed the dog down and asked, "Alan who?"

"Your cousin Alan. Alan Warner," said the man.

Rita suddenly realized who it was. Alan lived in the Muswell Hill district of London, just ten miles away; she hadn't seen him since his father's funeral two years ago. "Hang on," she called. Rita undid the bolts and took the chain off the lock. She opened the door and Alan stood there with his distinctive goofy grin.

"It's twenty-five to two in the morning," Rita complained She was bleary-eyed and naturally wanted an explanation.

"She threw me out because I found out she was having an affair," said Alan, and he practically shoved his way into the house. Cally growled at him and then howled. Rita left the dog in the hall and made Alan and herself a cup of tea.

"Will you be all right down here if I go back to bed?" Rita asked her cousin. "I've got to get up at eight for work you see," she explained.

"Yes, of course," said Alan, and for some reason, he kept going to the front room where he peeped out of the window, as if he was looking for someone.

"Are you on the run or something? Sit down and stop making me nervous," said Rita, and she asked him to go through his story once more. Alan said he had found a gold cigarette lighter in the bedroom of his home, and that it had started an argument between him and his young, twenty-five-year-old common-law wife. She had taunted him by saying that she was having an affair with a man her own age who was a better lover than Alan, who was forty-five. As Alan's partner owned the house, she had decided to throw him out. Alan said he had walked almost ten miles from Muswell Hill to his cousin's Wimbledon home, yet he didn't seem fatigued and remained on his feet, pacing about and behaving nervously.

Rita said things would look better in the morning, and urged Alan to sleep on the settee. She brought a duvet down to him and two pillows, and even tucked him in. As Rita was leaving the living room, Alan said, "Thanks Rita. I'm sorry about calling on you at all hours in the morning."

"It's okay. Get some shuteye, eh?" Rita replied, and she turned out the living-room light and retired to her bedroom.

The Problem Child

The Sad Tale of The "Haunted Boy" Nobody Wanted

In 1990 a childless couple in northern England jumped at the opportunity of fostering an eleven-year-old boy named Gary. The authorities told the couple that Gary had been put up for adoption twice before, but had been returned to the care of the social services for being "unusually hyperactive". The couple took Gary home a fortnight before Christmas and spoiled him rotten. The child said he wanted three Christmas stockings and was given them. The couple put up a huge Christmas tree and laid bundles of presents for Gary under it. The child opened some of these presents before Christmas Day, but the couple didn't scold him, they just laughed about it, and allowed the boy to take the gifts – a box of soldiers and a little drum – up to his room.

At 3 a.m. the couple were woken by a strange noise which was coming from Gary's bedroom. The foster parents jumped out of bed, rushed into Gary's room, and were shocked at the bizarre sight which greeted them. The drum was beating all by itself, and all the little tin soldiers were hopping along the floor in single file in time to the drumbeat. A sleepy-eyed Gary was sitting up in his bed, giggling and clapping his hands as he surveyed the eerie spectacle. The couple – who were very religious – took the poltergeist-like phenomenon as a manifestation of the Devil and promptly decided they didn't want to adopt the child. During the journey to the social services department, strange knocking sounds were heard on the roof and side windows of the couple's car. Once again, Gary spent his Christmas without a mum and dad, because he probably possessed the psychic gift of telekinesis: the ability to move objects by the power of the mind. The "problem child's" present whereabouts are not known.

At about 3 a.m., Rita awoke to the sound of a dog barking. It was her Labrador, Cally. The barking was coming from somewhere in the distance outside the house. Rita jumped out of bed and opened the curtains. She saw to her horror that Cally was running along the end of the street, chasing a cat. She wondered how the dog had got out, then remembered that Alan was downstairs. She turned to switch on the bedside lamp – and there was Alan, lying on the bed wearing only a pair of underpants. He smiled at Rita in a sinister way, and said, "Come back to bed, love."

Rita was puzzled, then frightened. She ran out of the room and Alan ran after her, saying, "What's the matter, love? Don't you like men?" And he grabbed at Rita's long hair as she ran down the stairs. There was a struggle in the hall; Alan forced kisses on the terri-fied woman and ran his hands all over Rita's body. Rita let out a scream and Alan rushed into the living room and grabbed his jeans. As he struggled to put them on, he gritted his teeth and shouted to Rita, "I'm going to kill you now!"

Rita ran out of the house and down the street. She turned a corner and made straight for a public phone box. She dialled the police and, as she was put through to them, Alan came running down the street towards her. Rita screamed and blurted out where she lived and what was happening, just seconds before the enraged Alan arrived at the phone box. He pulled Rita out of the telephone box then grabbed the receiver and tried to smash it against the perspex panels of the box. Rita ran off again and hid behind a hedge further up the street. Alan walked off, and the police quickly turned up, thinking a so-called domestic incident was in progress. Rita came out of hiding with tears streaming from her eyes and told the police officers what had happened. "Which way did he go?" asked one of the officers, and Rita just pointed to the end of the street. Two officers ran in that direction and a patrol car followed them. A policewoman escorted Rita back to her home. The police never found a trace of Alan.

But there was a mysterious twist to the proceedings. It transpired that Rita's cousin, Alan Warner, could not have attacked her, because he had been in Coppetts Wood Hospital recovering from open heart surgery, and had been there hovering on the brink of death for over a week because of complications. Stranger still, on the night Rita was allegedly visited by her cousin, Alan had been saying some strange things while he was in a semiconscious state. Nurses told police that Alan had kept mumbling something about his wife having an affair, and of a journey he was making to a cousin in Wimbledon named Rita. Another strange incident also came to light which only served to deepen the mystery even more. A charity worker who was a close friend of Alan Warner said he had spoken to his friend outside a public house in Highgate – at the very hour when Alan was in fact being operated on. This extraordinary case attracted the attention of the Psychical Research Society in London, and investigators from this organization theorized that, through some bizarre biological process, Alan Warner somehow projected an etheric double of himself as his body was being subjected to the trauma of an operation. But how would a projection be solid enough to attack Rita? Rita said she thought that there was something evil about the impostor who assaulted her, and she also said she regretted not taking notice of her dog, Cally, who had reacted with such unusual hostility towards the night-caller, as if she had known there was something sinister about the man.

Mysteries of the Human Body

• •

"A healthy body is a guest chamber for the soul;
a sick body is a prison."

Francis Bacon

Einstein's Brain Was Different After All

In 1955, seventy-six-year-old Albert Einstein's health
was rapidly deteriorating. Doctors diagnosed a hard-
ened aorta which was evidently leaking blood.
Einstein had suspected his heart was failing for
several years, but now the doctors were really worried,
because they thought the troublesome artery would
develop an aneurysm and possibly explode with pressure. When Einstein was given this grim news he
shrugged and said, "Let it burst." Not long afterwards,
it did.

Einstein was admitted to Princeton hospital, and
his son flew in from California to be with his father in
his final hours. Einstein's stepdaughter, Margot, was
already at the hospital. At first it seemed as if the
aneurysm was healing, but at eleven o'clock that night
in April 1955, Albert Einstein became very pale and
exhibited irregular breathing. He began to say something in German to the nurse, Alberta Roszel, but she
did not speak the language. It seemed as if the world-

famous physicist was trying to convey something of importance. Less than a minute later he took two deep breaths and died.

After the post-mortem, Einstein's 2 lb 10 oz (1.2 kg) brain was saved for study. It was photographed, preserved in formalin, then chopped into 240 numbered cubes. The body meanwhile, was cremated at Ewling Crematory in Trenton.

Most neuroscientists laughed at the idea of seeking physiological evidence of genius by examining the convolutions in Einstein's brain. It was generally thought that all brains were basically the same, differing only slightly from person to person, just as faces vary from human to human. However after some forty-four years of studying the physicist's brain, a plethora of curious features were found which set his grey matter apart from the average brain.

In 1999, Professor Sandra Witelson of McMaster University, Hamilton, Ontario, found that in one area, the inferior parietal region, there were many substantial differences. That part of the brain was extensively developed on both sides, giving this region of Einstein's brain 15 per cent more capacity than average. Spatial and mathematical thinking are strongly dependent on the right and left posterior parietal regions. Neurologists examining the physicist's brain also discovered that it did not feature a particular groove (known as a "sulcus"), and it was speculated that the absence of this groove may have been the key to Einstein's genius. Without the groove, which exists in all other brains, more neurons would have been able to fit into the area, in effect permitting the development of an extraordinarily large expanse of highly integrated cortex. This is now seen as proof

Einstein's brain was different after all.

that there were physical advantages in Einstein's brain which probably gave rise to his genius and unique world view of reality.

Bodily Elongation

In the annals of psychical research there are many references to the unusual phenomenon of "bodily elongation" where, under certain circumstances, usually during religious ecstasy or in the midst of a poltergeist attack, the human body is seen to elongate and morph into various shapes.

One early report of bodily elongation is found in Canon Buti's *Life* of Mother Maria Constante Castreca. He writes that in the year 1700, Maria was praying before a statue of the Infant Jesus when she suddenly stretched vertically as her body trembled. Another case of a body undergoing a dynamic physical change during religious devotion is mentioned in the biography of St Catherine of Genoa. During the torment prior to her death, St Catherine experienced agonizing sensations of an intense internal fire. Then she felt a sharp, painful twinge in her arm, and when she looked, her arm was lengthening slowly. It stretched five or six inches so that the elongation was quite noticeable.

In September 1880 a professor of pathology, Dr Imbert Gourbeyre, and five colleagues, witnessed the dramatic and repulsive bodily transformation of Marie-Julie Jahenny, a well-known stigmatic. Jahenny went into a trance, and minutes later her entire head sank into her body, below the level of her shoulders. When her head re-emerged, Jahenny's tongue came out of it and began to swell to an enormous size, revealing the bloated, rearmost tastebuds of the greatly enlarged organ. The girl's entire frame then underwent an astounding contraction into the thorax so that her body resembled a lumpy ball of flesh. The pathology professor and his five colleagues were understandably shaken by the grotesque transformation and one of them had to leave the room. None of them could explain how Marie-Julie Jahenny accomplished the metamorphosis.

A similar loathsome transfiguration took place during a poltergeist haunting at Amherst, Nova Scotia in August 1878. The poltergeist outbreak seemed centred on nineteen-year-old Esther Cox. One night Esther slept with her younger sister, who was terrified by the noisy activities of an invisible "ghost". During one of the manifestations, Esther was flung from her sister's bed into the centre of the room, with all the bedclothes still swathed around her. Suddenly, the girl's long hair shot up on end, and her face became blood-red. Then her eyes actually protruded out of their sockets. Esther's sister let out a scream at the sight of the bulging eyes and ruddy face, and the rest of the family came rushing into the room in time to witness the most amazing, but obnoxious, transformation of the pretty teenager's body. Esther Cox let out a groan and said to the shocked people present: "My God! I'm dying". Then the girl's arms, legs and trunk started to swell up as if she was inflating. When it seemed as if the unfortunate girl was about to burst, there was a loud booming sound in the bedroom which shook the foundations of the house, and suddenly Esther's body was back to normal, her long hair was hanging down over her shoulders again, and her peaches and cream complexion had returned.

Curiously, the "talent" of bodily elongation is actually listed as one of the eight "Siddhis" (magical talents) of the Indian Yogis, who can extend the length of their limbs through yoga.

The Mystery of Recapitulation

The human embryo, in the course of its development, passes through various stages when its aspects strongly resemble characteristics found in the embryos of other species of animals. For example, human embryos develop tails which usually disappear before birth, although a small percentage of babies are born with a rudimentary tail which must be surgically removed. Human embryos also develop gill pouches which disappear or are altered to produce other structures such as the ear canal. The gill pouches of shark and man bear a very close resemblance, and so do their circulatory systems, but no one knows why.

In its earliest stages the embryo of the human is almost identical to a starfish embryo, and in later stages, on the way to birth, the embryo resembles fish, reptile, and amphibian embryos. Recapitulation still has biologists and scientists divided in their opinions. Some think the similarities between the human embryo and the embryos of other creatures is coincidental, but there are others who believe that recapitulation hints that man had fish-like ancestors from which he descended millions of years ago. Could man's possible aquatic origins explain why millions of people the world over feel the urge to travel to the beach each year in the pursuit of leisure?

Human Incendiary Bombs

One October evening in the late 1950s, nineteen-year-old Maybelle Andrews was dancing with her boyfriend, Billy Clifford, at a London dance hall. One moment Maybelle was smiling and giving loving looks into the eyes of her partner, the next moment she was engulfed in a ferocious fire of unknown origin. The mysterious blaze seemed to originate from her back and then her chest. The flames raced upwards and suddenly enveloped her screaming face. Then the teenager's hair was aflame too. Billy Clifford was in a state of shock. The girl he loved was a human torch, yet no one had been smoking on the dance floor, and there were no naked flames anywhere in the building. Maybelle was severely burnt by the strange fire, and died on the way to hospital. When her grief-stricken boyfriend Billy was later asked to give a description of the "spontaneous combustion", he said: "I saw no one smoking anywhere on the dance floor, and there were no candles on the tables. I did not see her dress catch fire from anything. I know it sounds incredible, but it appeared to me that the flames burst outwards, as if they originated within her body." The official verdict was "death by misadventure, caused by fire of unknown origin".

We may never know how flames came to take the life of Maybelle Andrews, but it is likely that the cause of her death was "Spontaneous Human Combustion" (SHC), a bizarre but frequently reported phenomenon in which fire suddenly overwhelms the victim at such a speed, he or she rarely has time to call for help. In most cases the fire burns so fiercely that the majority of the body, including the bones, is completely consumed and reduced to powder.

The great mystery is the ferocity of the flames. In a crematorium, a temperature of 2,500–3,000°F (1,370–1,650°C) is needed constantly for up to four hours, and even then bones usually remain. However, the remains of victims of SHC have been found in a chair which has somehow survived an infernal blaze which reduced the body to a mound of smouldering ash. How can something so destructive be so localized? And where does the fire originate? These are questions which are continuing to baffle investigators.

On 22 March 1908, retired schoolteacher, Wilhelmina Dewar, died at her home in Whitley Bay, Tyne and Wear, from SHC. On this occasion, the victim was found dead in her bed. Her body and legs were charred but the bedclothes were undamaged and did not even bear a singe mark. The circumstances of her death were so peculiar that the coroner was stumped for an explanation. In all of his forty years as a coroner he had never come upon a case as bizarre.

SHC can strike so quickly that the victim rarely has a chance to dash for water (which probably wouldn't be effective in extinguishing the flames anyway). On a hot summer's day in 1922, Mrs Euphemia Johnson was consumed by flames as fierce as a blowtorch as she drank a cup of tea at her home in Sydenham, Greater London. Her remains – a small powdery pile of calcified bones – were found on the floor beside the victim's overturned chair. Despite the intense heat that must have been present to reduce a body to a heap of powder, the coating of varnish on the chair Mrs Johnson had been seated upon as she burned alive was hardly marked. The rubber tablecloth had been slightly yellowed by the weird but fatal inferno, which indicated that the tremendous heat energy had somehow been contained or focused upon Mrs Johnson.

In October 1964, Olga Worth Stephens of Dallas, Texas, USA, a seventy-five-year-old former actress, was sitting in a parked car when witnesses saw her burst into flames before their shocked eyes. Olga was burnt to death but the car was not damaged, and the vehicle was examined to see if it had contained anything that could have started the fire. The fire investigators drew a complete blank. A similar incident took place in October 1980 when Jeanna Winchester was riding along in her car in Jacksonville, Florida, USA. She suddenly burst into flames and crashed her vehicle as she made frantic attempts to put out the fire. On this occasion the victim survived the strange ordeal and, despite a thorough investigation of Winchester's vehicle, the origin of the flames could not be found.

Could the cocktail of chemicals within the human body be the cause of SHC? Plain water is made up of two of the most explosive elements known to mankind, hydrogen and oxygen, and both of these elements are used as fuel in space rockets and the space shuttle. Perhaps under certain conditions the elements in the human body become unstable or trigger a chemical reaction with devastating effects. Perhaps Billy Clifford was correct when he suggested that the flames which killed his girlfriend Maybelle originated within her.

Who Wants to Live Forever?

In 1997 the world's press reported that Jeanne Calment had died at the truly biblical age of 122. Born at Arles, France, on 21 February 1875, Jeanne remembered meeting the artist Vincent Van Gogh in her home town in 1888, when he came into her uncle's shop to buy paints. She recalled that he had been "dirty, badly dressed and disagreeable". Calment credited an occasional glass of port wine and a diet rich in olive oil for making her the world's oldest person. She started fencing lessons at eighty-five, and was still riding a bike at one hundred, but was forced to give up cigarettes at 120 because, she said with a girlish laugh in her voice, "the doctors feared for my health". Although her final year was spent in a wheelchair, blind and almost entirely deaf, Jeanne Calment never lost her sense of humour and remained spirited and mentally sharp until the end. "I dream, I think, I go over my life, I never get bored," Jeanne said, shortly before her death.

Ageing is a human process which many of us consider natural, but there is a growing consensus among gerontologists and biologists that what we call ageing can actually be looked upon as a disease, and a curable one at that.

If we look at nature we will see that there are various creatures that are, for all intents and purposes, immortal; they never die. The reproductive strategies for many creatures do not include mandatory senescence; as long as there is a sufficient supply of nutrients and a stable environment, then existence and reproduction will take place without interruption and without death. Of course, these immortal creatures are all very simple organisms, such as bacteria, slime moulds and viruses, but there are larger "creatures" that are seemingly eternal. A 5,000-year-old bristlecone pine which is growing in the White Mountains of California recently produced a pine cone containing seeds. These seeds were planted in a nursery and sprouted. The father of these tiny, delicate saplings germinated long ago, long before the foundation of Rome and the Golden Age of Athens, around the time the pyramids were built. What's more, as this tree is still growing, it is officially the oldest living thing on the planet. Early in January 2000, scientists and geneticists who analyzed the DNA of the Methuselah tree were astounded to see that its genetic code did not contain "programmed death" – unlike us humans. It is now known that the tips of human chromosomes are the molecular clock of ageing. Here's how we age. When a cell undergoes replication, most of the chromosome is duplicated, but the duplicating machinery operates in such a way as to copy only part of the chromosome; part of the tip is not replicated. Therefore, during cell division, one of the two new cells only gets a shortened segment of the copied chromosome. All these little missing bits of tips add up as progressive cell divisions occur, and the overall chromosomal length gets shorter and shorter. Studies have shown that the successive loss of chromosome length acts as a type of clock, and when the chromosome "fuse" is whittled down to a certain length, a self-destruct mechanism goes berserk and wreaks havoc on the cells.

Now for the good news. Gene sequences have been isolated that can control the lifespan of individual cells and even entire organisms. Dr Michael Rose of the University of California is an expert on ageing, and he recently stated:

> *I believe that in twenty-five years we could see the creation of the first products that can postpone human ageing significantly. This would be only the beginning of a long process of technological development in which a human lifespan would be aggressively extended. The only practical limit to human lifespan is the limit of human technology.*

Another expert who understands the genetics of ageing is Dr William Regelson, professor of medicine at the Medical College of Virginia:

> *With the knowledge that is accumulating now about the nutritional and neuroendocrine aspects of ageing, and if we develop ways to repair ageing tissues with the help of embryonic cells, we could add thirty healthy years to human life in the next decade. And beyond that, as we learn to control the genes involved in ageing, the possibilities of lengthening life appear practically unlimited.*

Dr Michael Jazwinski of Louisiana State University Medical Center concurs. He has also done a lot of research into the problem of winding back the clock of age. He comments:

> *Possibly in thirty years we will have hand in hand the major genes that determine longevity, and will be in a position to double, triple, and even quadruple our maximum life span of 120 years.*

It's possible that some people alive today may still be alive 400 years from now.

The aforementioned statements are not flights of fancy; they are the careful words of well-respected and prominent scientists who are all experts in the field of gerontology, the scientific study of age and ageing.

Does all this research mean that the fabled Elixir of Youth is at hand? The answer seems to be an unequivocal "yes". Even as you read, progress is being made in the study of ageing, especially on the genetic level, and there really is a possibility that life-extending drugs will be available in the not-too-distant future. However, the ecological and ethical repercussions will have to be worked out. Our planet is already overpopulated with transient humans who are born at a certain rate and die at a fairly regular rate. Should that death rate be impeded or ultimately stopped, we can envisage the cataclysmic strain that would have on the Earth's food and energy resources. However, the prospect of immortality is such a deeply-rooted desire that the pro-immortalists lobby will probably be willing to take on any ecological and agricultural crises in their pursuit of everlasting life.

My Victorian Father

A satisfactory conclusion has yet to be arrived at regarding the following peculiar episode, which took place in London in the 1960s. There were allusions to the story in the *News of the World* in 1967, and the story has also been briefly mentioned in *Fate* magazine in the United States. This is the first time the entire story has been pieced together into a tantalizing glimpse of a man who apparently outlived the normal allotted lifespan of threescore years and ten.

In 1965, a twenty-seven-year-old Kent man named Roger Drayton applied for a vacancy at Lechertier Barbe Ltd, an old art shop in Bloomsbury Street, London. The shop was frequented mainly by art school students who purchased paints, brushes, charcoal, paper and other art materials. Roger was taken on for a trial period at the store, and in his first week a local artist named Richard Jones came into the shop and bought a large canvas and a collection of paintbrushes. He chatted to Roger, and remarked that he would make an ideal model for his project, because he was quite tall and had an interesting profile. Roger was told that he would pose fully-clothed, and what's more he would be paid, even though it would only be a "few bob".

Roger was quite flattered and agreed. The artist gave him the Finsbury address of the house where the sitting would take place, and asked him to get there at 8 p.m. on the following evening.

Roger turned up at the appointed time and a young girl opened the door. She was very beautiful, but dressed quite dowdily in a black polo-neck sweater and a long, pleated, dark-brown dress. Even her shoes looked frumpy. She said, "You must be Roger?"

"Yes," Roger replied, and continued, "Richard asked me to come."

"My name's Virginia," said the girl, and self-consciously bowed slightly as she said, "Good evening."

"Hi," said Roger, and he accompanied the girl – whom he assumed to be Richard's girlfriend or wife – up the stairs. The flights of steps seemed to go on and on. Then Virginia showed him into the attic studio. The place was like an explosion in a paint factory, and the combined aromas of turpentine and varnish were stifling.

"Ah, Roger," Richard said, and he put down his palette and stopped painting a background scene on the large canvas he had purchased at the Bloomsbury Street store.

"That's quite a long hike up those stairs," commented Roger, out of breath, and Richard led him over to a chair and told him to sit with his legs crossed in a casual way. Richard then started to make a charcoal sketch of Roger, and Virginia just looked on, timidly smiling at the subject. Roger smiled back at her, but Richard told him to maintain a serious expression.

By about 11 p.m., Richard said he'd done enough, and showed Roger his work. It was a fairly detailed oil painting, but still needed quite a lot more work to be added. Richard paid his new subject the equivalent of about fifty pence in today's money, and told him to come back tomorrow at the same time. Roger was escorted down the flights of stairs by Virginia, and the two of them left the Finsbury house together. Roger learned that Virginia was not the artist's wife or partner, she was simply his assistant. Roger asked her where she lived and offered to walk her home. Virginia blushed and in a rather faint voice said she lived in Northington Street in Clerkenwell, but then coyly added, "I appreciate your offer to escort me home, but I must desist."

Roger thought the girl's choice of words was somewhat quaint. "Er, I take that as a 'no' then?"

The girl then said, "You don't know what father is like, Roger. He simply does not allow me to become involved with men."

"That's a bit strict isn't it?" Roger asked, and laughed. He grabbed Virginia by her elbow and looked into her eyes. He said, "You're only young, you have a life to live, you know?"

Virginia suddenly started to sniffle and tremble. She said, "I should have been back home at nine o'clock. He will beat me now."

"No he won't," asserted Roger, and then he announced, "Virginia, you're coming for a drink with me." Roger took the girl on a long bus ride to a pub he regularly frequented called *The Crown*, which was situated in Aberdeen Place near St John's Wood. The girl seemed very nervous and looked about at the drinkers. She had exhibited the same anxiety during the bus journey as if she suffered from agoraphobia. She told a startled Roger she had never been inside a pub before, and had never tasted alcohol. Roger said she should make up for lost time, and plied her with shorts and other drinks. When they left the pub, the girl was quite drunk, and started to cry, saying her father would beat her senseless when she got home. Roger hailed a taxi cab and said enough was enough. He was going home with the distressed girl to confront her bullying father. Despite Virginia's hysterical objections to his chivalrous intentions, Roger pushed her into the hackney and told the cabby to drive to Northington Street.

When the couple reached the destination at Clerkenwell, Virginia implored Roger to go home, as his presence would only make matters worse, but Roger insisted upon having a showdown with her chauvinistic father. Virginia stood rooted to the spot, trembling, and Roger finally relented when he saw how frightened she was. He embraced her, kissed her gently on the lips, then took her into the shadows of a tree, where he continued to caress her and reassure her that everything would be resolved soon.

Then they both heard footsteps coming down the street.

A tall man wearing a short cape and a deerstalker hat came marching towards them down Northington Street. He swung a cane as he strutted along. "That's him," said Virginia, and seemed terrified.

"That's your father?" Roger asked, and he ushered her into a doorway and turned his back towards the man, shielding Virginia from his view. Roger looked over his shoulder at the antiquated-looking man striding by. As the man passed the young couple, he seethed, "Where can she be? What the deuce has happened to her?" And he stopped for one heart-stopping moment, took an old fashioned watch on a chain from his waistcoat, and inspected it. He then walked on into the night.

Roger took the intoxicated girl to his basement flat in Chiswell Street. He said he'd sleep on the sofa and offered Virginia his bed, but the girl said she wanted him to sleep with her. Roger was about to get the biggest shock of his life. The girl stripped to her underwear – undergarments as equally outdated as the rest of her attire – and got into the bed. She begged him to get in with her, and when he did, he found himself running his hands all over her as he kissed her. But he couldn't make love to the girl – because she was wearing a chastity belt of some sort! Virginia said her father had the key and had fitted the belt to prevent her from losing her virginity.

Virginia then told a strange tale to Roger, who was still recoiling in shock. Her father said he was fifty-five years old, but an old woman she regularly visited in her neighbourhood said she had been an admirer of Virginia's father when they were both in their twenties. That woman was now in her eighties. Then one day Virginia had been rooting through her father's room when he was out of the house, and she had found an old sepia-toned picture of him wearing a top hat. The caption on the photograph said, "Birkenhead, 1892".

"Perhaps it was his father, or grandfather?" Roger suggested. The revelations were giving him the creeps.

Virginia said the man in the old photo had a mole on his left cheek, just like her father.

"What's your father's full name?" Roger asked; his curiosity had by now been aroused.

"George Moreland," replied Virginia, and she then told Roger about the collection of wedding photographs with dates ranging from 1895 to 1945 that she had also found. "He has married seven times," Virginia said, "He married my mother just after the War. I think he's a devil, Roger. It's as if he's always been alive."

"Don't be silly, Virginia," responded Roger, and he gave a sham laugh, but Virginia's story was very strange indeed. "He certainly acts Victorian – making you wear a bloody chastity belt," Roger remarked, "You must go to the police in the morning. I'll go with you. This is 1965 – not the Middle Ages."

And Roger later fell asleep with his arms round Virginia. But when he awoke in the morning she was nowhere to be seen. Roger went to the artist's studio in Finsbury, and he told Richard about Virginia and the antiquated father. Richard said he had always thought there was something weird about the girl's father, but had no idea he had been cruel enough to make his daughter wear a chastity belt. Richard gave Roger the girl's address in Northington Street, but when Roger called, the house was unoccupied, so Roger asked the neighbours where Mr Moreland and his daughter had moved to, but nobody knew. The neighbours in the street described Mr Moreland as an eccentric, reclusive man who used to stroll down the street pointing his walking cane at the television aerials, saying he'd never have a television or a radio in his home because they were "immoral".

Roger never saw Virginia again. Now for a strange ending to this bizarre tale. In the severe winter of 1980, Roger, who was then aged 42, was driving through north London in a blizzard. The car stalled halfway up Spaniard's Road, near Hampstead Heath, and as Roger was trying to restart his vehicle, he happened to glance at the taxi on his right, which was also lumbering through the thick snowdrift. The passenger in the taxi was talking to a woman and pointing towards the Heath. Roger's jaw dropped when he suddenly recognized the man. It was the mysterious Mr Moreland, Virginia's old-fashioned father. Roger saw to his utter surprise that the venerable man hadn't changed in the slightest in the fifteen years that had elapsed since he'd seen him – and he still wore the deerstalker hat. Roger felt a shudder when he looked at the man. He tried to restart the car so he could follow the taxi, but by the time the car did start to move, the cab carrying Moreland had vanished into the blizzard. The mystery of George Moreland continues to haunt Roger. He has tried to rationalize the apparent incredible longevity of a man who seems to be a surviving Victorian, but no rational explanations apply. Perhaps, somewhere in modern-day London, the enigmatic Mr Moreland is reading this intriguing but sadly incomplete account of his unnaturally long life with a wry smile.

The Man Who Led Two Lives

In January 1887, mild-mannered carpenter and local preacher, Ansel Bourne, left his home in Rhode Island, USA, then drew $551 from his bank account before setting off for Providence to discuss a land-purchasing deal with his nephew.

At 5 a.m. on the morning of 14 March that same year, Mr Bourne awoke to a loud report, which sounded like a pistol being fired close to his head. He jumped up off the bed but there was only the darkened bedroom. Mr Bourne felt strange, as if he had been drugged, and he staggered to the window for fresh air. He opened the window, looked out into the street and saw it was unfamiliar. Mr Bourne soon realized that he did not have a clue where he was, and worse still he later began to doubt *who* he was as well.

Mr Bourne met the owner of the house he was in, a Mr Earle, and he seemed very concerned about Mr Bourne's strange behaviour. "Are you all right, Mr Brown?" the landlord asked the confused lodger.

"Look here," Mr Bourne answered, "My name isn't Brown, it's Bourne."

"But you're Albert Brown," the puzzled landlord told him, and he also asked the bewildered lodger if he knew where he was. Mr Bourne didn't, so the land-lord filled him in on some highly unusual details. He revealed that Mr Bourne was in a room at the back of a small confectionery and stationery shop on East Main Street in Norristown, Pennsylvania.

"Pennsylvania?" Mr Bourne exclaimed, "What on earth am I doing here?"

A doctor was called and, after examining Mr Bourne, he suspected amnesia, possibly brought on by a blow to the head, even though there were no marks or bruising on Bourne's head. Bourne said that the last thing he recalled was leaving his nephew's shop on Broad Street, Providence, Rhode Island – which was 230 miles away.

It transpired that Ansel Bourne had arrived in Pennsylvania in February of that year and had set up the confectionery and stationery business as Mr Albert John Brown. But Mr Brown's alter ego, Ansel Bourne, could recall doing nothing of the sort. He had no interest in confectionery or paper and pens, and remained completely baffled at the missing weeks in his life. Mr Bourne's nephew was contacted and he later came to collect his uncle. Bourne learned from his nephew that he had been reported missing on Rhode Island and that the police had been making plans to drag the river to find his body.

Mr Bourne remained perplexed by the period of amnesia. Three years later a Professor William James of Harvard heard of the strange case, and offered to hypnotize Bourne in an effort to shed some light on the mystery. Bourne gave his consent and was duly put into a hypnotic trance. Under hypnosis, Mr Bourne became the mysterious Mr A.J. Brown once more, and he gave a blow-by-blow account of the journey he had taken three years ago, from Rhode Island to Pennsylvania. Mr Brown told the professor that he had set up a shop (with the $551 he had withdrawn) while being a little confused as to what his real identity was. All he knew was that his name was Brown and that he had lost his wife in 1881. Mr Bourne had lost his own wife that same year. As the days went by, Mr Brown felt his identity "evaporating" until it had vanished on the morning of 14 March 1887. That was the morning Ansel Bourne's ego had returned with the sound of a loud bang.

Professor James deduced that the personas of Ansel Bourne and Albert John Brown were two distinct entities with their own mannerisms, gestures and handwriting, but he never explained where A.J. Brown had come from and how "he" had taken over Ansel Bourne's life.

The Real Jekyll and Hyde

Most people have heard of Robert Louis Stevenson's disturbing tale of dual personality concerning Dr Jekyll and Mr Hyde, but there was a bizarre case of a real-life Jekyll and Hyde character at large in Victorian England in the mid-nineteenth century. Richard Rawlins was a fairly wealthy south Lancashire engineer who had shares in several Cornish tin mines and the Liverpool to Manchester Railway. He was said to be a tall, handsome, raven-haired man with a fine voice and a rather shrewd nature. He had been married three times, each marriage ending after a short period because of Rawlins's dramatic mood swings and strange dual personality. From his childhood, Richard Rawlins claimed he had a naughty "twin" inside him, and he often changed hands to write and draw when he "became" his alter ego. Richard's mother once asked Richard what his invisible twin's name was, and the boy shrugged. Mrs Rawlins laughingly suggested the name Ralph, and unwittingly christened the flipside of her son's personality. Ralph was a nasty, mischievous character who delighted in pulling the legs off spiders, while Richard was the thoughtful, sensitive boy who picked flowers for his mother.

A children's doctor was baffled at the child's dual personality disorder, and surmised it was just young Richard's way of getting attention. But in adolescence, Richard kept on becoming Ralph, usually when he had undergone an emotional time or had had an accident. When sixteen-year-old Richard broke up with his girlfriend, Lottie, he broke down in tears in Liverpool's Toxteth Park. A policeman approached the distressed young man and asked him what the matter was, but the rejected Romeo's angelic face became twisted and his eyes squinted at the police officer. Richard had become Ralph, and he spat in the policeman's face and ran out of the park shouting abuse at passers-by. Upon reaching his home, the mentally unstable teenager was attacked by his dog, Samson, a huge black Labrador. The dog loved Richard, but growled and ran from the boy when he became his nasty counterpart Ralph.

The teenager ran into the front parlour and suffered a fit. He was found by the maid biting the hearth rug with a foaming mouth. As the maid called for Richard's father, the boy passed out. When he was revived with smelling salts he told his parents that Ralph had spat at a policeman and had screamed abuse at people in the street on his way home. The weeks went by without Ralph putting in another appearance, and the boy seemed normal enough. Only occasionally did he swap his pen to his left hand when he wrote, and there were only minor variations in the teenager's handwriting style. As the years elapsed, it looked as if the rebellious Ralph had disap- peared for good into the depths of Richard Rawlins's subconscious. However, in 1845, a dramatic accident brought Ralph back into Richard's life with a vengeance. Richard Rawlins was now a twenty-five- year-old mining engineer who patented several explosive devices for blasting quarries and mines. On 1 November 1845, Rawlins entered the premises of Rodney Hart, a Liverpool gunsmith and gunpowder supplier. Rawlins intended to purchase 5 lb (2.3 kg) of gunpowder to test out a detonation device he was working on for the mines, but a young apprentice in the cellar of the shop dropped a flintlock he'd just loaded. The gun went off, and blasted a hole in a barrel of gunpowder. The apprentice was killed instantly and the ensuing blast was of such ferocity that the only part of the apprentice's body that could afterwards be found was part of his lower jaw. Rodney Hart was blown through the windows of his shop but survived, despite a great loss of blood. Richard Rawlins was blown up onto the first floor of the devastated building by the tremendous force of the blast. He was found hanging over a beam, barely alive, suffering from severe concussion.

Rawlins was treated at his palatial home by several distinguished physicians, and for a week it looked as if the young man would remain in a comatose state. But he pulled through – or at least, *Ralph* pulled through. Richard's personality was evidently destroyed in the shop explosion. As soon as the young man was able to get out of his bed he practically raped the maid and then assaulted the cook, who was a woman of forty. Ralph stole over one hundred guineas from his father's room and then escaped by climbing dangerously out of a garret window. He ran across the rooftops and went on a crime spree. He committed two burglaries in the Islington area of Liverpool, sexually assaulted three teenaged girls in the Everton district, and almost battered a pub land-lord to death because the ale he served tasted sour. Unlike the meek Richard, Ralph had the strength of a savage, and seemed to take delight in battling the police. The wayward Ralph Rawlins was finally cornered a week later by eight policemen armed with batons in Vauxhall Road. The mixed-up young man had just set fire to a soap warehouse, and the damage was estimated to amount to almost one thousand pounds.

Sadly, a blow on the skull from a policeman's riot baton killed Ralph instantly. The man with two personalities suffered a massive haemorrhage of the brain and died with blood gushing from his nose and ears. Surgeons at the British Medical Institute in Liverpool were eager to get to the bottom of the dead man's double personality, and sought permission to open his skull to establish if there were any cerebral malformations. At first Mr Rawlins refused permission, but later had a change of heart, as he was curious about his son's mental make-up himself.

A surgeon opened up Rawlins's skull and was flabbergasted by what he saw. There were two brains tightly pressed together in the skull case, or four hemispherical lobes in all. It was surmised that Richard had, in fact, been one half of a twin when he was conceived, but the other twin never developed into a foetus, yet retained its brain, which grew alongside the other. Undoubtedly, one of the brains contained the personality of Richard, and the other brain was the source of the spiteful alter ego who asserted himself as Ralph. The Rawlins family naturally didn't want society to know of their freakish son, so the findings of the Medical Institute were filed away for posterity.

The Story of a Severed Head

Back in the dark days of the French Revolution in 1789, there was a farmer named Jean St Justin who was incredibly strong and very athletic. St Justin was of average height and weight, and not particularly muscular, but delighted in outdoor exercise. It was said that he could carry a grown man under each arm and run the length of a field. When a neighbouring farmer was chopping down a leaning oak tree, the trunk of the tree fell on him and pinned him down. St Justin came to the rescue and lifted the oak tree off the farmer as if it were no more than a broom. On another occasion St Justin played a game of tug of war with a bull, and somehow managed to drag the animal over a marker in the field. St Justin could also swim underwater in the nearby river for amazing lengths of time. On one occasion he managed to hold his breath for about seven minutes, which is unheard of, even today.

The farmer was nicknamed "Samson" because of his phenomenal strength and stamina, and he was very popular with the country girls on the outskirts of Versailles. There was one beautiful maiden named Marie, from a neighbouring farm, who found herself falling for St Justin, but another man, Guy Damont, also had feelings for Marie, and he became insanely jealous of St Justin's physical prowess and popularity.

One morning when St Justin was ploughing the fields, Guy Damont approached him with his hands behind his back. St Justin sensed something evil in Damont's eyes, and asked him what he wanted. Damont was holding a sharp-bladed sickle behind his back; he suddenly lashed out just once, and the sickle took St Justin's head clean off his shoulders. A deformed man came over to the murderer and asked him why he had killed the farmer. The man was a hunchback, and had difficulty speaking. Damont suddenly noticed three figures approaching on horse-

For Louis XVI, decapitation meant a swift death – this wasn't always the case with some victims.

back in the distance. He put the bloodstained sickle in the hunchback's hand, and when the riders came across the field to the scene of the gruesome murder, they saw the hunchback leaning over the decapitated corpse of St Justin with the blood-soaked sickle in his hand. They naturally assumed the hunchback, who was renowned as the village idiot, had killed the farmer. The three men on horseback had been gardeners at the Palace of Versailles before the Revolution, and they knew the hunchbacked man was a kind and sensitive man, so they found it hard to believe that he had now turned into a violent killer. The men suspected Guy Damont, who was known locally as a misfit who was cruel to the farm animals; Damont had once been seen barbecuing a live rabbit with a look of delight on his face. One of the gardeners, a man named Anton, put it to Damont that he had killed the farmer, but Damont's face burned red with rage and he said, "I am an innocent passer-by! This cretin killed him. You must believe me."

Suddenly, something grisly happened. The severed head of Jean St Justin made a noise. It opened its mouth and closed it again, making a clacking noise with its teeth. Damont realized that, somehow, the head was still alive. The men on horseback looked afraid, and Guy Damont was terrified at the sight of the head, which was now biting the ground.

"Lord, my poor friend St Justin. If only you could speak," sobbed Anton, and his sympathy for his slain friend overcame his nervousness. The gardener lifted the head from the ground and looked at it. The eyes rolled about and the expression on the face was one of anger and desperation. Anyone else would have died long before with the shock, but apparently the farmer's incredible mental and physical stamina had enabled St Justin to survive the terrible decapitation for a while. Just as he could hold his breath under water for seven minutes, the farmer was also managing to live without oxygen for the same amount of time. If only he could speak, thought Anton, but he knew that was impossible; no one could speak without a throat. Then the gardener had an idea. He said to St Justin's severed head, "St Justin, if you can understand me, close your eyes."

The head immediately squeezed its eyes shut for a second or so, then opened them and looked at Anton.

"Did Martin the hunchback kill you? If he did not, close your eyes; if he did, open your mouth twice," said the gardener, with tears in his eyes. The blood was steadily dripping from the decapitated head.

Again, the head squeezed its eyes shut to answer "no" to the question.

"This is witchcraft!" Guy Damont screamed, objecting to the grisly proceedings.

Then Anton asked, "Did Guy Damont kill you?"

St Justin's severed head opened its mouth twice. Seconds later, the head became motionless, and Anton said, "May God take your spirit Jean St Justin. I promise, your death will be avenged." And Anton sadly read the lips of the dying head; they were trying to say, "I love Marie." Then the eyes closed. St Justin was dead.

Guy Damont made a run for it, but the two other men on horseback raced after the killer and apprehended him. Guy Damont was later put on trial for the murder of the popular farmer. He was found guilty and the revolutionary soldiers who acted as guards during the trial were instructed to take the killer to Paris. Anton accompanied the condemned man, and when Damont was guillotined, the executioner held the killer's head up to the crowd. Anton saw the eyes of the severed head roll about in horror as they looked at the cheering people. The last face the eyes of that terrified head glanced at was that of Anton, who cried out, "Now St Justin has been avenged!" Then the head was hurled into the basket.

Reincarnation

•••••••••••••••••••••••••••••••••••

"I am today, I am yesterday, I am tomorrow.
As I pass through recurrent births I am ever
young and vigorous . . ."
Egyptian Book of the Dead

Can We Really Have Another Go?

The concept of reincarnation is a fascinating one that
has intrigued humankind for thousands of years. The
possibility that the soul of an individual can survive
death and be reborn in a new body is a very attractive
idea, but is there any real proof of reincarnation?
Here's an intriguing account which, if we are to take it
at face value, indicates that some people at least have
lived through previous lifetimes stretching back over
millennia.

In 1937, a controversial book entitled *Winged
Pharaoh* was published. It was classed by scholars and
critics alike as a thoroughly well-researched and
above-average 120,000-word historical novel about a
priest-ruler in ancient Egypt. The literary reviewer of
The Times commended the book and wrote: "*Winged
Pharaoh* is in a class apart . . . glowing!"

The controversy surrounding the work had nothing
to do with the book's contents; it concerned the claims
of its author, an attractive thirty-year-old woman
named Joan Grant, because she maintained that she
hadn't researched a single historical detail to give her

work its authenticity. Instead, she had drawn on her own personal "memories" of a previous life she'd led as a priest-pharaoh thousands of years before.

Joan Grant was born in 1907 into a wealthy Edwardian family, living at Hayling in Hampshire, England. Even as a child Joan knew she had lived many lives before and often told bemused adults about her previous incarnations, using a curious phrase: "That was before I was Joan". Of course, the adults assumed Joan had nothing more than a vivid imagination, but there were many strange talents the girl possessed which did make some of them think twice about the little girl's claims.

When Joan was nine, World War I was still in progress, and the child suffered many nightmares about the conflict, even though she was not altogether sure what the war was about. One morning in 1916 she came down to breakfast and told her father – who was with a friend who had just returned from the Front on leave – about a curious, vivid dream she'd experienced the night before. Joan sat at the breakfast table and could hardly contain herself. She said, "Father, somehow I know you will not laugh at me. Last night I was with a man called McAndrew when he was killed. I can describe the regimental badge although I cannot remember the name of the regiment, except that it was not an English one. And I can even tell you the slang name of his trench."

The visiting soldier was truly amazed, because he was able to identify the regiment Joan spoke of as Canadian. The soldier later wrote to Joan's father, Jack:

Regarding Joan; for heaven's sake don't laugh at

the child. I cannot attempt an explanation, but I have checked what she said. A battalion of that regiment went over the top on a night attack a few hours before Joan told me about it at breakfast. A private called McAndrew was among those killed. She was even correct about the local name of the front-line trench.

The letter merely underlined what Jack already knew about his daughter: that she was somehow privy to information about events distant in space and time. However, Jack was a scientist, and he could not bend his rational mind to accept a supernatural explanation for his daughter's uncanny powers of distant sight.

On another occasion, a visitor came to see Joan's father. He was C.G. Lamb, a professor of engineering at Cambridge University. Mr Lamb had once been a close friend of Jennie Marshall, Joan's late grandmother and, because Mr Lamb was open-minded enough to have a secret interest in the paranormal, he became very intrigued by the unusual remarks of his friend's daughter.

On one occasion, Joan suddenly looked up at Mr Lamb and said, "Jennie gives me music lessons." Mr Lamb knew the little girl was talking about her long-dead grandmother, Jennie, whom he had been so fond of, and he returned an affectionate smile. Joan walked to the piano saying, "Father knows I would never be a first-class pianist so there is no point in my having lessons, but Jennie knows I need music lessons and she teaches me. Sometimes she plays the piano with me; music that is quite different from the ordinary tunes I have learned."

Then the child began to play those "different" tunes

and Mr Lamb was flabbergasted. Joan performed a medley of melodies that her grandmother had often played to Mr Lamb all those years ago, long before Joan was born. The old man mopped his brow and said, "Impossible. Extraordinary. Quite extraordinary but completely evidential. What you have just played was often played to me by your grandmother and I have not heard it since she died."

What baffled Lamb was the fact that young Joan could not have heard the pieces of music she had played from anyone else. All those years ago, when Jennie Marshall had learned she was dying from terminal cancer, she had decided – rather eccentrically – to burn all the manuscripts of her original compositions, because she wanted no one else to play her music after she had died.

At the age of sixteen, Joan Grant met another visitor to her home. The author H.G. Wells seemed very open-minded when Joan decided to tell him about her previous lives. Wells advised the girl to keep quiet about her past incarnations. "Keep it to yourself, Joan, until you are strong enough to bear being laughed at by fools, and when you are ready write down all you can recall," Wells told her, then added, "I think it's important that you should become a writer."

. In 1936, Joan came into possession of an ancient Egyptian scarab charm, and she soon discovered that each time she handled it, she was able to recall events of a previous life in ancient Egypt, when she had been Sekeeta, the daughter of a pharaoh (and later a priest-pharaoh herself). The recovered memories of Sekeeta were so vivid, Joan was able to write them down in a "posthumous autobiography" called *Winged Pharaoh*. According to Joan, many of the ancient Egyptian priests had learned through a hard mental discipline how to shift levels of consciousness in between the fuzzy sleeping and waking state. This shifting of consciousness to another state allowed a person to recall past lifetimes and also to come to terms with past deaths. For this retrospective analysis to be thorough, the person reliving past lives was shut in a dark tomb for four days.

Joan Grant contended that not only did every person alive today have lifetimes stretching back into the remote past, she also asserted that the present ills, psychoses and phobias of many people had their roots in traumatic incidents from the previous lives. The only way to resolve these psychological problems was to relive them and confront them. Joan Grant herself was forced to face her own deaths in various nightmares. She claimed that in her numerous lives she had been burned at the stake for witchcraft, had a spear driven through her eye during a joust, committed suicide, and had died from snake bites.

Joan also changed sex along the eternal road of life. Over 3000 years ago, during the reign of the pharaoh Ramesses II, Joan was a man named Ra-ab Hotep. In the sixteenth century she was a female. On this occasion she was born in Italy as Carola di Ludovici on 4 May 1510. Carola became a singer with a troupe of strolling players, but died at the age of twenty-seven. What was probably her last reincarnation was as a nineteenth-century girl named Lavinia who died after falling from a horse and breaking her back in 1875.

Those who interviewed Joan Grant at length in an effort to catch her out on some anachronism, some historical inaccuracy, were always unsuccessful, and would leave perplexed. The only explanation Joan could offer to account for her multi-lives was a strange analogy. She once commented: "Joan and Sekeeta are but two beads on the same necklace and the memory they share is contained in the string."

Joan also asserted that many of the people we are close to in this life have shared our lives in previous times. Sometimes they were husbands, sometimes they were wives, or brothers, sisters, sons or daughters. This was not as incestuous or controversial as it seemed, because the spirit, according to Joan, was androgynous; it contained both male and female characteristics.

In the Orient, death is viewed entirely differently from in the West. The Christian church rejects the concept of reincarnation, although both early Judaism and Christianity accepted the belief in rebirth (and since 1913 the Roman Catholic Church has readopted it). India, the subcontinent from which many of the world's languages, cultures and religious beliefs spread, may have been the origin of the doctrine of reincarnation. Lost in the mists of time there was the archaic belief in "the ever-returning Wheel of Life". The Hindus, Buddhists, Jainists, Vedantists and a myriad of other sects in India also have no difficulty in grasping the cyclic nature of the soul's journey through recurrent lifetimes. It is commonly believed in all the religions of the East that the soul has an almost endless round of lives to live out until it can see through the world illusion and enter the bliss of Nirvana. Even across the Pacific, the Okinawans preach that each person possesses a spirit, which vacates the body after physical death, and travels into the afterworld known as Gusho before returning to earth in the body of a newly-conceived baby. It is the same scenario with the Aborigines, and reincarnation is also deeply rooted in the belief systems of the North American Indians, the Eskimos, and Aleuts. The belief in rebirth after death is also widespread on the African continent, and may have given rise to a remarkable religious work of antiquity known as *The Egyptian Book of the Dead,* which is essentially a type of guide-book for the dying to lead them onto a safe path into the afterlife. By a strange coincidence, halfway around the world from Egypt there appeared another esoteric work entitled *The Bardo Thodol* or *The Tibetan Book of the Dead.* There are many remarkable parallels between this book and its Egyptian counterpart. The Tibetan book was translated by W.Y. Evans-Wentz, who was astounded at the similarity between the Tibetan and Egyptian books. Both books describe almost identical methods for raising the deceased person's "energy body" – called the "Ka" in Egypt, and the "desire body" in Tibet. Besides other textural similarities, Evans-Wentz was also intrigued at the way the great lamas of Tibet are embalmed and mummified in a fashion almost identical to the way Egyptian royalty were mummified after being embalmed. It was as if the two cultures, although widely separated geographically, had some common origin. Perhaps the nexus of the Egyptians and the Tibetans was some psychical connection between the two, but at present the similarities are unexplained by conventional anthropology and history.

The Bizarre Case of the American Knights

In August 1972 a respected New York hypnotherapist named Donald Ketticott regressed a retired property developer from Palm Springs named George Freemont. Freemont had been visiting a cousin in the "Big Apple" and had decided to pay a visit to Ketticott's surgery on East 26th Street to book an appointment, but was surprised when Ketticott asked him if he wanted to have a "quick taster" of hypnotic regression. Freemont said he would and that he'd like to be regressed to a certain summer's day in 1910 when he was just seven years old. Ketticott asked Freemont why he wanted to be taken back to that day, and the latter explained that on that date he had experienced a strange vision which had haunted him all of his life. He had been hiking with his father through the woods near Lake Tahoe in California when he had felt an intense urge to turn around. Upon turning, young George Freemont saw a knight in armour carrying a lance, mounted on a white horse. The apparition was shimmering with a golden light, and the knight, who wore a crown, smiled and said something. George had forgotten what it was the vision had said, and seconds later it had vanished, leaving the boy with an unbelievable tale to tell.

Ketticott acted strangely when Freemont related the strange episode from his childhood. He took out a notebook and scribbled something down, then enthusiastically went to the windows and pulled down the blinds. He told Mr Freemont to relax on the chesterfield and, within a couple of minutes, the retired Californian was in a hypnotic trance.

"Go further back, further to that day George. Fall through time, fall through the years back to that sunny day. You are there now," Ketticott intoned in a gentle but reassuring voice.

"I am there. I'm with my father. The sun's in my eyes," said Mr Freemont. His eyes were closed and his breathing rate was very slow.

"Move on to the moment when you see that vision. Move on," Ketticott told him.

"Wow!" George Freemont's mouth opened and his face looked like the face of a surprised schoolboy who was in awe of something.

"Now listen to the vision," said Ketticott softly.

George Freemont suddenly started speaking in an unknown language. It had elements of Latin and French in it, and as Freemont uttered the strange tongue, he lifted his hand and made a fist, as if he was saluting someone. In a deep voice Freemont said: "Arturus Rex."

At that point Ketticott brought the Californian out of the trance and asked him what he had learned. Freemont was quiet for a few minutes, then said that upon that summer's day long ago he had encountered a glowing vision of his "master" – King Arthur. Arturus Rex, the words Freemont had uttered when he "saluted" the vision, were Latin for King Arthur. Ketticott then asked him what the vision had said on that sunny afternoon.

"He told me that I was the reincarnation of one of his knights. He said I was Tristram, one of his most valiant men, and he told me that three other knights had been reborn in America and that I should try to seek them out." George Freemont expected the hypnotherapist to laugh at the incredible claim, but

Donald Ketticott told the retired Californian a bizarre tale.

Ketticott said, "Just over a year ago I regressed a policeman who works right here in New York. He had had recurrent nightmares since childhood about being run through with a sword. The nightmares were so lucid, the policeman could actually feel the agonizing pain and terror as the sword went through his torso. These nightmares began to affect his work, so he sought psychiatric help. A friend of mine tried psychoanalysis but that had no effect, so he referred the policeman to me. That policeman said that when he was a child of about eight or nine, he was woken on several occasions by a mysterious presence in his bedroom. The eerie glowing figure of a man in a crown would appear at the foot of his bed and smile at him. Well, I regressed the policeman and he told me that in a previous life he had died in a bloody battle as a knight, a knight of King Arthur's named Gareth. Under hypnosis he said that when he awoke from the night-mare he would see the golden vision of Arthur standing near his bed with a reassuring smile."

George Freemont was fascinated with Ketticott's story and asked if it would be possible to talk to the policeman in question. Dr Ketticott was reluctant at first but later arranged for Freemont to meet the policeman. According to Ketticott, the two men became the best of friends and made many visits to England to see the historical sites where King Arthur and his men lived and fought. The two "reincarnated knights" also travelled to what they claimed was the final resting place of their King – the Blessed Isle of Avalon – nowadays known as the Isle of Man.

Second Time Around

Several years ago, Liverpool hypnotist Joe Keeton treated a Liverpool housewife named Ann Dowling, and regressed her back over a hundred years. He asked Mrs Dowling where she was, and she said she was in the Liverpool of 1850, where she was living in a slum as a poor orphan named Sarah Williams. Keeton asked her what was happening in Liverpool in 1850, and Mrs Dowling said she was by the Philharmonic Hall, where there was excitement because a foreign singer was coming to visit. Keeton asked her about this singer, and Mrs Dowling said the singer's name had something to do with a bird. Research later showed that in August 1850, a Swedish singer named Jenny Lind had visited the old Philharmonic Hall – she was nicknamed "the Swedish Nightingale".

In the 1980s, a lorry driver from Manchester was driving past a cemetery near Newton le Willows, when he experienced *déjà vu* – the feeling that he'd been in the area before. He passed the same cemetery a few months later and got the same uncanny feeling; everything looked familiar but he'd never lived in the area. His friend urged him to visit a qualified hypnotherapist, and when the lorry driver was put in a trance he apparently remembered being a ghost at the Newton le Willows churchyard. He said he used to float up out of his grave and wander about, and it always felt as if he was in a dream. He said some people could see him, but they always ran away, and he felt very lonely. When he later went to the cemetery, he identified what he believed had been his grave. The gravestone stated that the person had died in August 1940, and that was the very month the man had been born.

One of the more well-documented accounts which seems to prove reincarnation is a reality is the case of a Warrington man who was born blind. Mr James had been blind from birth, but had recurrent dreams in which he could see a woman's face. When he was hypnotized, Mr James said, "I can see her face. She has rosy red cheeks, blonde hair and lovely blue eyes. She's my wife." He then went on to describe her sparkling jewellery and the sunset visible through a window behind her.

In 1977, a pub landlord in Morecambe, Lancashire, kept having recurrent dreams about being a highwayman. In the dreams he used to look in a mirror and see himself in a three-pointed hat and a black velvet mask of the sort worn by the Lone Ranger. In the end, his wife asked a hypnotist to come to the pub to look into her husband's strange dreams. The hypnotist put him in a trance, then asked him who the man in the mask was. The landlord said he was Edward Higgins, and began talking in a quaint rural accent. He said he was a gentleman by day, and a faithful churchgoer, but after dark he became a callous highwayman holding up coaches in Cheshire. After three hours of being in a trance, the landlord started screaming that he'd been caught, and he later turned pale, saying "they" were going to hang him. The landlord's wife asked the hypnotist to wake her husband up, but he reassured her, saying her husband would be fine. Suddenly, the man let out a terrible scream, then went deathly quiet. The hypnotist asked him where he was, and the highwayman said, "I'm in hell. I can see so many faces around me. All bad people." Then the hypnotist woke him up. It has now been established that there was a highwayman named Edward Higgins who operated near Knutsford, Cheshire in 1752. He was a classic Jekyll and Hyde character; a gentleman by day and a highwayman by night, until he was finally lynched.

In the 1950s, a Scottish man named Alfred Moberley was put into a hypnotic trance, and he said he was a servant of Pontius Pilate. When the hypnotist asked him to describe what was going on, Moberley said a man named Yeshua was causing trouble by preaching against the authorities. "Who is Yeshua?" the hypnotist asked, and Moberley calmly replied, "The one who says he is the Messiah." The hypnotist then asked him what Yeshua was like, and Moberley said, "Very tall, sullen-skinned, with a long pigtail."

Twenty years later, historians discovered that many of the Jews of Pilate's period wore their tapering hair in a pigtail, and they also discovered a reference to a "Teacher of Righteousness" named "Yeshua" among the Dead Sea Scrolls.

Ironically, Alfred Moberley had been an atheist.

Many hypnotherapists now believe that reincarnation could explain why people have irrational phobias and unfounded anxieties. A woman in St Helens who had a phobia of ships was regressed, and said she had died on the *Lusitania*. In a book called *The Children that Time Forgot* by Mary and Peter Harrison, there's an intriguing case of a boy in Blackpool who was terrified of aeroplanes. Whenever he saw one in the sky or heard the drone of a jet, he would fall to the floor and do a commando crawl under a table. When he was hypnotized, he said he'd been an American infantryman in a jungle and had been killed when a plane dived down and shot at him.

Several years ago, a Welsh woman gave her four-year-old son two large Easter eggs one Easter Sunday morning, and he told her: "Thanks Mum. You're better than my other mum; she never gave me Easter eggs." When the mother quizzed her son about this "other mum", he told her he had been in another family before his present one, but must have died, because he remembered everything "went black" one day. As the boy got older, he remembered less and less of his "former life", and today he cannot recall any memories of a previous existence at all.

Fate, Destiny and Coincidence

●●●

> "Kismet, Hardy."
> *Admiral Horatio Nelson's dying words to his friend and flag-captain Thomas Hardy after being mortally wounded by a sniper's bullet.*

Strange Twists of Fate

In August 1961, police were called to a domestic incident at a house in the suburbs of Vancouver, Canada. A large, overweight man named Edwin Plumley was battering his timid wife, Thelma, because his supper tasted "too salty". The policemen who turned up at the house asked Mrs Plumley if she was going to press charges against her violent husband – who had a history of wife-beating – but Thelma just shook her head and cried. The police reluctantly left the house and one the officers called back, "Remember now Thelma; if he hits you again, just give us a call. Next time he won't get off so lightly." Edwin Plumley shouted, "Get out of my house!" and slammed the door in the policeman's face. He turned to Thelma and said, "He's got the hots for you that's all. But you're old enough to be his mother."

On the following day, Thelma was ironing her husband's shirts, when the postman rang. He had a parcel and wanted her to sign for it. Thelma did, and the postman said, "Do you smell something burning?" "Oh God!" Thelma ran back into the house. She'd accidentally put the hot iron down on one of her husband's shirts and singed it badly. She paid for the innocent mishap that night. Edwin gave her a black eye and booted her across the bedroom. Thelma wouldn't come to bed, so her bully of a husband carried her into the bedroom and tied her to the bed, then made love to her against her will, before getting up and downing an entire bottle of whisky. At 5 a.m. he staggered into the bedroom naked, then practically raped his wife.

Thelma told her next-door neighbour, an old woman named Sally, about her ordeal. Sally urged Thelma to run away from home. "I've got nowhere to run," Thelma sobbed, but Sally suggested, "What about your cousin in Denver? She'd take you in. You said she was always asking you to visit her."

"Of course. My cousin Didi." said Thelma.

Sally went out of the room then came back with a brown envelope. She gave it to Thelma and said, "Here. There's three hundred dollars. You can fly down to Colorado. Get away from that monster."

"But I couldn't possibly take all that money from you, Sally," Thelma responded, pushing the envelope away.

"Just take it. One day you can repay me, when you can. Just get away from your husband, or he'll end up killing you," Sally insisted, and put the envelope in Thelma's hand.

Outside, just a few feet away, Edwin Plumley was fixing the television aerial on the chimney. His ladder was a bit rickety, so he tied a rope to it, then threw the other end of the rope over the roof. He walked round to the front of the house, grabbed the end of the rope and tied it to the bumper of his car. With the ladder now stabilized, he climbed it safely and began to tighten the brackets on the loose television aerial. As he did so, he heard a roll of distant thunder and saw storm clouds gathering on the horizon, so he decided to hurry up fixing the aerial in case lightning struck him. "Thelma would love that to happen," a neighbour heard him mutter to himself.

Then Mr Plumley heard his car door slam. It was Thelma getting into it; she had decided there was no time like the present, and was going to drive to Vancouver Airport to book a flight to Denver, Colorado. As the engine revved, Edwin Plumley realized with horror that the rope tied to his ladder was tethered to the bumper of the car. As Thelma tore off in the vehicle at high speed, the rope tightened and pulled the ladder – with Edwin clinging to it – over the rooftop. He screamed out as he was dragged headfirst across the roof. His body landed on a picket fence and he was impaled by three pointed pieces of the fence. One went through his lower back and emerged near his groin, another went through his lung and came out near his chest, and the third piece of railing went through his armpit. Edwin was probably still alive as he was pulled along with his smashed arm entangled in the rungs of the broken ladder. After driving a little way down the street, Thelma looked in the car's rear view mirror and saw the rope trailing behind and the bloody mess in the road.

When Thelma realized what had happened she couldn't even shed a single tear, and after the coroner had recorded a verdict of death by misadventure, she threw a party at her house and invited Sally round. Thelma wouldn't have to move to Colorado after all.

Here's another account of a strange twist of fate.

One sultry Saturday night in June 1957, a couple from the little town of Jennings in Louisiana, USA, were driving along a freeway, heading for New Orleans. The couple were Dean Backley, aged twenty-five, and his twenty-year-old girlfriend Jessica Davies, and they were planning to get engaged soon. As the car glided along the freeway, the couple were listening to the music on the radio when the programme was suddenly interrupted by a disturbing news bulletin. The radio announcer said: "This is a news flash. Police are warning the public of Louisiana to be on the lookout for the deranged axe murderer Nathan Webster, who has escaped from Baton Rouge penitentiary. Webster had been due to go to the chair next week for hacking a woman to death in her bed with an axe. We'll bring you more on this story as soon as more news comes in."

About an hour later, the engine of the car carrying Dean and Jessica started to make spluttering noises. Dean checked the fuel, but there was enough in the tank. Suddenly the car stalled just as it reached a deserted road that ran near the Mississippi river. Dean looked under the bonnet, then went to the boot of the car to get his toolbox after telling Jessica to switch the radio on. Dean wanted the radio on so he could hear some music to keep them company.

Jessica listened to the rock and roll songs on the radio for a while, and started thinking about her coming engagement. She really loved Dean. About five minutes later, two police cars came crawling down the road ahead, with their red lights flashing. Jessica turned off the radio and noticed that the cars didn't have their sirens on. She then heard a succession of thumps at the back of the car. The girl said, "Dean, it's the police." But the thuds at the back got louder. Suddenly, a sheriff got out of the first police car with a megaphone. Then three police marksmen also got out of the patrol cars and aimed their rifles towards Jessica. The rifles had telescopic sights. Two more policemen came forward training their torches on the girl.

The sheriff's voice boomed through the megaphone. He said, "Come on, Miss, walk towards me very slowly."

Jessica felt weak with shock. Why did the police want her? Or did they want Dean? Perhaps he had done something, the girl wondered.

She got out of the car and went to turn to look for Dean, but the sheriff said to the girl: "Don't turn round, come here now! Come on Miss!"

But Jessica did look round. And she saw a wild-eyed, grinning man in a convict's uniform. In one hand he held an axe that was covered in blood, and with the other hand he was beating on the boot of the car with Dean Backley's severed head. Jessica let out a scream, and the insane New Orleans axeman, Nathan Webster, raised his axe in a triumphant gesture. The police marksmen opened fire and killed him instantly.

Jessica never married and spent the remainder of her life as an eccentric recluse in a secluded shack in Georgia.

Someone else who had a close shave with death, but was spared because of a strange turn of fate, was West Point graduate, Colonel Frederick D. Grant, the oldest son of the American president Ulysses S. Grant. On 23

June 1876, he was enthusiastically making prepara-
tions to accompany the 7th Cavalry into the Black Hills
to locate and kill the Sioux Indians led by Chief Crazy
Horse. However, Colonel Grant received news that his
young wife was about to give birth to their first child,
so he was given compassionate leave. The 7th Cavalry
went ahead with its "Indian hunt" mission – under
General Custer. On that very day, Custer and his 266
men were ambushed at Little Bighorn by Chief Crazy
Horse and his 3,500 braves. None of the Cavalrymen
survived. Colonel Grant lived to the ripe old age of
seventy-two.

Another chilling lucky escape took place in August
1969. Novelist Jerzy Kosinski was fuming because a
French airline clerk had accidentally sent his luggage
to New York instead of Los Angeles. This meant that
Kosinski would be late for a Hollywood party he'd
been invited to by his friend, Voytek Frykowski. When
Kosinski did finally arrive at the party his blood ran
cold, because his friend Frykowski was dead, along
with the other party guests and the host, actress
Sharon Tate. Several disciples of the cult leader,
Charles Manson, had gatecrashed the party before
going on an horrific killing spree. One guest had been
decapitated and the others – including the heavily
pregnant Sharon Tate – had been stabbed to death.
But for the airline clerk's error, Jerzy Kosinski would
also have been murdered.

Changes in the weather have also been known to
affect historical events. The sudden gales that swept
the English Channel in 1588 and thwarted the Spanish
Armada are a case in point. There was a similar twist of
meteorological fate in August 1945, when the United
States Superfortress plane, *Boch's Car*, headed for the

skies over Japan with an atomic bomb in its hold. The target was the Japanese industrial city of Kokura, which had a population of 400,000. During the journey to destroy Kokura, a storm suddenly swept towards the target city, so the pilot, Charles Sweeney, headed for the secondary target: Nagasaki. The Superfortress released its atomic bomb and 36,000 men, women and children were killed. Over 60,000 were seriously injured. By a fluke of the weather, the 400,000 inhabitants of Kokura had been spared.

My Brother's Keeper

Around the year 1900, two brothers, Sean and Davy Murphy, were quarrelling in a Liverpool pub with the formidable sons of the O'Malley family. Young Mary O'Malley, who had just turned sixteen, had confessed to her father that the boy who had made her pregnant was nineteen-year-old Davy Murphy, so Gerald O'Malley had told his sons to teach the scoundrel Murphy a lesson he'd never forget. It had been three of the O'Malleys against Davy, until the latter's older brother came on the scene. Sean was something of a pugilist, and he thrashed the O'Malley brothers within inches of their lives, then told Davy to get out of Liverpool. Sean knew that the O'Malleys had a legion of cousins in the south end of Liverpool called the Fitzgibbons, who were one of the most feared and violent families in the city. Even the police were reluctant to intervene in feuds if the Fitzgibbons were involved, such was their reputation for belligerence.

Sean's fears of repercussions were well founded, and an army of Fitzgibbons arrived in the neighbourhood intent on wrecking the home of the Murphys. But for the intervention of a priest, there would have been "blood on the moon", to use an old Irish idiom.

Davy Murphy had been out courting another girl during all the trouble, and when he saw his brother Sean hobbling down the street towards him he barely recognized him. Sean's face was black and blue.

"You're the cause of all this!" Sean told his brother, and pointed at his own bruised and bloodied face.

"How's mother and father?" Davy said with a concerned look.

"They'd have been lynched only for Father O'Leary!" Sean bawled, and he gave his brother instructions. "You're to go to Uncle Desmond. He'll put you up for a while, then you're to leave Liverpool."

"Why should I back down to the O'Malleys?" Davy asked, feeling intimidated by Sean's extreme proposal.

"Because you're nothing but a liability to the family. Trouble follows you around no matter where you go and I'm tired of fighting your battles. I'm no longer your keeper," Sean answered.

Davy ran off in a temper. He went to his Uncle Desmond's, but wasn't with him long before he was causing trouble again. He told a beautiful girl he met that she should stay with him because his uncle had a fortune and had named him as the sole benefactor in his will. The girl told her brother, who in turn told a gang of petty housebreakers, and they broke into Desmond's house one afternoon and ransacked the place, looking for the non-existent fortune Davy had told the girl of. When Desmond learned that the break-in had been caused by a lie Davy had fabricated to impress a girl, he turfed out his troublesome nephew.

By 1905, Davy Murphy had emigrated to America; he was living in San Francisco and working as a labourer. He often wondered whether he should get in contact with his parents and brother Sean in Liverpool to patch things up with them, so one day he got a friend to write a letter on his behalf, as Davy could hardly read or write. Each day Davy expected a letter from Liverpool, but there was no reply. Surely his family had forgiven all the trouble he'd brought upon them by now?

A year later, something quite unexpected happened. At precisely 2 a.m. on the morning of 18 April 1906, a familiar voice roused Davy Murphy from his sleep.

"Davy! Wake up will you?" the voice bellowed from outside.

Davy opened his eyes and recognized the voice. It was Sean; he was outside the lodging house. Davy went to the window, opened it, and stared down at the familiar young man with the flat cap. It was Sean.

"Sean!" Davy was elated, and he put his trousers on and ran barefooted downstairs to let his brother in. As soon as he opened the door, Davy saw that Sean wore an anxious expression. Davy expected his brother to break some dreadful news, so he asked if his parents were all right.

Sean nodded and said: "For heaven's sake, Davy, get out of town or you'll never see the dawn!"

"What are you talking about?" Davy asked, and watched in amazement as Sean turned and ran off into the darkness, shouting: "This is the last time I'll save your neck, brother!"

Davy panicked. He had caused so much trouble with people across America in the few years he'd been there, and he wondered if someone was out for revenge on him again. Davy lost no time in packing his bags and hitting the road. He walked for miles, constantly looking over his shoulder, expecting to be lynched for getting that policeman's daughter into trouble, or receiving a hatchet in the head because of the time he'd painted the word "Tong" on the door of a Chinatown opium den he was refused entry to. Davy had made so many enemies on his travels, some of them were bound to catch up with him sooner or later – but how could Sean come to warn him? That was a real puzzler.

Minutes before the sun came up that morning, as Davy Murphy reached the outskirts of the city, San Francisco was shaken by a terrible earthquake. Buildings crumbled and around 700 people lost their lives. Most of the water mains were ruptured, so the raging fires were allowed to raze 4 square miles (10 square km) of the city to the ground.

Later on that apocalyptic day, Davy realized that Sean's warning had saved his life, and he prayed that his visiting brother had not been killed by the terrible earthquake. But three months later, Davy learned the strange truth from a man named Harris who had recently arrived in California from Liverpool. Harris said he was sorry to break the tragic news, but Sean Murphy had died from pneumonia – over a year ago.

"No, you've been misinformed," Davy told Harris. "Sean visited me on the morning of the earthquake."

"As true as God's in heaven, Davy," Harris asserted with a sombre voice, "Your brother died. I attended the funeral."

Davy Murphy heard the same tragic news from two other people who later arrived from Liverpool.

In the end, Davy returned to Liverpool and learned

that it was true. His brother had indeed passed away. Then how did Sean come to San Francisco to issue the warning that saved Davy's life?

"It was his ghost, Davy," said Mrs Murphy, "He was always worrying about you when he was alive, and even in death he was his brother's keeper."

Davy couldn't contain his sorrow and sobbed like a baby. He never courted trouble again after that day.

The Ashes

In 1985, a seventy-six-year-old pensioner named Maud lost her husband, Bill, to cancer. The couple – who lived in the Lancashire area of England – were inseparable, and Bill knew that when he died, Maud would feel so alone and lost. In the last conversation the couple had before Bill passed away, Maud said life without him would be unbearable, and Bill replied, "Keep your chin up love, because if there is a life after this one, I'll be there looking over you night and day. When the worst happens, just carry on and pretend I'm in the room with you."

Bill was cremated, and Maud kept his ashes in an ornamental urn which stood by her bed. Each night before she switched off the light, she would say good-night to the urn. She knew it was silly, but it was a way of coping with her terrible loss.

In the Christmas of 1985, Maud went into town to do some shopping. She entered a large department store, and during the shopping trip she went to the ladies toilet. Instead of hanging her handbag on a hook, she put it on the floor. Within seconds, someone had reached under the toilet door and snatched

Maud's bag. That bag had contained her pension book, £400 in cash that she'd saved to buy her grand-children Christmas presents, her late husband's wallet and his wedding ring, and a cashcard along with her PIN number, which she'd foolishly scrawled on a piece of paper in the purse because she never could remember the four-digit code. Maud reported the theft to the manager of the store and the police, who gave the unfortunate pensioner a lift home in a squad car. Because she didn't have the keys, a little boy in the street had to get in through the bathroom window so he could open the door for her.

Maud went upstairs to the bedroom and sobbed. She held the urn containing Bill's ashes and hugged it as she cried. She said, "Oh, Bill. How could someone do this to me? Help me, Bill."

On the following morning the phone rang, and Maud answered it. A man said he was the manager of the department store where her handbag had been stolen. He said he had found the handbag intact, with nothing missing. She only had to collect it and sign for it. What was more, the manager said, he'd give Maud a free Christmas hamper because of the trauma she'd been through.

Maud was elated. She used the money a sympa-thetic neighbour had given her to take a taxi to the department store – but when she arrived the manager was baffled. He said, "I didn't call you, and no one has reported finding your handbag. Someone must be pulling your leg. I'm so sorry."

Maud asked, "But how would they know my tele-phone number?"

"Oh dear," said the manager of the department store, and he looked at Maud and said, "I hope I'm wrong, Maud, but the person who phoned you could be one of the people who stole your bag. Perhaps he told you to come here just to get you out of the house so he and his associates can empty it; because I assume they have the keys. They were probably watching you as you left the house."

"Oh no," Maud started to shake. The manager ran to the nearest phone and alerted the police. By the time the police got to Maud's house, the robbers had already paid a visit and had stripped the place of anything valuable. Jewellery, the video, the television, everything that was worth something was gone – even the phone. Maud was led to the bedroom to survey the way the robbers had left it in a mess and she saw, to her complete horror, that the ornamental china urn containing her husband's ashes had also been taken. Maud actually felt faint when she realized that the urn had gone; she collapsed onto the bed and was later taken to hospital. Maud's blood pressure rose because of the shock and she spent a restless night in the hospital.

At around 3 a.m. Maud awoke and saw her husband Bill standing at the foot of the bed. He was surrounded by a silvery aura of light, and was smiling at her.

"Bill. Is that you?" Maud said, raising her hands to the vision of her late husband.

"Yes, dear. Everything's going to be just fine. Go to sleep. Everything will be okay in the morning. Now go to sleep," said Bill, in a very calm manner.

"But, Bill, you're . . ." Maud couldn't finish the sentence.

"I know, but I'm waiting somewhere very near. I still feel very much alive. I gave those cowards who took your bag quite a scare. Now go to sleep. You need rest," said Bill, and he started fading away. Suddenly, there was no one at the foot of the bed any more.

Maud closed her eyes. She felt much better after seeing Bill, and she slept soundly.

At 10 a.m., two policemen called in to the ward and told Maud some strange news. The criminals who had taken the handbag and robbed the house were a woman named Jackie and her boyfriend, Giles. They had confessed to stealing the handbag and the house-breaking after something strange happened. Giles had been blinded, and was still being treated in hospital. He had opened the burial urn and was peering into it with his girlfriend, laughing, when some of the ashes literally shot out of the urn and blasted Giles in the eyes. Jackie washed her boyfriend's eyes, but still Giles couldn't see. In the end she took him to the hospital, and the doctors in casualty asked him how he had got the suspicious-looking ash in his eyes. Giles was in agony and he told medical staff the whole heinous story. The police were called in and charged the couple.

Then Maud remembered the vision of her husband in the wee small hours, and how he'd told her that he had scared the people who took her handbag and ransacked her home. The incident was investigated by the Psychical Research Society and, as is usual in these cases, the whole episode was filed away for posterity. It took three months for the robber's eyesight to return, and an ophthalmologist who treated him said he could not explain the blindness.

Maud was later reunited with the urn, and still talks to it.

I Saw What You Did

The following incident happened in Seattle in the United States in the early 1970s, and illustrates the often spooky nature of coincidence. One Saturday night in July 1974, two fifteen-year-old girls, Diane Chester and Carolyn Berry, were babysitting at the home of the Keel family. Mr and Mrs Keel were visiting relatives 20 miles (32 km) out of town and weren't due back until two o'clock in the morning.

Diane was the mischievous one, and her friend Carolyn was always telling her to stop playing pranks on people. Around 9.30 p.m., Diane suddenly picked the phone up and dialled the number of a boy she liked at school. When he answered, Diane started breathing heavily down the phone, then said, "I think you're the hottest, sexiest boy in my school and I want to make out with you right now. My name is Carolyn Berry," then Diane hung up and fell about laughing. Her friend Carolyn told her to act her age, and was very upset about the nuisance call her friend had made. Diane said she was sorry to her friend, then announced, "I've got a really cool idea; we phone up someone at random and pretend we know some secret they're keeping. Everyone's got a skeleton in the cupboard. Shall we?"

"No," said Carolyn, "It's an offence to misuse the telephone. Grow up and watch television or get into a book." Then Carolyn went into the kitchen and looked for some ice cream in the freezer. While Carolyn was in the kitchen, she heard her friend messing about on the phone again. Carolyn ran into the living room and heard Diane say, "Hello there, mister. I saw what you did the other night and it wasn't very nice."

There was a pause at the other end of the phone, then a man said, "What do you want?"

Diane covered the mouthpiece of the phone and giggled. She then continued her bluff. She said, "I want money. Or I'll go to the cops."

Suddenly the grandfather clock struck 10 p.m., and Diane started laughing. Carolyn rushed over to the phone and slammed her hand down on the receiver, disconnecting Diane.

"You are a complete bore, Carolyn," said Diane, all annoyed.

The two girls then settled down to watch a movie on the television.

About twenty minutes later, the front doorbell rang. The girls were a bit nervous, because the Keel family had told them that no one would be calling tonight.

Diane went to the door and shouted, "Who is it?"

There was no reply. After a few tense moments, a voice answered, "The police."

Diane opened the door – and saw that it wasn't the police. It was a big, overweight man aged around fifty, with a shock of white hair. He barged into the house and pushed Diane backwards. The girl screamed and fell to the floor, and the man closed the door behind him and bolted it.

Carolyn ran over to the phone and dialled 911 for the police, but the line was dead. The man had cut the phone wires outside.

The man produced a gun and said, "Sit down on the sofa. Go on!"

The girls sat there, trembling. Suddenly the man asked, "What did you see?"

The teenagers looked at him with a blank expression. What was he talking about?

"Come on!" shouted the man, "You phoned me up and said you'd seen what I did! You tried to blackmail me – didn't you?"

Diane realized with horror that her prank on the phone had backfired, and she quickly explained: "No, sir, that was just me fooling about. I never saw you do anything."

"Liar!" screamed the man, and he pointed the gun at the girl, saying, "I'm gonna count to five, and if you don't tell me what you saw and how you saw me, I'll blow your brains out! I'll do it! One ... Two ..."

"I didn't see anything," sobbed Diane, and her friend started crying too. Suddenly the baby upstairs started to howl, disturbed by all the shouting.

Meanwhile, the crazy gunman continued counting: "Three ... Four ..."

"I swear I don't know! I swear!" Diane pleaded to the man with tears steaming down her face.

"Right, you're dead," said the man, and he stood there, ready to pull the trigger.

But he never fired. The man put the gun in his pocket and sat on an armchair, then he began to sob. He said, "I didn't mean to kill her. I just hit her, and she fell and knocked her head." The man then became incoherent and buried his head in his hands, crying. Carolyn tiptoed over to the door and unbolted it. She opened the door and ran for her life. The man still didn't look up, so Diane ran out of the house too.

The girls alerted the police, and soon the house was surrounded. The gunman didn't resist arrest, and calmly accompanied the police officers to a squad car. It turned out that the man had accidentally killed his wife a week before, after slapping her across the face during a heated argument. The woman had fallen and hit her head on a coffee table, and had died instantly. The man had put the body in a bag and driven to a refuse tip to dispose of it. Then, of course, young Diane phoned him saying she'd seen what he'd done and, by pure coincidence, the killer had heard the distinctive sounds of a rare nineteenth-century grand-father clock chiming in the background as the girl spoke. The man had mended that very same clock for the Keel family two months ago, and also knew the family quite well. He knew that Mr and Mrs Keel would be away while their regular baby-sitters were in the house. There was also another chilling coinci-dence; the murderer lived less than 100 yards (91 m) from the home of the Keels, and could even see the silhouette of Diane talking to him on the phone that summer night.

Astounding Coincidences

In 1938, the playwright A.J. Talbot wrote a one-act comedy called *Chez Boguskovsky*, which was about a man called Boguskovsky who steals a painting from the Louvre in Paris. Months later, in August 1938, a painting was stolen from the Louvre and when the thief was caught, police discovered that his surname was Boguskovsky.

On 13 February 1746, a Frenchman named Jean Marie Dubarry was executed for the murder of his father. Exactly one hundred years later on 13 February 1846, another Frenchman named Jean Marie Dubarry was also executed for killing his father.

The dreadful day of 30 May 1867 wasn't likely to be forgotten by Princess Maria del Pozzo della Cisterno. It was the day of her wedding to the King of Italy's son, Amadeo, the Duke of D'Aosta. On what should have been the happiest day of her life, the princess's wardrobe mistress hanged herself, then the palace gatekeeper slashed his own throat after a bout of depression. Then the colonel leading the wedding procession fell down dead from the effects of sunstroke. Hours later, the stationmaster fell under the wheels of the honeymoon train and was horribly crushed to death. Not long after that, the king's aide fell from his horse and died, and then the best man became emotionally unstable because of a personal problem and shot himself.

The nineteenth-century pioneering French science-fiction writer, Jules Verne, certainly had more hits than misses when he described the future of space travel. In his stories *From the Earth to the Moon*, and its sequel, *Round the Moon*, Verne gave uncannily accurate descriptions of the Apollo Moon missions which lay one hundred years ahead. Verne launched his rocket from Cape Town, Florida, USA, which is only miles away from the actual place where NASA launched its moon rockets – Cape Canaveral, Florida. Verne's rocket was named *Columbiad*, and NASA's first rocket to take Apollo 11 to the moon was named *Columbia*. There were three men in Verne's fictional rocket and there were three astronauts in the Apollo command module too. The rocket in the French author's book travelled at 25,000 mph (40,000 kph) and reached the moon in four days and one hour, whereas NASA's rocket travelled at 24,000 mph (38,400 kph) and reached the moon in four days and six hours. Furthermore, Jules Verne seems to have foreseen the near-fatal disaster concerning Apollo 13; in one of his space travel tales, the spaceship *Columbiad* is prevented from continuing on its voyage to the moon because of an oxygen explosion. The *Columbiad* then has to perform a complicated "slingshot" manoeuvre to catapult it back towards the Earth, where it splashes down in the Pacific to be rescued by a ship. All of the aforementioned events actually took place in April 1970 when Apollo 13 roared into the blue. There was an explosion on board the craft caused by an electrical short circuit which ignited an oxygen cell. The craft had insufficient power to complete its mission and had to perform a complicated slingshot orbital manoeuvre around the moon in order to gather the momentum needed to return it to Earth. The craft, like all the Apollo spaceships, then splashed down in the Pacific to be rescued by a US Navy ship.

On 5 December 1664, a ship sank with eighty-one passengers on board in the Menai Strait off north Wales. There was one survivor: a red-haired man named Hugh Williams. On 5 December 1785, a ship sank with eighty passengers on board, again in the Menai Strait. The only survivor was a red-haired man named Hugh Williams. On 5 December 1800, a ship sank in the Menai Strait with twenty-five people on board, and all the passengers drowned except for one: a red-haired man named Hugh Williams.

In 1911 three murderers were hanged in London for killing Sir Edmund Bury at Greenberry Hill. The surnames of the executed men were Green, Berry and Hill.

In April 1975 in Detroit, USA, Joseph Figlock was walking past an apartment block when something landed on him, almost knocking him unconscious. It was a baby that had accidentally fallen fourteen storeys. The baby survived, and as if that event wasn't

incredible enough, it took place again a year later
when Figlock was once more strolling past the high-
rise block. Once again Figlock was hit on the head by
another baby, and both he and the child survived the
astounding incident.

Who Played Cupid?

The following strange but true incident took place in
Los Angeles in the spring of 1994. It concerns a
condition most of us have experienced in our younger
days: the pangs of unrequited love, the emotional
agony of being infatuated with a person who doesn't
even know you exist. But this tale of unanswered love
has a bit of a twist to it.

In March 1994, Lance Warren, a twenty-three-year-
old burglar alarm installer from Orange County, just
outside Los Angeles, became intensely infatuated with
a twenty-five-year-old divorcee, Hannah Shulkind,
who lived in Santa Monica. Lance had only spent a day
in the woman's company, installing a burglar alarm,
and he had fallen head over heels in love with her. Lance
had sensed that Hannah was a lonely lady, disappointed with the way her life had gone after a messy
divorce. The alarm installer really had found his version
of Miss Right in Hannah Shulkind: she was as beautiful
inside as she was on the outside; like Lance, she loved
animals, and had adopted four dogs. Hannah had told
Lance that she thought her soulmate was somewhere
out there in the big city, perhaps even in another
country somewhere, but reckoned she would never find
him. Lance had wanted to tell Hannah there and then
that he might be that guy, but Lance was the introverted

type, and never said a word. He wished he could turn back the clock so he could tell Hannah how he had been looking for someone like her for so long.

In the meantime, Lance couldn't stop thinking about Hannah. He drove his car past her home most days, just to catch a fleeting glimpse of his secret object of devotion. His stomach turned over whenever he caught sight of the young woman. He even dreamed of her. Lance never even told his closest friend Danny about his secret crush, because he knew his mate would tell him to grow up and snap out of it, or something insensitive along those lines.

Then one Saturday afternoon, something quite bizarre happened. Lance's phone rang. He answered it and an English-sounding voice said: "Hello, is that Mr Lance Warren?"

"Yeah," said Lance.

"Are you still interested in Miss Shulkind?" the well-spoken caller asked.

"Hey?" Lance recoiled with shock.

"Do you still have romantic aspirations regarding Miss Shulkind?" said the Englishman.

Lance glanced about suspiciously, wondering if he was on *The All-New Candid Camera Show*. The young man really did think it was a wind-up of some sort. "Who is this?" Lance asked.

"That isn't important, but you can call me George," said the mysterious caller.

Lance was naturally intrigued. He hadn't told anyone about his feelings towards Hannah, so how did the caller know how he felt about her? It was really baffling. Lance asked "George" to explain how he knew so much.

"I'm not allowed to say actually, and it's really

beside the point. Are you still in love with Miss Shulkind?"

Lance's face burnt with embarrassment, and he finally muttered: "Yeah, I suppose so."

There was a pause, then George said: "Right. We've made arrangements for you to dine with Miss Shulkind on Monday evening at eight o'clock. We will mail further details to you soon. Good day."

Lance said: "Hey! George! What do you mean?"

But George hung up. Lance keyed in the trace code on his phone, but the caller's number was evidently untraceable. Lance was suddenly very nervous. He racked his brains trying to fathom out how anyone could know about his love for Hannah. It just didn't make sense. Lance was standing at the front of his house first thing Monday morning, waiting for the postman to arrive with his mail. The bemused postman handed Lance the mail and asked: "Waiting for a love letter?" Lance was so paranoid he said: "Are you in on this too?"

The postman didn't know what Lance was talking about. He turned and quickly left.

Among Lance's bills there was a manila envelope. Lance carefully opened it. On a pink card there was the message: "A table has been booked for you and Hannah Shulkind at the Matsuhisa Restaurant. Please arrive at eight p.m. All the expenses are on me."

Below the unsigned message was a small diagram showing where the restaurant was. Then Lance noticed a piece of A2 sized paper in the manila envelope. A message on it said: "Here is a copy of the letter forwarded to Miss Shulkind on your behalf." And what followed was what can only be described as a long-winded love letter, telling Miss Shulkind how much he loved her. It contained sophisticated words Lance hadn't even heard of before, but it was a very touching letter, and read like the work of some romantic novelist. Lance's stomach turned. He felt as if some interfering snooper was watching him. The alarm installer had to tell someone. So he told his friend Danny about the strange developments, and he showed him the letter from the mysterious George character who had phoned him. Danny was a rather imaginative person who loved talking about government conspiracies and UFO cover-ups, and he excitedly told Lance that he was probably being used by the CIA. Lance said that was ridiculous and didn't make sense. Danny advised his friend to go along to the restaurant just to see what happened.

Lance became more nervous as the hours ticked by. He borrowed his cousin's tuxedo, and Danny drove him to the restaurant, which was situated on La Cienaga Boulevard in the Beverly Hills area. Lance entered the upmarket restaurant and Danny watched from his car, which was parked further down the boulevard. Literally seconds later, a sleek black Mercedes with gold-tinted windows pulled up outside the restaurant and out stepped Hannah Shulkind in a beautiful red flowing satin dress. She looked absolutely stunning. She entered the restaurant and Lance's stomach got the butterflies. He rose from his seat at the reserved table and held out his trembling hand. Hannah giggled and reached out, and Lance kissed her hand. They both then sat at the table. The waiter came over with the menu and after the couple had ordered, Hannah told Lance that he was very romantic and imaginative. But Lance felt uncomfortable because of the bizarre events which had brought them together. Hannah looked at he young man in surprise as he just sat and stared at his hands, feeling like a fake and a failure. But Lance then added that he agreed with everything the love letter had stated. He said he had fallen in love with Hannah the moment he had first set eyes upon her. Hannah started to smile, and by the end of the night, the couple were holding hands and kissing like schoolkids on a first date. In the following year, Hannah and Lance were married. They spent many hours trying to work out who had been the mysterious Cupid who had gone to so much trouble to bring them together. They never did find out, but at the wedding reception in Los Angeles, a parcel arrived containing a gold-plated electric toaster. The gift-tag simply said it was from "George".

There's a strange epilogue to this unusual but touching incident. In 1997, a nurse who worked in the world-famous Cedars Sinai Medical Center in Beverly Hills, heard of the apparently supernatural match-making skills of the enigmatic George on a local radio programme, and she telephoned the radio station to tell how she too had met her husband through the strange intervention of an old man who called himself George. The nurse was shocked to receive a Valentine card from a literary agent named Richard, who lived in the Fairfax area. That same day, Richard received a Valentine from the nurse, yet neither of them had sent the other a card. The finger of suspicion couldn't be pointed at friends either, because the nurse had told no one about her feeling towards the literary agent, and Richard had certainly never discussed his interest in the nurse. When they both discovered that someone had duped them they were a bit uneasy, yet glad in a way that the unknown person had brought them together. About three months later, Richard found a Ray Bradbury book on his study desk, which struck him as strange, because he had never read the fantasy writer's works. In the book there was a slip of paper that had been inserted at the title page of a romantic tale called *A Story of Love*. A message on the slip of paper, inscribed in impeccable calligraphy, simply stated, "I sent the Valentines, Richard" and it was signed, "George".

There was no one who could have had access to the agent's home, which was not only alarmed with motion detectors, but also under the constant watch of a closed-circuit television system. Richard patiently checked the five hours of videotaped footage which showed the driveway and rear entrance of his home but there was nothing amiss. No one had come anywhere near his home, so Richard was left with the uneasy assumption that George had been some sort of paranormal entity, even though the agent was highly sceptical of anything remotely connected with the supernatural. Out of burning curiosity, Richard contacted a friend who worked in a forensic lab for the Los Angeles Police Department, and he asked him to scrutinize the book he'd found in his study for finger-prints. Richard's friend scanned the paperback for prints, and the only ones he could detect belonged to Richard, which really unnerved the literary agent.

The Erdington Murders Coincidences

On 27 May 1817, the body of a murder victim, twenty-year-old Mary Ashford, was found in a flooded sandpit at Erdington, a village lying five miles (8 km) outside

Birmingham, England. Exactly 157 years afterwards to the very day and hour of the Ashford murder, history repeated itself in a most brutal and chilling way when twenty-year-old Barbara Forrest was strangled and left in the long grass near to the children's home in Erdington where she was employed as a nurse. This may seem nothing more than a coincidence, but more intriguing similarities and parallels between the two murders came to light when the police were investigating the Barbara Forrest murder. As a police archivist officer read through the Ashford murder of 1817 he shook his head in disbelief. Whit Monday had been on 26 May both in 1817 and 1975 – the year of the Barbara Forrest murder. Like Ashford, Barbara Forrest had been raped before being murdered and both victims were found within 300 yards (274 m) of one another. Ashford and Forrest shared the same birth date, and the coincidences didn't stop there. Both girls had visited their best friend on the evening of the Whit Monday to change into a new dress for a local dance party. After each murder a suspect was arrested whose name was Thornton and, in both instances, this Mr Thornton was charged with murder but subsequently acquitted.

Let us take a closer look at these uncanny coincidences. At 6.30 a.m. on 27 May 1817, a labourer on his way to work in Erdington came upon a heap of blood-stained clothes belonging to a woman, near to Penn's Mill. He informed the police and during a search of the area around the suspicious find, they saw two tracks of footprints made by a man and a woman which led towards a flooded sandpit,

The police followed the two sets of footprints and saw that they ended at the edge of the water around the pit. The pit was searched and the corpse of a well-known and well-loved local girl named Mary Ashford was recovered. Her arms were heavily bruised and her remaining clothing was bloodstained. Police made enquiries with the locals and soon established Miss Ashford's last movements on the previous day. On Whit Monday – 26 May – Mary had travelled from Erdington to Birmingham to sell dairy produce at the local market. She had then made arrangements to visit a friend's house where she would change into a new dress. Then she and her friend, Hannah Cox, would go to the Whitsuntide dance at the Tyburn House Inn in the evening. Mary had arrived at her friend's house at six in the evening. She had changed into the new dress and had then gone to the dance with Hannah, where the two girls seemed to have enjoyed themselves. They'd had no shortage of male admirers, although for a majority of the evening, Mary had been in the company of a young bricklayer named Abraham Thornton, while her friend had been dancing with a boy named Benjamin Carter. The dance ended around midnight, and the foursome headed towards their respective homes as far as a place known as the Old Cuckoo, which lay just a short distance from Erdington village. Hannah and Benjamin then separated from Mary and Abraham and went off in another direction.

Later on, about 3.30 a.m., Mary Ashford was seen walking towards the home of Hannah Cox's mother. A witness mentioned that the girl was "walking very slowly and alone". At the house of Hannah's mother, Mary took off her new dress and changed into her working clothes. She told Hannah she was going home then said goodbye to her friend and left the house at 4 a.m. On two more occasions that morning Mary Ashford was seen. A Joseph Dawson testified that he had set eyes on the girl in Bell Lane around 4.15 a.m., and about ten minutes after that, Mary had been seen again in that same lane by Thomas Broadhurst. Both witnesses noted that Mary had been alone in Bell Lane.

Not long after these inquiries into Mary Ashford's last movements, the police interviewed Abraham Thornton, who seemed in a state of shock after being told that Mary had been raped and murdered, probably by strangulation.

Thornton told detectives: "I cannot believe she is murdered; why, I was with her until four o'clock this morning."

Thornton seemed sincere enough and apparently didn't grasp the fact that he was the chief suspect in the murder investigation. However, he soon understood the situation when he was taken into custody later that day and searched. Detectives grilled him about every detail of the events which unfolded after he had left Tyburn House Inn with Mary. Thornton admitted that he'd had sexual intercourse with Mary, but he denied he had raped and murdered the girl. In a deposition the bricklayer stated that when his friend Benjamin Carter, and Mary's friend Hannah Cox, had left them, he and Mary had strolled hand in hand over a field to a stile. The couple sat talking for about fifteen minutes then went to the Green at Erdington where Mary went into her friend's house to change her dress. Abraham had waited for quite some time but Mary did not come out so he went home alone. Thornton's statement was backed up by three other witnesses who had seen him at that time. One witness, a game-keeper named John Haydon, had even chatted to the young man for over a quarter of an hour. The police continued their investigation into the murder of Mary Ashford, but came up against a brick wall. No one had seen the murder victim and Abraham Thornton together after they had been sighted at the stile at the top of Bell Lane at three in the morning, a fact which provided the police with a real headache.

Thornton was brought to trial in August that year at the Warwick Assize Court before Mr Justice Holroyd. Hundreds of people who believed Thornton had killed Mary Ashford had waited outside the courthouse from six in the morning. All of them hoped they'd be the first to hear that a verdict of guilty had been reached, but they were to be disappointed. After just six minutes of deliberation, the jury returned a verdict of "not guilty". In modern English law that verdict would have been final, but in the early nineteenth century an ancient law existed which enabled Mary Ashford's brother, William, to appeal against the jury's verdict and thus demand a second trial. This was duly done and on 17 November 1817, Abraham Thornton once again stood in the dock, this time before Lord Ellenborough at the Court of the King's Bench. By now interest in the Mary Ashford murder had reached fever pitch in every corner of Britain, and the Fleet Street news hounds were delighted at this dramatic turn in the case. Legal history was made when Lord Ellenborough allowed Thornton to take advantage of an archaic law called "Trial by Battel". This ancient right necessitated Thornton renewing his plea of "not guilty" before throwing down a gauntlet from the dock. This signified a challenge to William Ashford for a fight to the death, unless one of them surrendered or was incapacitated during the fight.

There were objections to the Trial by Battel option,

but Lord Ellenborough proudly announced to the court: "It is the law of England!"

If Ashford accepted the challenge and won, Thornton would be executed immediately, but if Thornton won, he would have to be freed and would no longer have to appear in court in connection with the Ashford murder.

Abraham Thornton held what resembled a heavy leather mitten with a trailing feather attached, and invoked the ancient English law. He declared he was innocent and that he was ready to defend his innocence with his body. He lifted the gauntlet above his head, then hurled it down from the dock as the pressmen scribbled furiously.

William Ashford's counsel disputed Thornton's right to Trial by Battel and criticized Lord Ellenborough for allowing such an alternative to a proper second trial, but the protestations came to nothing. Because William Ashford had not responded to Abraham Thornton's challenge by 21 April in the following year, the latter was thoroughly discharged. He would no longer have to stand trial for Mary Ashford's murder, but because of the adverse publicity no one would employ the bricklayer, so he later emigrated to the United States.

To this day, criminologists have tried in vain to determine who murdered Mary Ashford. Now for the facts of the eerie case which has strange echoes of the Ashford murder.

On 27 May 1975, twenty-year-old Barbara Forrest was found dead in the long grass of a ditch near Erdington. She had been raped and strangled, and her body, which was partly clothed, had lain undetected for over a week. Barbara had worked at the nearby

Pype Hayes Children's Home. Her facial features bore an almost identical similarity to those of Mary Ashford and, like Mary, Barbara had been strangled after being raped. The police made inquiries and later arrested Michael Thornton, a Birmingham child care officer who worked at the home where Barbara had also worked. Like the Thornton who stood accused of murdering Mary Ashford in 1817, Michael Thornton was tried for the murder of Barbara Forrest, and he too was later acquitted. Both murders had taken place around the same time of day and, furthermore, both victims had been to a friend's house to change into a new dress before going out on the evening of Whit Monday to a dance.

Stranger still, days before each victim was murdered, they made prophetic remarks about their impending fate. The week before Mary Ashford was murdered, she told Hannah Cox's mother that she had "bad feelings about the week to come", but was unable to elaborate on her sense of dread, and ten days before Barbara Forrest was killed, she told a colleague at work of a strange premonition. Barbara's words had been: "This is going to be my unlucky month. I just know it. Don't ask me why."

Were the "twin" Erdington murders just a spate of uncanny coincidences, or were more sinister forces at work?

The Italian King's Double

In July 1900, King Umberto I of Italy arrived in the town of Monza, near Milan, with his aide-de-camp, General Emilio Ponzio-Vaglia. The king and the general went to a restaurant, and the proprietor approached. He bore an amazing likeness to the monarch, and the king asked the *padrone* what his name was. The proprietor replied that it was Umberto. The king laughed and said, "That is my name also." During the resulting conversation, more bizarre coincidences connecting the king and the restaurateur emerged. Both men had been born on the same day (14 March 1844) in the same town, and they had even married on the same day, both to a woman named Margherita. Each had a son named Vittorio, and on the day of King Umberto's coronation, the other Umberto had opened his restaurant.

The king found these coincidences staggering, and asked his "twin" if they had ever met before. Umberto said that their paths had crossed on two occasions: in 1866 they had both been decorated for bravery, when the king had been a colonel and Umberto had been a private, and in 1870, when each had been promoted to sergeant and corps commander respectively. The restaurateur then returned to his duties, and the king told his aide: "I will make that man a Cavalier of the Crown of Italy tomorrow."

The following day the king summoned his double, but was shocked and saddened to learn that he had just died in a shooting accident. The king sent his aide to Umberto's relatives to find out when the funeral would be held. Shortly afterwards, an assassin opened fire on the king and killed him instantly with two shots through the heart. The funerals of the two Umbertos were subsequently held on the same day.

Saved by the Bell

The following true story, which happened in the early 1970s, suggests that some benevolent force intervened to save scores of schoolchildren from death and serious injury.

One wintry morning in 1973, hundreds of children poured through the gates of St Anne's Roman Catholic Primary School in Adelaide, Australia, quite unaware of the strange event that lay ahead. The road outside the school was coated with sheets of black ice, and the grey heavy skies were laden with snow. Cars slid about as they passed the school, and the children impatiently made their way to the school playground to build snowmen and hurl snowballs at each other.

At nine o'clock the children went from assembly to their classes, but because there was a heavy snowfall that morning, playtime was cancelled, and the children were led into the assembly hall and shown cartoons on an old projector.

At 11.30 a.m. one of the prefects was sent down to the headmaster's office to press the button which activated all the electric bells in the school. The sound of these bells was eagerly awaited by the pupils, who were desperate to get outdoors into the thick snow before going home or going to school dinners. But for some curious reason the bells didn't ring, and one of the teachers glanced at his watch and saw that the time was almost 11.35 a.m. The teacher went down to the headmaster's office and saw the headmaster pressing the bell button repeatedly. "You must have broken it," the headmaster commented to the sulking prefect.

"I haven't, sir," protested the prefect.

"What's the matter?" the teacher asked.

"The bells won't ring," replied the headmaster, rapidly pressing the button set into the wall.

The headmaster's secretary came in, and she said, "There's an auxiliary back-up switch which rings the bells in the storeroom next door."

The headmaster, teacher and the prefect went next door and located a small lever which was housed inside a box mounted on the wall. The headmaster pulled this lever, but still the bells wouldn't ring. "Damn!" shouted the headmaster. He shook his head and turned to the prefect, "You'll have to go to each class and tell them it's lunch break."

As the prefect went to leave the storeroom, there was a terrible crashing noise which literally shook the foundations of the school. The headmaster, the teacher, and the secretary went outside to see what was going on. Two enormous juggernauts that were on their way to the fruit warehouse round the corner had collided with each other on the black ice and they had smashed into the playground and the school gates. One of the juggernauts had turned over and flattened the school railings, but the drivers of the vehicles escaped with only cuts and bruises. However, the headmaster and the teacher soon realized that if the lunchtime bell had rung out, scores of children would have been milling about at the scene of the lorry crash, and many of them would have certainly been killed. In other words, the schoolchildren had literally been saved by the bell.

Out of curiosity, the headmaster later tried out the electric bells of the school. He pressed the button, and all the bells rang, so why hadn't the switch worked at 11.30? An electrician examined the button and the wiring and confessed that he couldn't explain why the bells hadn't rung out on that fateful wintry morning. Was it just some weird coincidence or did someone up there intervene to prevent a tragedy?

Jinxes and Curses

∙∙∙

> "There is no redemption from Hell."
> *Jode*

Curses

Throughout the ages, in all nations, curses have been feared. A curse is an invocation of malevolence, a psychological weapon drawn from the routine armoury of the magician, shaman, or ill-wisher. Today, the psychologists would be quick to dismiss a curse as a simple form of suggestion and explain that a "hex" would only be capable of harming a person who was superstitious, gullible, and expecting trouble in the first place. That would seem to be the rational explanation; the only trouble is that this interpretation fails to account for the many cases of curses that have taken effect on a victim despite his disbelief in the mumbo-jumbo world of the supernatural. Take the case of Robert Heinl, a retired US Marine Corps colonel, who had served on Haiti for six years as the chief of a naval mission. Shortly after his retirement, Heinl wrote a book about the history of Haiti that criticized the ruling dynasty of François "Papa Doc" Duvalier. Heinl was later amused to learn from the newspapers that a curse had been placed on his book. Heinl dismissed the curse as a poor example of psychological warfare – then a streak of misfortune fell upon him. The manuscript of his book went missing; the ex-colonel fell through a stage while giving a speech, badly injuring his leg; a *Washington Post* journalist who was about to interview Heinl about his book was struck down with acute appendicitis; a large, stray dog attacked Heinl near his home and inflicted a serious bite; and finally, on 5 May 1979, Heinl was on holiday with his wife on St Barthelemy Island, near Haiti, when he suddenly dropped dead from a suspected heart attack. Heinl's widow later remarked, "There is a belief that the closer you get to Haiti, the more powerful the magic becomes."

In the mid-1930s a similar fatal curse was made not by a Voodoo magician, but by an elderly, well-respected pearly king called John Goode. The story begins in Bermondsey, London, in the political turmoil of January 1935. It was the year that London became the backdrop to a series of angry marches and provocative rallies. Sir Oswald Mosley led a procession of uniformed anti-Jewish bigots from the newly-formed British Union of Fascists through the East End, and the pacifists marched through the city to demonstrate against the brown-shirted National Socialists in Germany who were sowing the seeds of what would obviously be a major war. In the midst of those turbulent times the pearly kings and queens of London took to the winter streets, and the resplendent glitzy Cockneys were a welcome sight in the depths of the depression.

One famous member of the traditional procession was seventy-five-year-old John Goode. Although plagued with rheumatoid arthritis, the old costermonger from Bermondsey limped on in great pain with the parade until they reached a stopping-off point at a public house near Covent Garden. While enjoying a glass at this pub, Goode met a Geordie labourer, Derek Walker, who had recently moved from Wallsend to Riley Road in Bermondsey. Walker seemed an amiable fellow, and he and Goode conversed and quaffed pint after pint of ale. When the pearly king was leaving, he happened to notice that his wallet was missing. The barman locked the doors of his pub and Derek Walker became very nervous all of a sudden. A quick search of the pub resulted in the discovery of Goode's empty wallet in the toilet. Someone opened the door and called a policeman in, and Goode told the officer that he believed Walker had taken all the money from his wallet, which amounted to £6. Walker was searched and his wallet was examined. It contained £12, which was a lot of money for a labourer to be carrying around in those times. Nevertheless, theft could not be proved, and Walker was free to leave the pub, but the policeman advised the Geordie not to show his face in the area again. As Walker was leaving, John Goode yelled out, "Pay heed to me, you thieving git, for I truly curse you and your family, and it will not end for twenty long years! You'll know it's over, for I'll make your entire world turn to ice!" There were gasps of astonishment from the pearly kings and queens around the public bar, because the curse was so uncharacteristic for a person like Goode, who was renowned for his warm-heartedness. Walker shook his head, confused at the meaning of the old man's words, then promptly left and ran off.

The following January Walker fell on hard times. When he was offered a poorly-paid job at a building site in Westminster, he jumped at the opportunity, but three days after he started work King George V died and Walker was laid off, because the site was near to Westminster Hall. For some obscure reason, Walker was never recalled to work on the site. In January 1937, Walker had an altercation with five members of the British Union of Fascists in an East End pub. It ended with Walker having his ribs cracked, his two front teeth kicked in, and his nose broken. In January 1938, Walker's wife left him and took their two children with her. In January 1939, Walker was at the Southwark offices of the Central Electricity Board paying his bill when an IRA bomb exploded nearby. The bomb blast sent Walker sailing through the air and left him unconscious for two hours. Fragments of glass that were embedded in his face left five unsightly scars. While strolling down Wapping High Street a fortnight after the blast, Walker bumped into a grinning John Goode. Walker remembered the old man's curse, and realized that the theft of the wallet had taken place during the accursed month of January four years previously. Walker darted down a street and ran off. Then in January 1940, the Geordie received his call-up papers. He desperately tried to evade World War II by falsely asserting that he had health problems, but his claims were ignored and he subsequently joined the Cheshire Regiment. While serving with the Cheshires on the South Coast in January 1941, Walker received a letter informing him of the total destruction of his house by German bombers. The following January in Italy, Colin Hunter, Walker's best friend, was blown to smithereens when one of his own mortars detonated itself for no apparent reason. Walker witnessed the tragedy at close range and was severely traumatized for months. In January 1943, Walker caught a sexually transmitted disease from a prostitute while on leave in London. Walker's testicles became so badly infected by the disease, he had to have them removed. Twelve months later the ill-starred Walker dreaded the arrival of another unlucky January. This time, misfortune struck when a German prisoner Walker was guarding suddenly produced a pistol and whipped him across the face, smashing in his nose.

Ill-fortune and calamity continued to plague Walker every January as regular as clockwork. Finally, by January 1955, the star-crossed Geordie was a complete nervous wreck. He had moved back to Tyneside in an effort to escape retribution, for he knew that it was the last year of John Goode's curse, which was prophesied to end with his world turning to ice. Strangely enough that winter was the coldest one on record. Temperatures plunged to an unheard of low, leaving the River Tyne frozen over. Throughout that January, the anxiety-stricken Walker took the utmost care when he journeyed to and from his job at the steel stockholders situated on the waterfront of the frozen river. Each day Walker crossed off the date on the calendar, wondering if he would ever make it out of that troublesome month alive. He finally crossed out the final day of January and tore down that month's page from the calendar. He crumpled the page and tossed it into the fire triumphantly. John Goode's curse had failed; at least that's what Walker thought. On the following day – the first day of February – Walker was on his way to work when he slipped on ice. He crashed to the ground, striking the back of his head. He was rushed to hospital but died of his freak head injury four months later.

In the mid-1980s, a similar fatal curse was made by a middle-aged busman from Cheshire, England, named Frank Macready. In 1986, Frank scrimped and saved to buy a brand new, front-loading video recorder and colour television for his autistic twelve-year-old nephew, Richie Lewis. Richie was overjoyed with the gift and Frank got the boy a couple of Disney videos.

One evening at 9 p.m., Frank returned to his flat and saw that the front door was partly open. At first he thought that his nephew had left the door open, as Frank had given him a key to the flat so he could use the video. Frank had asked Richie to put the video in his own home, but the boy loved Frank's company and preferred coming to his flat to watch the videos. When Frank went into the living room his heart missed a beat. The video had gone, but the new television the video had rested on was still there. There was one curious clue. The glass covering a framed photograph of Richie had been cracked. The photo had stood on the new video, so it seemed that the thief had knocked down the picture during the robbery and cracked its glass, but for some reason had taken the trouble to put the photo back in its place. Frank wondered if his nephew was the culprit, but the child broke down and burst into tears when he learned that his cherished video had been stolen.

Frank went to his local public house and told his best friend Derek about the robbery. Derek patted him on the back and bought him a pint of bitter. Derek said he would keep his eyes open for a second-hand video to replace the stolen one. Frank suddenly said, "I can't understand how anyone could do such a thing. I hope something terrible happens to the coward who took that video!" Most of the drinkers in the pub and the landlady were looking at Frank, who continued to rant about the robbery. Derek told him to calm down and went to the toilet. "I put a curse of death on the person who stole Richie's video! I hope he drops down dead! I do!" Frank shouted.

Seconds later, another friend of Frank's, named Andy, came into the pub and ordered a pint. He noticed that Frank looked irritated and red-faced, and asked him what the matter was. Frank told Andy about the video theft, but Andy just gave him a side-long smirk and said, "Come off it, Frank. You must think I was born yesterday."

"What're you on about?" Frank asked with a perplexed look.

"Everyone knows it was an insurance job," Andy said, quaffing his pint of mild.

"What?" Frank recoiled. He wanted to give Andy a thump for the audacious claim.

Andy smiled and leaned forward to whisper to Frank. He said, "I saw Derek coming out of your place with the video this evening at eight."

"You're kidding," Frank said with a shocked expression. But it made sense. It was Derek who had put the cracked picture of Richie back on the television. Then Frank realized something else. Two weeks ago, the spare Yale key to his flat had gone missing: Derek must have taken it during one of his visits. Andy had presumed that Frank had arranged for his best friend to fake the robbery so he could get the insurance money and sell the video. Frank was furious, and he stormed off to the toilets to have words with his so-called friend, but when he went into the gents, he found Derek dead on the floor. A post-mortem recorded the cause of Derek's death as natural causes, but Frank was convinced that the curse he had put on the video thief had taken Derek's life.

That is not the end of the story. In 1992, Frank's car was stolen as he was visiting his cousin in the Cheshire town of Prestbury. When Frank came out of his cousin's house he glimpsed a red-haired man driving off in his car. When police found the vehicle, the thief had removed the radio-cassette player. The callous criminal had also taken an envelope from the glove compartment of the busman's car which had contained a set of photos of Frank's mother, who had passed away just a few weeks back. The thief had scattered and ripped up the prized photographs. The keys to the car were also missing. Frank was more upset about the torn-up photographs of his late mother than the state of his car.

Two days later, Frank was driving his bus through Bramhall, when an old friend boarded the vehicle and said he had heard about Frank's car being stolen. Frank said, "I hope whoever ripped up those photographs of my Mum meets a terrible death."

Frank uttered those words at precisely 4.30 in the afternoon. At that exact time there was a car crash on the single carriageway almost directly in front of Frank's bus. The driver of the crashed car was catapulted through the windscreen as the vehicle smashed into a concrete lamp post. He bounced along the pavement and Frank stopped the bus and he and his friend ran to the man's aid. The casualty on the pavement was the red-haired man who had stolen Frank's car a couple of days back and torn up the pictures of sentimental value. The man was dead from his injuries. The police later confirmed that the dead man had indeed taken Frank's car because he still had Frank's car keys with him. At the dead man's home, police found twelve radios ripped from various cars, including the radio cassette-player from Frank's car.

Once again, Frank had the eerie impression that he had put a fatal curse on another person who had wronged him.

Were the two deaths just coincidence, or the result of the ancient and well-documented powers of the death curse?

"You're All Going to Hell"

In 1902, a twenty-five-year-old sailor named August Siparis was sentenced to hang for murder in the town of St Pierre on the island of Martinique in the West Indies. Siparis swore at the judge during his trial and said God knew he was innocent. The judge laughed, put on the black cap and said, "You're guilty – you will be hanged."

Siparis became so enraged, he actually broke the chains of his shackles and he cried out, "I am innocent! You are all going to hell! You're all corrupt on this island. You're all going to hell!" As Siparis was blurting out all these condemnations, a part of the courthouse roof fell in and a shaft of sunlight shone upon the condemned man.

Siparis was locked in a tiny prison cell measuring 4 ft by 6 ft (122 cm by 183 cm) with a low ceiling 5 ft (152 cm) from the floor. Siparis was left in total darkness without food or water while the authorities erected a special gallows in the prison yard which would allow the sailor's execution to be seen by most of the island's 30,000 inhabitants. One of the prison guards heard Siparis sobbing in the cell and said, "Don't cry in there. Your ordeal will soon be over." And this sympathetic guard slid two biscuits under the cell door. The prisoner said to the guard, "Thank you. Listen, please take heed; leave the island tonight, or you will be burnt alive." And Siparis explained to the guard that he had dreamt that the Isle of Martinique had been engulfed in a terrible inferno. The guard just laughed and said it had been a nightmare.

On the following morning at six o'clock, a deep rumbling was heard throughout the island. Half a mile (just under 1 km) away, the tip of Mount Pelee then started to glow until it was yellow-hot, and the smell of sulphur filled the air. The guard who had heard the warning from the prisoner told his superior about the strange dream Siparis had experienced, but the head of the prison took no notice. Suddenly, at precisely 7.52 a.m., the glowing mountain of Pelee exploded with the force of an atomic bomb. A hurricane of white hot rock fragments and lava showered the town, and a cloud of superheated steam blasted down on everyone and everything. In the space of two minutes, 30,000 people on the island – including the prison guard Siparis had warned – were burnt alive. People never even had a chance to run from the infernal nightmare; they were simply ignited in their tracks, and then the firestorm which followed blew their ashes away like a giant blowtorch. The town of St Pierre was reduced to smouldering rubble. Only two people survived the catastrophe, a black shoemaker whose house somehow remained standing, and August Siparis – the man in the condemned cell who had told everyone that they were going to hell.

The cell he had been in had been demolished by the volcanic upheaval, but he had somehow survived to witness the horrific scenes of death and destruction.

The prisoner was afterwards reprieved, and the black shoemaker who also survived the tragedy told the authorities that Siparis had warned everyone that they would burn because he was innocent of the murder charge. The authorities seemed afraid of Siparis, and for many years people on the other islands of the West Indies talked about the prisoner of St Pierre who had condemned the bloodthirsty and wicked inhabitants of Martinique to a hell on earth.

Brunel's Jinxed Supership

Mariners are renowned for their superstitions. To the seafarer, the sight of an albatross over a ship is a warning of an approaching storm and, as Coleridge recounted in *The Rime of the Ancient Mariner*, to kill the same bird would bring an eternity of bad luck. Even today there are fishermen who will stay ashore if they happen to meet a priest or nun on the way to their boat, and there are still some seadogs who will refuse to set foot on board a ship that has had its name changed – a superstition that is said to date back to 1867, when a Nova Scotian brigantine named *The Amazon* was renamed *Mary Celeste*. The re-christened ship suffered a catalogue of calamities and was finally found abandoned, drifting near the Azores, in 1872. To this day, no one knows what became of her crew.

Sailors are also cautious about unlucky cargo. When

an allegedly sinister mummy of an Egyptian princess was transferred from the British Museum into the hold of a famous liner in April 1912, many seamen believed their vessel would be jinxed. It may have been sheer coincidence, but the same liner sank on her maiden voyage. She was the *Titanic*.

Another ship which had an unlucky maiden voyage was the 2000-ton steel barque *Hinemoa*. During the voyage in 1892, four apprentice seamen died of typhoid. Then the captain later went insane. The second captain of the barque turned into a ruthless thief and ended up in prison, the third became an alcoholic, the fourth died of "natural causes" in his cabin, and the fifth captain committed suicide by blowing his brains out. The sixth captain of the *Hinemoa* survived the jinxed ship, but under his command the vessel capsized, and two sailors were swept to their deaths when the ship righted itself. Finally, in 1908, the ship became a write-off when she drifted ashore on the west coast of Scotland. An engineer who worked on the barque believed the ship had been jinxed for using tons of soil from an East London graveyard as ballast.

Without a doubt, the unluckiest ship that ever sailed was built at the yards of John Scott Russell in Millwall, London, over a period of three years in the late 1850s. The *Great Eastern* was the brainchild of one of the greatest engineers of all time, Isambard Kingdom Brunel. At 19,000 tonnes, the gigantic ship was the most ambitious engineering project of the nineteenth century. The colossal 692-ft (211-m) long iron-plated double hull of Brunel's supership surpassed the dimensions of Noah's fabled Ark, and she was capable of carrying 4,000 passengers. The ship the maritine world called "wonder of the seas" sported an unheard-of six masts, and since traditional maritime nomenclature could not be applied to them, they were referred to as Monday, Tuesday, Wednesday, Thursday, Friday and Saturday. Motive power was to be supplied by a 24-ft (7-m) steam-driven propeller or gigantic paddle wheels, and should her steam engines fail, the ship would simply unfurl her gargantuan sails. The Herculean vessel would also stockpile enough coal to accomplish a journey from England to Australia and back without the need to refuel.

While the *Great Eastern* was under construction at Millwall, two hundred rivet gangs worked on the ship's novel double hull until all three million rivets had been hammered into place. The outer hull was separated from the inner one by a gap of 3 ft (1 m). Within the hulls there was an innovative arrangement of sixteen watertight bulkheads, designed to make the ship virtually unsinkable. One day in January 1857, during the round-the-clock racket of hammering and banging, somebody noticed that a riveter and his apprentice were missing. The weeks went by, but the two missing men were nowhere to be seen. One riveter, an Irishman, said he had heard a strange pounding coming from within the double hull, but no one took him seriously.

The width of the Thames at the Millwall shipyards was too narrow to allow the *Great Eastern* to be launched lengthways, so the ship had to be ushered into the river sideways, an operation that took an agonizing three months of trying to solve the technical difficulties. During the long wait, Brunel became ill through overwork and worry. He was only fifty-three but looked twenty years older through working for years without adequate sleep. He opened *The Times* one day to discover that the newspaper thought his time-consuming project was a white elephant:

> *There she lies on the very brink of the noble river which is to carry her to the ocean, but she will not wet her lips.*

But the leviathan finally did wet her lips on 31 January 1858 after being eased 330 feet (101 m) down a slipway by buckling hydraulic jacks. Brunel himself remarked that "putting St Paul's to sea would have been easier".

On the very day the *Great Eastern* was launched Brunel was standing on her deck, unable to believe that his creation was finally in service, when he suffered a massive stroke and collapsed. He remained gravely ill for the remaidner of his life, and on 15 September 1859, he died after hearing that a steam pipe had burst on the *Great Eastern* during her trial run to Weymouth. The explosion had destroyed a funnel and the searing cloud of escaping steam had boiled five stokers to death. In a separate tragedy around the same time, another crewman had fallen onto a paddle wheel and been instantly killed. Three members of the ship's crew had talked of hearing pounding noises within the hull before the two tragedies.

The astronomical costs of the delayed launch – over £1 million – ruined the Eastern Navigation Company, which had planned to employ Brunel's ship on long voyages to India and Australia. The Great Ship Company took over the affair and opted for the quick profits of a North Atlantic run. From then on, the unlucky career of the *Great Eastern* started in earnest.

The first planned voyage to the United States in 1861 was cancelled because repair work to the ship's damaged funnel and boiler took longer than expected. The frustrated directors of the Great Ship Company were eager to get some return on their troublesome investment, so they moved the *Great Eastern* to Holyhead, Wales, to put the ship on display to paying sightseers. Shortly after arriving at Holyhead, one of the fiercest gales in living memory blew in from the Irish Sea and tore the *Great Eastern* from her moorings. For eighteen hours she was tossed about in the coastal waters, but she rode the storm well while other ships sank around her, thanks to the vessel's newfangled double hull and waterproofed bulkheads. After the gale had moved away, the *Great Eastern* was an awesome sight as she steamed back from the storm-clouded horizon to Holyhead. However, the storm had caused thousands of pounds worth of damage to the ship's grand salon. Three months later, the *Great Eastern*'s first captain, William Harrison, the coxswain, and the nine-year-old son of the chief purser were drowned when a sudden violent storm swamped their gig as they were going ashore. In the seafaring world, nothing casts a darker shadow over a ship's character than the death of a captain prior to a maiden voyage. So when the news of the three deaths reached London, the directors of the Great Ship Company resigned immediately.

The new board of directors, eager to restore the public's confidence in the seemingly jinxed ship, announced that the *Great Eastern* would leave Southampton for New York on 9 June 1860. It was a financial disaster. All the adverse publicity had earned Brunel's ship a bad reputation. People opted for the smaller, more reliable Cunard ships. Hundreds of tickets for the *Great Eastern*'s voyage were printed, but when 9 June arrived, the ship still wasn't ready because of technical difficulties with its engine. Finally, on 16 June, a mere thirty-five passengers boarded the mammoth vessel. The new captain, who had never made an Atlantic crossing before, commanded a crew of 418. During the twelve-day crossing, poor-quality economy coal caused thick carbonaceous deposits to form on the linings of the funnel casings, which in turn caused the engines to overheat, and this resulted in the main dining room area becoming intolerably hot.

When the *Great Eastern* arrived in New York she was greeted by thousands of cheering sightseers, but things soon turned sour when some of these onlookers attempted to go on board the British ship. They were told that they would have to pay a one dollar admission fee. People who paid the fee were determined to get their money's worth, and they pocketed anything on the ship that was not bolted down for souvenirs.

It was announced that the ship was to make a two-day excursion, and 2,000 people were soon queuing for tickets. But the two-day outing turned into a nightmare when it became apparent that only 300 beds were available. As a result of this, over 1,000 passengers had to sleep on the deck, where cinders and a steady drizzle of soot from the damaged funnels rained down on them. To make matters even worse, a pipe burst in the ship's storage room and soaked the food supplies. The only foods that were salvaged were dried chicken, over-salted meat and stale biscuits and, even for these unsavoury items, passengers were charged extortionate prices. By the time the burst pipe was fixed, all the ship's drinking water had leaked away. The infuriated passengers looked forward to a speedy landing, but even that wasn't straightforward; through some unaccountable navigational error, the *Great Eastern* had drifted way off course during the night and was over 100 miles (160 km) out to sea. When the ship finally reached New York, the hungry, weary passengers fought to disembark. Not surprisingly, when a second excursion was announced only a handful of tickets were purchased. New Yorkers were disappointed with the steamship, so she returned to England, and even this voyage was plagued by misfortune. The screw shaft gave out in mid-Atlantic, and at Milford Haven the ship fouled the rope of a small boat and drowned two of its passengers. Hours after the tragedy, the *Great Eastern* smashed into the frigate *Blenheim*, seriously damaging the latter's hull.

In September 1861, the liner was struck by a hurricane in mid-Atlantic. Both side paddles were ripped off by the storm, which also tore the lifeboats away from the deck and unhinged the rudder. The repairs cost over £60,000. In the following year, the *Great Eastern* was steaming through Long Island Sound near New York harbour, when the ship struck an uncharted rock which created a gash 83 ft (25 m) long and 9 ft (nearly 3 m) wide in the outer hull. The repairs this time cost in excess of £70,000.

The ill-starred liner was put up for auction in 1864, and was bought for a mere £25,000. Her buyers put her to work as a cable layer, but bad luck still bedevilled the vessel. In 1869, the *Great Eastern* steamed from Ireland to Newfoundland, laying a telegraph cable on the seabed as she went, but when she was 1,186 miles (1,898 km) out into the Atlantic, a minor accident caused the cable to snap. The severed end sank 3 miles (nearly 5 km) to the ocean bed, and all attempts to retrieve it failed.

Further commercial missions were dogged by disaster, and so the ship was brought back to Milford Haven and literally abandoned by her owners. For twelve years the *Great Eastern* was left to rust. By 1886, it was decided that the derelict ship (now coated with a layer of barnacles 6 ft (nearly 2 m) deep) was nothing but an obstacle to the shipping lines, so the dilapidated hulk was brought to Liverpool, where she was anchored in the Mersey and emblazoned with advertisement signs. Brunel must have turned in his grave when his "wonder of the sea" was exploited in this way.

The *Great Eastern* was sold at auction by Messrs Dixon and Moore – two Liverpool businessmen – to a firm of metal dealers. Even during her final voyage to a scrapyard near Birkenhead, the *Great Eastern* was involved in a collision with a tug in the Mersey which almost sank after sustaining heavy damage.

It was no easy task to break up the reinforced hull of the ship, so the wrecker's iron ball was invented for the task. Three days into the formidable demolition job, the wrecker's ball smashed into the hull, dislodging a large plate. When the ball impacted into the ship again, something was seen to fall from a hole in the hull. Two demolition experts gave orders to cease work and went to have a look at what had fallen out of the ship onto the piles of scrap at the quayside. It was a skeleton of a man in musty clothes. Another skeleton, that of a much younger male, was later found in a compartment sandwiched between the two hulls. The skeletons were later identified as those of the missing riveter and his apprentice by members of their families who had travelled from Canning Town, London, and Dagenham. Many believed that the chilling discovery explained the *Great Eastern*'s jinx.

The Crying Boy Jinx

In 1988, a mysterious explosion destroyed the home of the Amos family in Heswall, England. When firemen sifted through the burnt-out shell of the house they found a framed picture, entitled "The Crying Boy", a portrait of an angelic-looking boy with a sorrowful expression and a tear rolling down his cheek. But the picture was not even singed by the blaze. Not long afterwards in Bradford, there was another blaze, and again a picture of the crying child was found intact among the smouldering ruins. The head of the Yorkshire Fire Brigade told the national newspapers that pictures of the weird Crying Boy were frequently found intact in the rubble of houses that had been mysteriously burnt to the ground. Journalists asked him if he thought that the picture was evil and could somehow start the fires, but the fire chief refused to comment.

Claims that the unlucky painting causes fires are still occasionally reported (there was a Crying Boy picture found at a gutted house in Dublin in 1998, for example), but no one has ever found out just who the child is in the supposedly cursed painting. One well-respected researcher into occult matters, a retired schoolmaster from Devon, George Mallory, claimed to have uncovered the truth in 1995. Mr Mallory asserted that he had tracked down the artist behind the controversial portrait, an old Spanish postcard artist named Franchot Seville, who lived in Madrid. Seville said the Crying Boy was a little street urchin he had found wandering around Madrid in 1969. He never spoke, and had a very sorrowful look in his eyes. Seville painted the boy, and a Catholic priest told him that the boy was Don Bonillo, a child who had run away after seeing his parents die in a blaze. The priest told the artist to have nothing to do with the runaway because, wherever he settled, fires of unknown origin would mysteriously break out; the villagers called him "Diablo" (Devil) because of this.

Seville ignored the superstitious priest and looked after the boy. The paintings of the little sad orphan made Seville fairly rich, but one day his studio was mysteriously burned to the ground. Seville was ruined, and he accused the little Don Bonillo of arson. The boy ran off crying, and was never seen again. Then, from all over Europe came the reports of the unlucky Crying Boy paintings causing blazes. Seville was also regarded as a jinx, and no one commissioned him to paint, or would even look at his paintings. In 1976, a car exploded into a fireball on the outskirts of Barcelona after crashing into a wall. The victim was charred beyond recognition, but the victim's driving licence in the glove compartment was only partly burned. The name on the licence was one nineteen-year-old Don Bonillo; could this have been the same Don Bonillo who had been the subject of the Crying Boy paintings eight years earlier? We will probably never know, as no friends or relations ever came forward for the body.

The Curse of the Green Eye

For thousands of years, the belief has persisted that certain people and objects can bring misfortune. In 1830, a British banker and gemstone collector named Henry Thomas Hope bought a large blue diamond which became known as the Hope Diamond. The origins of the oversized diamond are not known with any certainty, but it is thought that the gem was cut from an even larger diamond in the Golconda mines of India, and there is a brief reference to the Hope Diamond being in the possession of King Louis XIV of France in the eighteenth century. It was later lost in the turmoil of the French Revolution. Today, the Hope Diamond is kept at the Smithsonian Institute in America, but the gemstone is regarded as a jinx because every person who owned it in the past either dropped dead of unnatural causes or committed suicide after buying the diamond.

In England there is another example of an unlucky diamond: a spectacular emerald-like gemstone folk-lorists have nicknamed the "Green Eye". On 21 October 1839, the night skies over western Wales lit up with a blinding blue flash, and scores of people saw a meteor fall to earth. On the following morning, a farmer near Hollowmoor Heath in the neighbouring county of Cheshire discovered a small crater in his field. None of the cows would venture near the crater, and the farmer saw that there was a black object the size of a billiard ball embedded in the centre. The farmer showed the object to a clergyman and he passed it on to a friend named Ibbotson, who was an amateur astronomer. Ibbotson cleaned the meteorite and sawed it in half. In the middle of the globe there was an object that was so hard, the blade of the saw glanced off it. Ibbotson cracked the meteorite open and saw that the object was a precious stone which was white, like opal. The unearthly gemstone was the size of an egg and had a peculiar flaw: the stone contained a circular, green emerald-coloured crystal which made the stone resemble a human glass eye with a green iris. Ibbotson sent a report of his find to the Royal Astronomical Society in London but never received a reply. He decided the "Green Eye", as he called it, would be an unusual birthday gift for his niece who lived in Dublin.

Five months later Ibbotson boarded the Dublin-bound steamer *William Huskisson* at Liverpool Docks, but the ship never reached Ireland. The steamship sank in the middle of the Irish Sea, and no one has ever explained why. The ship was in excellent condition and its captain and crew had made the crossing hundreds of times, yet forty passengers – including Mr Ibbotson – perished beneath the waves. Weeks later Ibbotson's suitcase was washed up on the English coast at Hoylake, and a man named William Peters opened the case and saw the strange Green Eye stone. He took the gemstone to a valuer who couldn't identify the material that the stone was made from, so Peters went over to Liverpool to sell it. Twenty-four hours later he died from a typhoid-like fever which claimed 15,000 victims in the town. So-called "Fever Sheds" were opened in the port, and the body of William Peters was literally thrown onto a heap of corpses in one of these sheds. A poor Irishman named John Law, who stripped and searched the plague corpses, became the next owner of the Green Eye, and was naturally delighted at his lucky find. He showed it to his friends at a tavern in the town and said he intended to get it valued soon. The landlord of the inn was very superstitious; he said the gemstone had an aura of evil about it, and told Law to take it off the premises. Law laughed at the landlord's comments and went home. Half an hour later, a boy ran to the pub and said that Law was dying outside his lodging house. Law was impaled on railings in front of the house, and was barely alive. Two railings had gone through his back and were protruding from his chest. Law was barely alive, and coughed up blood as he gave an account of what had happened. He said a man had run into his room and demanded the diamond. There was a struggle, and the man pushed Law through his open window. He had landed on the railings. Law's friends made the fatal mistake of trying to lift their companion off the railings, despite Law's terrible screams. But their well-meant intentions killed the man. As they lifted him, a railing severed a major artery and the other railing ruptured his liver.

Then the so-called Green Eye gemstone fell out of Law's hand. One of the bystanders picked up the stone and a fight later broke out over who should have it. Law's cousin – a man named George Wishart – claimed it and he later emigrated to the Isle of Man. One day, Wishart decided to have the Green Eye mounted in a gold locket, but on his way to the jewellers, he literally dropped dead in the street. A pathologist said he had died from cardio-congestive failure, but couldn't fathom out why, as Wishart had a legendary cast-iron constitution.

Wishart's niece, May Allen, took possession of the seemingly jinxed gemstone and, within a year, five of her friends had died in tragic accidents, although Mrs Allen refused to believe that the Green Eye was cursed. In December 1909, she decided to visit relatives in Liverpool with her son, Ernest. They both boarded a steamship named the *Ellan Vannin*, and yes, you've guessed it: that ship sank in mysterious circumstances on its way to the port in Liverpool Bay. Lookouts on the Wirral lighthouse were horrified to see the *Ellan Vannin*'s lights go out, then suddenly the ship went under the waves within a couple of seconds. Everyone on board the ship was drowned, and the cause of the sudden sinking has never been found. The bodies of May and Ernest Allen were buried at Liverpool on the western side of St James's Cemetery next to the Anglican Cathedral. Relatives of Mrs Allen said she had definitely taken the Green Eye diamond with her to show her Liverpool cousins, but the diamond was never found on the body. We must therefore presume that the cursed Green Eye gemstone is somewhere in the River Mersey, probably within the wreck of the *Ellan Vannin* which still lies beneath the waves of Liverpool Bay. Considering its dark history of tragedy to all those who have owned it, perhaps the Green Eye should be left where it lies.

The Cars of Doom

Over the years there have been many reports of ships and planes being cursed and jinxed. The following two stories are well-documented, and concern cars that seemed to have been nothing short of cursed.

In 1914, a French motor manufacturing firm named Phaeton built a long, open-topped vehicle that could carry six people. The car was painted blood-red, and this colour turned out to be very appropriate, because the vehicle was later surrounded by death and tragedy. In July 1914, the Archduke Franz Ferdinand and his wife sat in the rear seats of the red car, and in the front of the vehicle with the chauffeur sat a general and two other notables. The brand new car was on a tour of Sarajevo. Halfway through the tour a man ran from a line of people who were waving little Bosnian flags, and hurled a bomb at the red car, obviously intending to destroy it and its passengers. The bomb didn't go off, but bounced off the car's bodywork and rolled behind the vehicle, where four guards were following on horseback. The bomb suddenly exploded, and the blast took down the four unfortunate horses and sent the guards flying into the crowds. The red car carrying the Archduke speeded up and drove on. Minutes later, for some strange reason that has never been explained, the driver of the red car turned the vehicle into a dead-end street which was not a part of the planned route. Seconds after the unscheduled stop, a young Bosnian student ran from a doorway in the street and crossed the cobbled road. He drew a pistol, jumped onto the running board of the red car and emptied six bullets into the shocked Archduke and his wife at point-blank range. The Archduke's wife was dead, and blood was gushing out of her mouth turning her white dress the same colour as the car – blood red. The Archduke also began to cough and splutter, and blood cascaded from his mouth and the other bullet holes that dotted

The Cursed Locomotive

In 1981, British Rail officials were amused to receive a telephone call from a frantic woman named Angelina, who said she had seen a terrible tragedy in a dream about a locomotive. The customer enquiries officer at BR asked Angelina what she had seen, and the caller said that unless a Brush diesel locomotive with the number 47216 was immediately withdrawn and scrapped, it would cause death and destruction. The BR official traced Angelina's number and informed the police, but the police backed up the woman's claims because Angelina was a reliable and respected psychic whom the police regularly consulted themselves. British Rail officials merely changed the number on the supposedly jinxed locomotive from 47216 to 47299, but they received another telephone call from Angelina. She said she knew that they had not scrapped the locomotive, but had just changed its number, and she said that the locomotive would kill people in a matter of days unless it was scrapped. BR refused to take any further calls from the psychic, and three days later the allegedly cursed locomotive ploughed into a passenger train in Surrey. The locomotive was carrying 18 tons of oil, and over thirty people died in the crash and resulting inferno. Angelina's prediction had tragically come to pass.

his body. In those days it was customary to sew up the uniform, so the Archduke had bled to death by the time his coat was opened up to treat him. The student who had killed the Archduke and his wife was Gavrilo Princip, and the double assassination he committed was solely responsible for sowing the seeds to World War I, which claimed the lives of millions.

In 1914, an Austrian general took command of the red car that the Archduke had been assassinated in, and nine days later suffered a catastrophic defeat against the Serbians, after which he was sent to Vienna in disgrace. He couldn't take the shame and he later went insane and died mysteriously. The red car then passed into the hands of Captain Raska, another Austrian. During his first trip in the car, Captain Raska was rounding a bend on a mountain when he suddenly saw two peasants in the road ahead. The captain swerved to avoid them and crashed into a tree. His final agonizing screams were horrifying; the steering wheel had gone through Captain Raska's chest, and he begged the peasants to shoot him as he almost choked on his blood. A few minutes later he stopped screaming and died.

The unlucky car then came into the possession of the Governor of Sarajevo, a man named Alexandrovac, who was a vintage car enthusiast. He had four accidents with the car in four months, then crashed and lost his right arm in the impact. Six months later the car was found upside down in a ditch, and the governor was inside, crushed to death. The next owner of the red car was a doctor. He laughed at all the local talk about the car being cursed, but within months his body was found under the car's tyres. No one knows how the doctor came to be under the car, but the vehicle had somehow rolled over the doctor and had crushed his spine. The car was then purchased by a wealthy landowner named Graco. One day the red car stopped dead. Graco got a farmer to tow the vehicle with a horse-drawn cart, but halfway through the journey, the car suddenly started up again. It killed the farmer and his horse, and the driver was thrown through the windscreen and bled to death. The car was repainted a blue colour and purchased by a man named Tiber Hirschfield. He was taking five passengers on a short journey in the jinxed car one day when he suddenly lost control of the vehicle. The car smashed into a wall and all six people in it were killed instantly. The car was repaired and five more people died while driving it over the next six years. The vehicle was finally put on display at a Vienna transport museum. One morning, in 1944, the curator of this museum arrived at the building and told work colleagues he had experienced terrible nightmares the night before about losing his head. Later in the evening, an English bomber plane dropped its load on the museum, and the jinxed car was blown into thousands of tiny pieces. In the explosion, part of the panelling from the car flew across the room and decapitated the curator of the museum who had earlier talked about the nightmares he'd had about losing his head.

Another unlucky car was the one the Hollywood actor, James Dean, died in after a tragic motoring accident in September 1955. After the crash, when the wreck of Dean's car was being towed to a garage, the engine slipped and fell onto a mechanic, breaking both his legs. The engine was then bought by a doctor, who put it into a racing car. The doctor was killed when his car crashed within days. A man who had bought the drive shaft from Dean's car also died the same day in a car crash. As Dean's car was later being repaired in a garage, a fire of unknown origin broke out and almost destroyed the vehicle. The jinxed car was then put on display at Sacramento, but it mysteriously fell off its mount and landed on a teenager, crushing his hip. The car was then taken to Oregon, where it fell off a truck that was carrying it, and smashed through a shop front. Finally, in 1959, for reasons that were never explained, Dean's car suddenly broke into eleven pieces while sitting on stationary steel supports.

The Lions and the Witch Doctor

Even today, witchcraft and magic still play an important role in the lives of many tribal Africans. In many parts of the African continent there are people who still believe that a death curse will take a life, and that a witch doctor has magical powers that enable him to summon up the spirits of the dead.

In Rhodesia (now Zimbabwe) in 1949, a witch doctor named Ohsoo Kamadi appeared before Salisbury High Court accused of practising witchcraft and killing two victims through reinforced suggestion, by telling them they had been cursed to death. Kamadi was found guilty and sentenced to two years' imprisonment. The witch doctor shrugged, and muttered something to his interpreter. The judge asked what the tribal magician was saying, and the interpreter said, "He just says, 'So be it'; he accepts your judgement." The judge then said, "Tell Mr

Kamadi that his so-called medicines and hocus-pocus charms and dolls are to be destroyed as well."

The interpreter told Kamadi about the judge's intentions, and Kamadi became very angry. He started shouting and pointing at the judge. The interpreter told the judge, "Your Honour, Mr Kamadi says he will curse you if you destroy his charms and medicines. He says that lions will come through your town and kill you, unless you leave his charms and medicine alone."

The judge laughed nervously and said, "Tell Mr Mumbo Jumbo that he will now be serving three years, and that I will *personally* destroy his paraphernalia." And shortly afterwards the judge broke up the witch doctor's charms, and smashed his collection of medicine bottles containing various potions and plant and animal extracts.

Later that week, a pride of lions strolled into the town. The first people to see the wild animals were the judge and his family. They gazed at the animals with a horrified look, and watched one of the lions tear apart a goat that had been tethered to a pole. The animals seemed very hungry and unusually savage, as if they'd been disturbed by something. Then the judge remembered the witch doctor's curse, and went downstairs to lock the doors. He grabbed a 12-bore shotgun and loaded it, then went up to the veranda to take a shot at the lions – but they were nowhere to be seen. Later that day, the lions were seen walking the city centre streets, past the very High Court where the witch doctor had been sentenced. The beasts slaughtered two Alsatians and tore the arm off a soldier who tried to shoot at them. When the authorities surrounded the area, the lions seemed to vanish.

The judge sent his family to another town, and he sat up all night in his bed with the loaded shotgun. About 3 a.m. he thought he heard the sounds of a strange drum, beating in the distance, and that marked the beginning of a series of weird incidents. Thuds were heard on the front door, and animal sounds, such as strange grunts and snarling noises. The judge crept downstairs in his slippers and night-gown and looked through the letterbox; he saw a pair of fierce green eyes staring back. They belonged to the lion which was leading the pride, and it roared when it saw its prey peeping at it. The judge fired through the letterbox, and the lions scattered. He then fired through the door again, but blasted one of the hinges off. As he ran back up the stairs to get more shotgun cartridges, the door behind him burst open, and in came the large muscular lion he had fired at. It roared and charged up the stairs after the terrified judge. He never reached his room. The lion seized him, grabbing his head in its enormous jaws and cracking his skull. At that moment, two policemen entered the judge's house and fired at the lion, but it fled back down the stairs and ran out into the darkness to join the rest of the pride. The judge died in agony two days later. The grisly incident was thought to have been caused by big game hunters who had disturbed the lions, but the tribesmen in the area knew better. They believed that the witch doctor's curse had taken effect.

The Witch Doctor's Curse

In the eighteenth century, the English city of Liverpool became prosperous through the so-called "ships of shame", which transported millions of black African slaves to America and the West Indies. The rapidly-growing colonies of the New World were in need of a massive labour force, and the unprincipled businessmen of England thought that the black men, women and children of Africa could fulfil the demand for workers. Around ten million African slaves were shipped across the Atlantic in appalling conditions. Each slave was confined to a space in the ship's hold which was smaller than a coffin. They were shackled to one another and therefore had to wallow in each other's dirt for months on end. Not surprisingly, fever, dysentery and a high mortality rate were common-place on the slave ships during the hazardous voyage from Africa to the western side of the Atlantic. Sick and dying slaves were regarded as a dead loss to the slave-sellers, so many of the kidnapped Africans suspected of being ill were thrown overboard to be eaten by the sharks. In November 1781, a Captain Collingwood of the slave ship *Zong* ordered his men to take turns in throwing 133 slaves into the ocean. Just a few of the poor souls jettisoned into the shark-infested waters were ill, but Captain Collingwood thought the cruel measure would be an effective way to conserve the ship's fresh water reservoir.

Against this evil backdrop of cruelty and disregard for human life, the following strange tale unfolded. It began in the year 1783, when a Liverpool slave ship, the *Amelia* sailed with its captured human cargo from the port of Old Calabar in Nigeria. Among the men, women and children who had been abducted and taken by force from their country, there was a young boy named Abu, and his uncle, Obah, a partially blind, grey-haired old man who curiously knew a little English. During the *Amelia*'s voyage to the West Indies, the boy Abu suffered a fit, and his uncle Obah called out to the crew to give his nephew water. The old man's frantic request fell on deaf ears, and so he and a number of other slaves down in the hold started to rattle their chains in protest.

The master of the *Amelia*, Captain Mallard, was enraged, and he had the protesting slaves brought up on deck, where they were subjected to lengthy flogging sessions. The thirteen-year-old Abu was also flogged, and fainted. His Uncle Obah threw himself over the boy and begged the captain to give the child water. Obah struggled to explain who the boy was and, through an interpreter, he stated that young Abu was prone to strange fits which gave him visions, that the child was the only son of his tribe's witch doctor, and that if he was not taken back to Nigeria, a terrible curse would fall upon the captain of the *Amelia*. When Captain Mallard heard this, he grabbed the boy by his ankles and started to swing him round. The boy screamed, and his elderly uncle cried out and tried to attack the captain. Suddenly, Mallard let go of the child and he went head first over the ship's rail and plunged into the waves. There was a roar of protest from the slaves below deck who had witnessed the captain's cowardly and callous act. The murmuring below continued for a while, and angry eyes full of hatred stared up through the slits in the deck's barricado. The old man Obah sobbed, and was promptly taken down into the hold and chained up again. As the shackles were put on him, the old man pointed an accusing finger at Captain Mallard and said, "Curse you! Curse you, captain and family!"

The Blood Runs Cold

In 1950 in the state of Texas, USA, the police found a seventy-year-old man lying in a pool of blood at his home. He had been shot twice in the chest at close range, and there was one macabre clue to the killer's identity. The dead man – George Stafford – had traced out the name Dan in his own blood on the floor shortly before he died. A detective paid a visit to a petty local criminal named Dan Edwards who had been seen hanging around old Mr Stafford just days before the shooting. Dan Edwards protested his innocence, but couldn't account for the $100 he had in his possession, so he was promptly arrested on a charge of murder. Edwards got off on a technicality but, not long afterwards, strange things happened to him. One night in a hotel, Edwards was lying on a bed asleep when something cold splashed on his face. It was blood, dripping from the ceiling. Edwards summoned the manager, but the source of the blood could not be determined or explained. The room above Edwards's room was empty and, stranger still, the bloodstain on the ceiling faded before the eyes of Edwards and the hotel manager. The same gruesome phenomenon followed Edwards for the next fifteen months, and was witnessed by dozens of horrified people. On one occasion in a diner, the imprint of a bloodstained hand appeared on the back of Dan Edwards's jacket. On another occasion, Edwards found the dollar notes in his wallet soaked with the same mysterious blood. In 1952, Edwards put a pistol to his head and committed suicide, perhaps to end his grisly persecution.

Ten months later, all the slaves from the *Amelia* had been sold; all except the half-blind slave Obah. Old slaves were almost impossible to sell, and old slaves who could hardly see could not be given away. Obah, therefore, was taken to Liverpool and offered to anyone who would have him. He was put on exhibition on the steps of the Liverpool Custom House. Obah was adopted by a well-to-do couple from an affluent district of Liverpool, George and Catherine Hughes. The couple looked after Obah until he died ten years later from a fever.

Not long after Captain Mallard's return to the port of Liverpool, bad luck and weird occurrences seemed to haunt him and his family. His eldest son, Matthew, who had a cottage overlooking the shore at Formby, went insane after telling his wife that an enormous black dog with glowing red eyes had stalked him during his evening walk through the sand dunes. The hound was jet black and left no tracks in the sand as it chased after him. Matthew's wife watched him turn into a shambling, nervous wreck over the next few days, and ended up deserting him. Matthew Mallard was later committed to a lunatic asylum.

Weeks later, Captain Mallard was woken in the middle of the night at his home by the sound of a strange drum beating in the distance. Even his neighbours heard the peculiar thumping sound, but no one could tell where the noise was coming from. Three nights later, the infuriating rhythm of the drum ceased abruptly at precisely 4.15 a.m., and Captain Mallard later learned that his elderly mother – who lived in the next street – had died at that exact time after screaming out once in her sleep. A month later, the same eerie drumbeat disturbed the sleep of

Captain Mallard once more. This time he awoke in his four-poster bed to find his wife lying in a pool of blood beside him. She had suffered a life-threatening miscarriage and almost died as a result.

Then something chilling took place one Sunday after Mallard had been entertaining a Captain Slater at his home. Mrs Mallard found a strange object on the mantelpiece of the drawing room. She thought it was a doll's head, but when she picked it up and inspected it, she saw that it was too lifelike and had a hideous quality about it. She screamed and threw it in the fire. Captain Mallard retrieved the object from the glowing coals with a pair of tongs, and saw to his horror that it was the shrivelled head of a real human. It was one of the so-called shrunken heads, which are allegedly used by shamen and witch doctors as black magic talismans. Mallard thought Captain Slater had planted the head in his drawing room, but Slater swore that he had never set eyes on the shrunken head before. Mrs Vaughan, the maid-of-all-work in the Mallard household, later reported hearing the sound of the strange drum again, and said that she had been having vivid nightmares about a black man's grinning face painted with white stripes.

Captain Mallard decided to go back to sea in an attempt to get away from the ghostly goings-on at his home. He captained a vessel called the *Moonrise* which was bound for Littleton, New Zealand. Mallard was to bring back a consignment of wool and frozen mutton from New Zealand, but his ship vanished without a trace. Twenty-six years later, a British ship called the *Horizon* caught sight of a large sailing vessel drifting off the coast of Chile. As the ship drew nearer, the crew of the *Horizon* could see that the vessel was apparently unmanned but, stranger still, the masts and ragged sails of the ship were covered with thick deposits of a green mould. On the prow, faded with the weather and the passage of time, the crew of the *Horizon* could see the name *Moonrise*. A boarding party from the *Horizon* investigated the apparently abandoned ship, and when one man jumped onto the deck he found that the timbers had decayed to such an extent that they crumbled beneath him. The other men hauled their shipmate out of the hole and walked carefully around the deck. In the captain's cabin a skeleton in ragged clothes was found, and the atmosphere had an intense putrid smell. Thirteen more skeletons were found elsewhere on the *Moonrise*; they had all presumably died from some sickness long ago. The captain of the *Horizon* inspected the damp, mouldy pages of the ship's logbook to examine the last entries but the ink had become too blurred by the moisture to be legible.

Suddenly, a loud groaning noise echoed down the length of the *Moonrise*, followed by a loud crack. The captain and his men rushed onto the deck and watched in horror as the main mast crashed down into the waters. In a state of panic, the men dashed back to the lifeboat and rowed like mad. As the boat moved away, the ship with the "skeleton crew" started to break up. The remaining two masts toppled onto the *Moonrise* and, within seconds, the rotting ship started to sink at the stern. The men of the *Horizon* rowed away just in time to avoid being sucked down with the rapidly sinking vessel.

When news of the strange discovery of the long-lost ship reached the ears of Captain Mallard's wife, who was now in her sixties, she fainted. She told the doctor treating her that her husband had been cursed to death for killing a witch doctor's son, then became incoherent. The doctor administered laudanum, but Mrs Mallard broke out in a sweat and her eyes rolled about. At the minute of her death, which came at three o'clock in the morning, seven people attending her sickbed heard the howl of a dog out in the street.

The strange tale was reported in the local newspaper, and when Mr and Mrs Hughes – the couple who had looked after the old slave Obah – read about the discovery of Captain Mallard's old ship and the ensuing sudden death of his wife, they knew that the witch doctor's curse had done its work.

Cursed Places

We've all heard of voodoo curses put upon people, but can a whole village be cursed? That seems to be the case in the following story, which was reported in the media in the early 1970s.

The English village of Fosdyke is situated on the River Welland near the Wash in Lincolnshire. A documentary was made about the small fishing community of Fosdyke in 1973, and the programme's contents angered thousands of viewers because one villager, sixty-year-old Len Lineham, gave graphic details about the 300 baby seals he had caught and clubbed to death in the previous year. The interviews with villagers were intercut with shocking footage of the seals being battered to death and naturally, as the British are said to be a nation of animal lovers, there was a public outcry. Most viewers wrote letters of protest to the television company which made the disturbing documentary, but hundreds of other people wrote poison pen letters to individual fishermen in Fosdyke who had been named in the film. Among the hate mail were several chilling death threats and curses. The media picked up on the curses and were soon reporting a number of strange deaths in the so-called "Cursed Village of Fosdyke".

Nine days after the programme went out, Len Lineham – the man who confessed to the mass clubbings of the seals in the documentary – reacted to the pressure he was under by blowing his brains out. Then Lineham's grandson was killed in a horrendous road accident. Shortly after that tragic incident, Lineham's niece choked to death while eating a meal. Two other fishermen were also killed in a car crash a week later. Not long afterwards, something even more bizarre occurred: seven people in Fosdyke's fishing community suddenly died from "natural causes". Days later, Colin Runnals, another seal-hunter, was found floating face down in a shallow river. He had drowned in the shallow waters even though he was an expert swimmer. The newspapers and television reporters had a field day with the spate of unaccountable deaths in the fens, and hysteria swept through Fosdyke. Begging letters were sent to Canon Cooper, who was then chaplain to the Archbishop of Canterbury. The villagers pleaded for him to come to their community to exorcise the terrible curse. Canon Cooper visited the village and told the people that no evil powers could prevail against the power of God, and he blessed Fosdyke with his staff.

But the strange deaths continued as soon as the chaplain left the village, and by the end of that year, the chilling death toll stood at 666. The mystical significance of this number was not overlooked, and many thought it was proof that Fosdyke was in the grip of a Satanic hex. The curse gradually lifted, although even today the people of Fosdyke recall the year 1973 with a sense of horror. They still regard it as the year the nation cursed their village.

Another English village which is said to be cursed is Coggeshall in Essex. The endearing picturesque appearance of the village's thatched cottages and magpie-coloured Tudor façades belies an aura of evil which dates back to the sixteenth century, when the village was allegedly infested with black magicians and witches. It was upon Market Hill in Coggeshall in the 1640s that Matthew Hopkins, England's officially-appointed Witchfinder General, hanged scores of men, women and children who had been accused of being sorcerers. In 1647 Hopkins was cursed by one of the "witches" and weeks later he came under suspicion of being a warlock himself. Hopkins was subjected to his own witch-detecting test by being bound and lowered into a river. He floated, of course, which was taken as sign of being guilty, and was duly hanged.

Four centuries later, Coggleshall was the centre of media interest following a series of chilling events which took place in the 1980s. The first of these was the mysterious disappearance of Diane Jones, a thirty-five-year-old doctor's wife. She vanished without a trace in Coggeshall after enjoying a drink with friends in a local pub. Diane's battered corpse was later found in a wood in Brightwell, 35 miles (56 km) from her sixteenth century home. The post-mortem estab-lished that Diane had been two months pregnant and had been battered to death on the night of her disappearance. The killer was never found. Diane's grief-stricken husband, Robert Jones, was briefly interrogated by police, who wanted to know why he hadn't informed them of his wife's disappearance until nine days had elapsed. Mr Jones explained that he had initially assumed that his wife had walked out on him.

Less than two years after the Diane Jones murder, there was another violent killing in Coggeshall. This time the victim was Patsy Bull, the wife of a millionaire antiques expert. Patsy had been blasted at point-blank range in the family's antiques warehouse, and police initially suspected that the murder had been a cold-blooded execution carried out by ruthless robbers. However, Patsy's husband Wilfred was later questioned and subsequently charged with the murder. At the murder trial, it was learned that Wilfred Bull had been having an affair with a widow, and a row with Patsy over his infidelity had led to the fatal shooting. Mr Bull was sentenced to life imprisonment.

In 1985, just 2 miles (just over 3 km) from the outskirts of Coggeshall, five bodies were found at a farmhouse at Tolleshunt D'Arcy. The dead – who had all been shot – were Neville Bamber, his wife June, their six-year-old twins, Daniel and Nicholas, and Sheila, an adopted daughter. The police had been alerted to the scene of what was obviously a multiple murder by Sheila's brother, Jeremy Bamber. He had told the police that his sister had gone crazy with a gun. The police were suspicious of Bamber's account and shortly afterwards they charged Jeremy with murder. He was later convicted of killing his parents, sister and nephews in a bid to inherit the family wealth. Jeremy had shot his father nine times and clubbed him with a rifle butt. His mother had been blasted at close range between the eyes. Sheila had been shot twice (one bullet had ripped through her jugular vein), and the twin boys had five and three shots to the head respectively.

A year after the Bamber murders, Coggeshall was rocked by yet another violent killing when the clay pigeon shooting champion Jimmy Bell shot his wife and then himself. In 1988, there was another tragic death in the vicinity of Coggeshall when a restaurateur named Peter Langan killed himself in a fire he had deliberately started in a dramatic effort to stop his wife from leaving him. A year after that, a murder attempt was made on the Vicar of Nayland by his wife, who had plotted with her lover to shoot him.

England is by no means the only country with cursed sites. Standing over 1,100 feet (335 m) above the bone-dry plains of Alice Springs in Australia's national park, is the amazing spectacle of Ayers Rock. Each year, thousands of tourists flock to Ayers Rock, known as Uluru to the Aborigines. At sunset, the amber rays of the sinking sun turn the rock pink and ruby red, and many of the sightseers who have witnessed the beautiful flushed radiance of the stunning landmark are keen to take mementoes from the rock, such as pebbles or other loose stones. But for some sinister reason, such keepsakes have an evil reputation for bringing misfortune to those who take them. Time after time, park rangers at Ayers Rock have received parcels from visitors containing pebbles and rocks taken from the rock with accompanying notes telling how their souvenirs had brought them nothing but bad luck, illness, and even death back home.

Lightning Persecution

There is an old, but incorrect saying that "lightning never strikes twice in the same place". There are many park rangers in America's Yellowstone Park who have been struck more than three times by lightning while patrolling the wide open parkland, and some have been killed by the searing bolts of electricity. In north Wales, in the middle of the last century, there was one unfortunate man who was literally victimized by lightning.

In 1857, Horace Pym, the twenty-year-old son of Sir Walter Pym, a wealthy landowner and ruthless businessman, left his family's sprawling mansion on the outskirts of St Asaph. He rode on horseback round the Welsh countryside and came upon a beautiful girl named Megan, who was standing on a hill and throwing corn to the birds. Horace Pym rode up to Meg and dismounted. He told the girl he was the son of Sir Walter, but the girl could hardly understand English. Horace thought she was ignoring him, and raised his hand to her. Megan flinched, but Horace didn't hit her. He enjoyed the way the girl looked so afraid of him and relished the moment. The girl cried out something in Welsh, and a bird of prey resembling a falcon swooped down and attacked the young man. Horace fell to the ground and rolled down the hill. The girl shouted out more words in her native tongue, and Pym's horse bolted away. Pym then assaulted the girl. Some accounts say that he raped her. As Pym turned away, Megan started crying and pointed to the skies, shouting something Pym could not understand. When Pym ran off, the clouds overhead darkened, and soon it was raining heavily. Thunder rumbled through the hills, and suddenly a bolt of forked lightning struck Pym. The bolt pierced his scalp and burnt holes in his feet. Pym fell to the ground, unconscious. When he awoke it was night, and he felt seriously ill. Upon his return home, he told his father he'd been attacked by a mob of Welsh peasants who had tried to rob him. Pym's father was furious, and sent a posse of men armed with shotguns to the area, but all they found was young Megan and her mother, who lived in a run-down cottage. One of Pym's men knew that Megan and her mother were regarded as notorious witches, and left them well alone. Megan's mother, Sian, was known throughout the valleys as a horse-whisperer, someone who could communicate with the animals and beasts of burden, and she had evidently taught her magical gift to her daughter, who had been seen talking to foxes and birds.

The men returned to their master's estate and told Sir Walter there were no peasants in the area where young Horace said he'd been set upon. Sir Walter hit his son with a riding whip and ordered him to stay in his rooms in the mansion for a week. A few days later, a terrible thunderstorm descended on St Asaph and ravaged Sir Walter's estate. Several of his men were killed by the lightning and, during the fearful storm, young Horace hid under his bed, terrified of being struck by lightning again. When the storm cleared, Horace went to the window and peeped out at the clouds – and a powerful flash of sheet lightning exploded in his face, temporarily blinding him. The surge of electrical energy was of such ferocity, it actually scorched an image of Horace's face on the window pane, and this "lightning picture" as it became known, remained etched on the window until the mansion was demolished in 1900.

Horace was later sent to Preston to supervise his father's printing business, and died a year later after falling from his horse in 1860. A week after his burial, a particularly violent thunderstorm raged over Preston, and a bolt of lightning came down from the sky and shattered Horace Pym's gravestone.

Mystical and Forbidden Knowledge

· ·

"What you do not understand cannot
be yours."

Goethe

The Akashic Records

Throughout the history of human civilization there
have been individuals who have claimed to be the
possessors of arcane knowledge that has allegedly
been accessed from unknown sources. The Masons,
Mystery Schools and various other esoteric groups
have professed to possess secrets of the occult; but
where did these secret societies get their clandestine
information from in the first place?

Some of the occult knowledge was probably carefully passed from generation to generation by initiates
of the fabled Ancient Wisdom; this was a vast collection of books about cosmic law, the hidden powers of
mankind and other mystical matters, supposedly
written by the scientists of a super-civilization in antediluvian times.

But for centuries, occultists have claimed that there
is another source of hidden knowledge called the
Akashic Records. These records are said to contain
data on everything in the universe; every thought and

deed of every life form from the beginning of the cosmos to the present.

The word "akashic" derives from the Sanskrit "akasha", meaning the fundamental etheric substance of the universe and of which the records consist. The substance is said to fill all space and to link every atom of animate and inanimate matter.

The Akashic Records are therefore like some colossal databank (similar to the Internet but unimaginably more extensive) that contains information about every person and event from the dawn of time to the present day. The Western counterpart of these records would be the Book of Life, where all the details about a person's conduct are recorded by their attendant angel.

If you think the notion of vast amounts of information existing in the ether is a bit far-fetched, consider this: gigabytes of data are passing through you and surround you at this very moment as you read these words. Television, satellite and radio signals carrying pictures, music, chat, classified and encoded military information, messages from mobile phones etc., are radiating through your body at the speed of light. This modern-day continuous chatter of the electromagnetic spectrum is a good analogy when referring to the Akashic Records. The same thing happens in both cases; unless you know how to tune in and decode the signals around you, they are undetectable and of no use.

How then, do you tune in to access the records? Mystics use meditation or visualization techniques where you simply picture a blank chalkboard and wait for the information you need to appear on it.

Sometimes it would seem that the records are

unconsciously accessed at random by people who believe that they have been inspired. For instance, Mozart claimed that he often heard new symphonies playing in his head which didn't seem to be of his making, while Sir Paul McCartney has always maintained that his most popular song, *Yesterday*, came to him from the depths of his sleep. Many writers and poets, such as Samuel Taylor Coleridge and Charles Dickens, have made the same curious assertions about novels and poems that seemed to have been dictated to them from some invisible author in their unconscious minds. In fact, Coleridge dreamed the whole of his poem *Kubla Khan* and simply wrote it down in the morning.

Scientists have also made many discoveries in the time-honoured tradition of "sleeping on the idea". In 1863, a young German scientist named August Kekule experienced such a dream of discovery while dozing on a bus. The scientist dreamt that he was watching chains of carbon and hydrogen atoms slithering about like snakes. Suddenly, one chain formed a type of loop which instantly revealed to the dreamer what the molecular structure of benzene was. Kekule awoke excited; he had been wracking his brains trying to work out the structure of benzene for months and now all had been revealed to him in a dream.

Of course, all the previous cases could be rationalized as the products of a fertile subconscious. However, if the Akashic Records do exist on some higher plane of existence, then the information they contain could often be accessed by more than one person simultaneously. It is often said that when the time is ripe, ideas, inventions and discoveries usually appear in different parts of the world at the same time.

For example, in 1900, three scientists in Holland, Germany and Austria, Hugo de Vries, Carl Correns, and Erich von Tschermak respectively, independently discovered the laws of genetics on the same day.

In 1876 the same thing happened when Alexander Graham Bell patented the telephone. Another inventor named Elisha Gray sent a detailed description of his telephone to the US Patent Office a few hours after Bell's invention had been patented. More and more patents for a telephone poured into the office and, within a few years, there were some 600 lawsuits over the Bell telephone patents.

But how could something as new as the telephone be a part of the Akashic Records? Some occultists maintain that, because the records are universal, they therefore contain the history of other planets in the cosmos that are more technologically advanced than the Earth. The scientists of these older worlds will have progressed further in physics than Earth's scientists, and will doubtless have long ago accomplished telephonic communication and other technological advancements. Thus, all such achievements would be recorded in the Akashic repository.

How could the Akashic Records store such a phenomenal amount of universal data? No one seems to have an answer to that question but that doesn't mean that there isn't an explanation, simply that it is not known, or perhaps not recognized for what it is, at the present moment. After all, a laser hologram is a not dissimilar concept, yet this would have baffled scientists of the 1950s completely. We now know that if a photographic plate containing the interference patterns of an object that has been recorded as a three-dimensional hologram is shattered, the whole

3-D image can be recreated by shining a laser through one small sliver of the smashed plate. All the information about the total image of the object has been recorded somehow onto every point of the plate. This discovery was not made until 1965 and was totally unexpected, so who are we to dismiss the possibility of something similar on a far grander scale?

The Akashic Records are reputed to exist as a network of "etheric space" which science has yet to discover. All the same, most scientists would no doubt scoff at the concept of this mysterious ethereal archive. Yet Einstein himself once observed how science is unable to work out just what empty space actually is, with a very profound remark. He said, "What does a fish know about the water in which he swims all his life?"

The Necronomicon

Never has a book been surrounded by such controversy as the *Necronomicon*, an archaic work that is said to be the ultimate repository of forbidden lore, containing formulae and incantations to summon forth the Great Old Ones, dark and poorly-understood entities from dimensions outside space and time. Many ancient religions have referred to these archetypal beings as enemies of mankind who swore to take possession of the Earth in revenge against the Elder Gods or "Shining Ones" – the ancient guardians of humanity.

A piece of timeworn codex was discovered in Cairo in the 1940s which allegedly contained an incomplete excerpt from the *Necronomicon*, copied down by an

Arab named Abdul Alhazred in AD 730 at Damascus. For decades the delicate codex was kept under lock and key in various places in the Middle East, but in 1971 an alleged copy was faxed to an antiquarian book dealer in Paris by a Californian named Howard Meakes. The text of the faxed document was written in a code with glyphs reminiscent of Hebrew letters. Upon decoding, the following narrative was extracted:

"Of Ye Old Ones and their Spawn

The Old Ones were, the Old Ones are and the Old Ones shall be. From the dark stars They came ere man was born, unseen and loathsome They descended to primal earth.

Beneath the oceans They brooded while ages past, till seas gave up the land, whereupon They swarmed forth in Their multitudes and darkness ruled the Earth.

At the frozen Poles They raised mighty cities, and upon high places the temples of Those whom nature owns not and the Gods have cursed.

And the spawn of the Old Ones covered the Earth, and Their children endureth throughout the ages. Ye shantaks of Leng are the work of Their hands, the Ghasts who dwelleth in Zin's primordial vaults know Them as their Lords. They have fathered the Na-Hag and the Gaunts that ride the Night; Great Cthulhuis Their brother, the shaggoths Their slaves. The Dholes do homage unto Them in the nighted vale of Pnoth and Gugs sing Their praises beneath the peaks of ancient Throk.

They have walked amidst the stars and They have walked the Earth. The City of Irem in the great desert has known Them; Leng in the Cold Waste has seen Their passing, the timeless citadel upon the cloud-veiled heights of unknown Kadath beareth Their mark.

Wantonly the Old Ones trod the ways of darkness and Their blasphemies were great upon the Earth; all creation bowed beneath Their might and knew Them for Their wickedness.

And the Elder Lords opened Their eyes and beheld the abominations of Those that ravaged the Earth. In Their wrath They set their hand against the Old Ones, staying Them in the midst of Their iniquity and casting Them forth from the Earth to the Void beyond the planes where chaos reigns and form abideth not. And the Elder Lords set Their seal upon the Gateway and the power of the Old Ones prevailest not against its might.

Loathsome Cthulhu rose then from the deeps and raged with exceeding great fury against the Earth Guardians. And They bound his venomous claws with potent spells and sealed him up within the City of R'lyeh wherein beneath the waves he shall sleep death's dream until the end of the Aeon.

Beyond the Gate dwell now the Old Ones; not in the spaces known unto men but in the angles betwixt them. Outside Earth's plane They linger and ever awaite the time of Their return; for the Earth has known Them and shall know Them in time yet to come.

And the Old Ones hold foul and formless Azathoth for Their Master and Abide with Him in the black cavern at the centre of all infinity, where he gnaws ravenously in ultimate chaos amid the mad beating of hidden drums, the tuneless piping of hideous flutes and the ceaseless bellowing of blind idiot gods that shamble and gesture aimlessly for ever.

The soul of Azathoth dwelleth in Yog-sothoth and He shall beckon unto the Old Ones when the stars mark the time of Their coming; for Yog-sothoth is the Gate through which Those of the Void will re-enter. Yog-sothoth knowest the mazes of time, for all time is one unto Him. He knowest where the Old Ones came forth in time long past and where They shall come forth again when the cycle returneth.

After day cometh night; man's day shall pass, and They shall rule where They once ruled. As foulness you shall know them and Their accursedness shall stain the Earth."

In 1583, John Dee, astrologer to Queen Elizabeth I and a practitioner of the occult sciences, wrote to a friend, telling him that he had come into possession of an ancient and potent scroll called the *Necronomica*, which contained terrifying magical techniques for raising the dead, controlling the weather, causing widespread death at a distance, and many other workable methods for invoking powers that are currently lying dormant in man. Dee enigmatically claimed that the text of the strange book, which had once belonged to a wizard in Devon, was written in Enochian, the language spoken by the angels. What became of Dee's fascinating book is not known. Dee died wretchedly poor in 1608 and his books were either burned by ignorant peasants or stolen by rivals.

Numerology

In the first century BC, the Greek philosopher and mathematician Pythagoras (only known nowadays for his theorem concerning right-angled triangles), developed the idea that there was a grand design to the universe which interconnected everything in a numerical relationship. The followers of Pythagoras believed that numbers were the key to the cosmos, but long before the Pythagoreans, Abraham, the father of the Hebrew peoples, is said to have compiled *The Book of Formation*, a kabbala of mystical number-based knowledge dictated to Abraham by God.

The kabbala was passed to Abraham's son Isaac, who in turn bequeathed the esoteric work to his son Jacob, and he subsequently transmitted the teachings to the twelve tribes of Israel. Seven generations after Abraham, the revelations of God were also manifested in the form of the Torah on Mount Sinai and given to Moses. The Torah today is a scroll on which the Pentateuch (the first five books of the Old Testament) is written, and it relates the history of the Jews from the Creation to the death of Moses. The Torah scroll is always kept in synagogues.

Down the centuries, the Torah has been studied both by rabbis and gentile students, and there have been many curious claims about encoded messages and revelations contained within the sacred texts. The basis of these intriguing claims is the way in which each letter of the Hebrew alphabet is assigned a numerical equivalent. According to the kabbalists who have scrutinized the texts, the very name of a person encodes truths about their inner nature and even data regarding their destiny. This system of decoding names is called "gematria". The method of conversion based on the kabbalistic system is as follows:

1	2	3	4	5	6	7	8
A	B	C	D	E	U	O	F
I	K	G	M	H	V	Z	P
Q	R	L	T	N	W		
J		S			X		
Y							

To determine your own number, add up the numerical equivalent of each letter of your name, then add together the numbers of the resultant number, and so on, until the addition produces a single-digit number below 10. For example, if your name is John Jones: J=1, O=7, H=5, N=5, J=1, O=7, N=5, E=5, S=3. So, 1+7+5+5 plus 1+7+5+5+3=39. Now, 3+9=12, and 1+2=3. Three is the "name number" of John Jones.

Once you have ascertained your name number, consult the following interpretation list of the kabbalists to discover your true nature.

One
The number of purpose, ambition and intense motivation. If the negative side of a One person takes hold, they are very selfish and egotistical. They are often dominating and inconsiderate, and in extreme cases, tyrannical, but are often born leaders.

Two
The number of balance, open-mindedness and sensitivity. Twos are good-natured and easygoing, yet very secretive. However, if their negative side dominates them, they can be very malicious in a devious way.

Three
The number of versatility, harmony and conformity. Threes are popular, fast-thinking, and able to integrate quickly into a group. Their negative side is the tendency to be showy and conceited.

Four
The number of endurance, reliability and dedication. Fours proceed slowly but surely to reach their goals, but usually not until middle life. Their negative side is the proclivity for bottling up emotions and being unable to communicate clearly in relationships.

Five
The number of mystery, sexuality, and the supernatural. Fives are often charismatic and sexually attractive, and have an avid interest in the paranormal. They shield their innermost fantasies and thoughts from even their closest partners, and their only negative trait is recklessness.

Six
The number of loyalty, abiding affection and domesticity. Sixes are happiest at home, and hate changes in their routine. They are often introverted in their public life, but highly sexed in their private life. Their Achilles heel is gullibility, as they are always taken in by dubious sob stories.

Seven
The number seven has long been associated with magic and luck, but is also the number of knowledge, insight, and creative imagination. Sevens have a knack of seeing solutions which others easily overlook. Their

only negative characteristic is the way they often with-
draw into themselves in lengthy contemplation.

Eight
Eight is the number of worldliness, material success
and practicality. Eights live in the here and now, are
only concerned with the mundane and secular and
not given to flights of fancy; they are only interested in
living and dealing with the real world. The only negative aspect of their nature is the tendency to spend too
much time weighing up the pros and cons instead of
taking a risk.

Nine
The number of achievement, empathy, and inspiration. Nines often succeed on every level, but have difficulty finding the right partner. They find inspiration in
the unlikeliest of people, and have a penchant for pets.
There are several negative traits to Nines: the
tendency to be a little whimsical about their aims in
life, their lack of self-discipline, and their susceptibility
to unshakeable obsessions.

Unlucky 13

Long before the Hollywood "slasher movies", Friday
13th was already regarded as an evil and unlucky day,
supposedly because there were thirteen people at the
Last Supper. Also, according to the Bible, Adam and
Eve ate the forbidden fruit on a Friday, and in the holy
Book of Apocrypha, it is foretold that the Antichrist
will appear on the thirteenth day of a month which
begins with a Sunday – the thirteenth day of any

month beginning with a Sunday will of course be a Friday 13th. According to a growing number of historians, Christ was crucified on Friday 13th September. The number thirteen is venerated by occultists and Satanists and, according to superstition, anyone with thirteen letters in their name is thought to have the Devil's luck. Much has been made of the fact that over thirty of history's most infamous serial killers have all had thirteen letters in their names. People like: Jack the Ripper, Charles Manson, Albert De Salvo (the Boston Strangler), Theodore Bundy, and Jeffrey Dhamer all had thirteen letters in their names, and several killed a victim on a Friday 13th. There are thirteen members in a witches coven, and the coven meets on the nights when the moon is full: there are thirteen full moons in a year.

Weird Incidents Connected with the Number 13

On Friday 13 June 1930, Sir Henry Seagrave was advised not to make an attempt on the world water speed record because of the unlucky date. He said: "I defy superstition." At 13 minutes past 1p.m. (13th hour), Sir Henry was killed when his boat overturned on Lake Windermere.

On a Friday 13th in 1972, a pilot was told not to fly his passenger jet until the 14th by a gypsy. The pilot said he didn't believe in mumbo jumbo about Friday 13th and went ahead with the flight. He was killed when his jet crashed into the Andes on that date, and the surviving passengers who were left stranded without food were forced to resort to cannibalism to survive.

On a Friday 13th in 1979, Prince Charles was inter- viewed on the radio programme *Desert Island Discs*, and he said he thought the so-called unlucky date was "pure bunkum". After he left the BBC, Charles went to view renovation work at Exeter Cathedral; he acciden- tally walked into scaffolding bars and was almost knocked unconscious.

On Friday, 13 January 1984, a Thames television programme ridiculing the Friday 13th superstition had to be abandoned when a hurricane destroyed the studios at Teddington. Nine people were killed in the freak hurricane, including the driver of a number 13 bus in Surrey.

On Friday, 13 March 1987, a man named Monty Sterling, who had suffered bad luck and serious injuries on twelve occasions in the past when Friday 13th arrived, decided to stay in bed all day. Incredibly, Mr Sterling still became a victim of the Friday 13th curse, even in bed, because a transit van skidded off the main road and ploughed into his living room. A fire broke out and Monty was taken to hospital suffering from the effects of smoke inhalation. He was cared for in Ward 13 of Frimley Hospital, Surrey.

Apollo 13 Coincidence

On April 13, 1970 at 1300 hours, 13 minutes and 13 seconds, there was an explosion on board Apollo 13, which was 213,000 miles (340,800 km) from Earth on its way to the moon. It was a fault in circuit 13 which had caused an oxygen cell in the spacecraft to explode.

Astronaut Jim Lovell saw indicator lamp 13 flash. Later, when the ship was ready to re-enter Earth's atmosphere, Jim Lovell jettisoned the lunar service model – and he could see that the explosion had blown a panel away from the ship. That panel measured 13 ft (4 m) by 13 ft (4 m). Back on Earth a month later, Lovell entered a charity raffle – and he won with ticket number 13.

A Fatal Investigation

In March 1947, a respected English scientist named Edward Morton decided to embark on one of the most controversial ghost-hunting programmes in the history of psychic research. Dr Morton and a team of film cameramen and sound recording engineers moved into an old seventeenth-century mansion called Potterdene Hall, situated in the picturesque landscape of the Cotswolds. Morton had been invited to the allegedly haunted hall by its owner, a rich, elderly industrialist, who gave the scientist and his team two months to carry out their investigations while he spent a vacation abroad.

According to local legends, Potterdene Hall was haunted by several ectoplasmic apparitions, including the "Wild Cavalier" who, after a night of fruitless gambling, returned to the hall to murder his wife. It was said that the cavalier's wife had cursed her murderous husband with her dying breath, saying that his soul would remain earthbound within the walls of Potterdene Hall until the place crumbled. Many families who had lived in the hall over the centuries had subsequently witnessed the chilling re-enactment of the murder. The accounts of the ghostly murder were so consistent that Dr Morton was convinced some unexplained phenomenon was taking place, and by June 1947 he and his team of ghost-hunters had moved into Potterdene Hall. Infrared cameras and sensitive microphones connected to tape recorders were set up at the scene of the spectral re-enactment, a large ground-floor room with French windows which opened on to a terrace. Single-lens reflex (SLR) cameras rigged to trip wires were also set up around the room to take still pictures in case a hoaxer got up to any tomfoolery.

The ghost watch soon began. Two of the team waited in a room next door to the haunted one, listening intently through earphones to the amplified sounds from the tape recorders. Meanwhile, two other men patrolled the hall, and Dr Morton sat in a room he'd converted into an office, co-ordinating the para-normal investigation.

For over thirty days, nothing out of the ordinary was heard then, in the first week of July, a professional psychic investigator named Frederick Redfern, who had recently been enlisted by Dr Morton to join the team, said he had detected a dramatic change in the atmosphere of Potterdene Hall. Redfern became very uneasy and said he felt that something was about to manifest itself.

On the following night, something eerie did take place to back up Redfern's hunch. At 11 p.m., weird sounds of raised voices and laughter reverberated through the house and startled the psychical investi-gators. Heavy footsteps were also heard throughout Potterdene Hall, and by midnight the temperature in the mansion had fallen to a chilly 41°F (5°C). Then a ghost put in an appearance in the ground-floor room, and the cameras rolled, capturing the amazing materialization of what appeared to be a young man wearing seventeenth-century clothes. He marched through an open door in the room, apparently unaware of the film and sound crews' presence. An array of SLR cameras automatically flashed and whirred as they snapped the solid-looking phantom. Morton, Redfern and the rest of the team hurried after the ghost into the next room and continued to film him. On the floor of the adjoining room was another apparition, that of a young blonde woman, and she and the male spectre were less than 20 ft (6 m) away from their dumbfounded observers. The scene made everyone's stomach turn, because the phantom of the man they'd followed was repeatedly stabbing the woman in the chest with a dagger. The victim tried to grab her assailant's clothes after the final thrust but he tore away and then vanished. Seconds later, the whole scene faded away, and only the woman's sobs could be heard for a moment – then silence.

The team continued to film and record, but the ghosts never reappeared. Morton was ecstatic, and hours later he was driving to London with several canisters containing the undeveloped footage of the ghostly murder and the soundtrack. Morton was certain that he now had the proof in the can to show that ghosts did exist, but alas, for some unknown reason, Morton's burnt-out car was later found in a ditch. The scientist's body was almost unrecognizable when it was removed from the twisted wreckage of the vehicle; in his hands he was still holding the film canisters, as if he had survived the crash and had been attempting to crawl to safety with the precious proof of the paranormal events which had taken place at Potterdene Hall. Unfortunately, the flames from the crash had destroyed the celluloid in the canisters and the only photographic evidence of the Potterdene Hall apparitions that survived were the still pictures taken by the other members of the team. These photographs showed nothing but blurred figures and unfocused lights, nothing conclusive. The cause of the crash which killed Dr Morton and destroyed his unprocessed film was never ascertained, and some thought that the cause of his death had come from the spirit world; perhaps something supernatural which had reclaimed the evidence – with fatal results.

The Terrible Secret

Grim, forbidding Glamis Castle stands in the great vale of Strathmore in Tayside, in the north-east of Scotland. For centuries the vast fortified castle with its pointed towers has had a sinister reputation for housing an unspeakable, terrible secret, but just what is this dreadful mystery? It is said that only certain members of the British Royal Family know, but there have been whispers and bloodcurdling rumours circulating about the secret of Glamis Castle for hundreds of years, and these strange claims are the subject of the following accounts.

It is known that the Glamis Secret has nothing to do with a stubborn bloodstain that cannot be removed from the floorboards in one of the castle rooms. That stain is the blood of King Malcolm II, who was cut down by the swords of his rebellious subjects in the castle in the year 1084; nor is the secret anything to do with the fact that a Lady Glamis was burnt at the stake outside the castle for practising witchcraft, although her ghost still walks the corridors of Glamis as the Grey Lady. No, the secret of Glamis Castle lies in solving the following grotesque jigsaw puzzle of weird events.

If you stand outside the castle and count the number of windows, and compare the total with the number of windows inside the building, you will always be two windows short; in other words, there seems to be a walled-up secret room in Glamis, and what this room contains has been the subject of much debate for over six hundred years. No one knows where this secret room is, although some say it is on the top storey of the castle inside a tower. Then there is another clue; over the centuries, servants have claimed to have heard strange thuds on the walls of the building, and one of the Earls of Strathmore said he once overheard King James V mentioning the *thing* locked up in its room. Many servants at the time speculated that the *thing* was a deformed overgrown child, the product of continual inbreeding within the aristocracy over the centuries. Some researchers believe this might just be the case, for there is an oil painting at the castle depicting the green-clad figure of a child with a strangely deformed torso. The identity of the painting's subject has never been established.

In the year 1486, a particularly nasty event occurred at Glamis Castle when a party of neighbouring aristocrats, the Ogilvies, came to Glamis and begged for protection from their sworn enemies, the Lindsay family. The Ogilvies were escorted to a chamber under the castle and left there without food or water for over a month. When the chamber was opened, only one of the Ogilvies was still alive. He had eaten the other members of his family through starvation. In the seventeenth century, it was said that an unfortunate black slave was stripped naked and hunted "for fun" by the earls and their dogs. The slave was repeatedly impaled with lances and the dogs literally ripped him apart while the ladies of the castle looked on and laughed. The murdered slave's ghost may be the strange figure known as Jack the Runner, who has been seen darting about the castle, screaming as if in agony.

Around the time the slave was hunted to death, a young maiden from the local village, involved with one of the earls, was said to have stumbled on the secret chamber in Glamis. Whatever she saw must have been terrifying, because she ran screaming from the castle and was later captured by two royal henchmen. One of these henchmen took a pair of iron tongs, ripped out the young lady's tongue and threw it on the fire. This is known as the ritual of silencing, and had been performed on several servants over the years who had inadvertently stumbled upon the Glamis secret. The shock usually killed the victim or they bled to death. But the poor young woman ran out of the castle dungeon, minus her tongue, in a state of terror and with blood spurting out of her mouth. The henchmen went after her and one of them grabbed her in a headlock and twisted her head until her neck broke. The body was then carefully sawn up and fed to the wild boars in the forest.

The unmentionable secret of Glamis was briefly touched upon in 1904 when the thirteenth Earl of Strathmore, Claude Bowes-Lyon, told an inquisitive friend, "If you could only know the nature of the terrible secret, you would go down on your knees and thank God it were not yours." The Earl's cryptic remark only deepens the mystery, although the friend he spoke to later claimed that he had found the secret chamber, whereupon he was quickly bundled off to the colonies – some say he was sent to Australia.

Earlier this century, when the daughter of the four-teenth Earl of Glamis asked what the secret was, her father told her, "You cannot be told; for no woman can ever know the secret of Glamis Castle."

It is claimed that certain members of the Royal Family know of the terrible secret, and they are all males. It is said that they are traditionally told on their eighteenth birthday, but none of the royals has ever commented on or denied the secret of Glamis Castle.

Secrets of the Vatican Letter

In a subterranean labyrinth of corridors and vaults beneath the Vatican in Rome there is a large safe containing various documents which the Vatican has hidden from the light of day. Most of the records in the Vatican Archives are hundreds of years old and are classed as heretical. Among the yellowed, timeworn manuscripts are Henry VIII's application for divorce, a dossier on the subversive activities of one Galileo Galilei, compiled by the spies of the Inquisition, and, according to an enduring legend, the Vatican safe also holds a small azure-coloured envelope that bears the Papal seal. Within this innocuous-looking envelope is alleged to be a mysterious document known as the Vatican Letter, reputed to contain prophesies of a terrifying, apocalyptic nature.

The story of the Vatican Letter began in the year

1917. In the little Portuguese town of Fatima, three youngsters were looking after their families' sheep. The shepherds, Lucia dos Santos, aged nine, Francisco Marto, aged eight, and his six-year-old sister, Jacinta, were astounded to witness the appearance of the radiant figure of a boy who looked about fifteen years of age. The vision told the children to pray, then vanished.

The youngsters were sure they had encountered an angel, but decided to keep the unearthly meeting a secret. As Portugal's irreligious political leaders had vowed to stamp out Catholicism "within two generations", it was hardly the time to report the sighting of a heavenly messenger.

On 13 May that year the children were out in the fields again, tending their families' flocks, when they witnessed another apparition that appeared after a flash of strange summer lightning lit up the skies. The shepherds expected thunder and rain, and ran for shelter, but no thunder rolled and no rain fell. Instead, a woman in white suddenly appeared, inexplicably, nearby. The "lady" told the children that she was from heaven and said, "Continue to come here on the thirteenth of each month. In October I will say who I am and what I desire and will perform a miracle all shall see so that they believe."

As soon as the heavenly visitant had vanished, the children agreed that the encounter with the lady must be kept secret. However, upon reaching home, little Jacinta could not contain her excitement and blurted out her account of the meeting with the unearthly woman, whom she believed to be the Virgin Mary. News of the vision quickly spread and crowds descended on Fatima. They followed the shepherd children everywhere and, on the thirteenth day of each month, the multitudes pursued them to the site of the rendezvous with the apparition. When the lady appeared, as she had promised, most of the crowd couldn't see her, although many did report seeing "a strange bright cloud" hanging low in the sky directly over the shepherds.

When 13 August arrived, Lucia, Francisco and Jacinta could not keep their appointment with the lady; the children had been kidnapped and jailed by the civil authorities. The youngsters were interrogated over their conversation with the invisible entity and, when the young shepherds remained tight-lipped, an official warned them that they would be "boiled alive" if they refused to denounce their vision. The brave children remained silent and were subsequently released. Six days later, the lady appeared to the young shepherds again, telling them that they would only see her one more time on this planet.

On 13 October a raging rainstorm hit Fatima, but the 80,000 people who had made a pilgrimage to the town endured the inclement weather and concentrated on the three shepherds. The observers were not disappointed. The rain stopped, the skies glowed and flashed with incandescent colours that were much richer than those of the usual rainbow. Shortly afterwards, the children appeared to be talking to an unseen presence. When the skies darkened again, a sensational rumour rippled through the crowds; the lady had handed a letter to Lucia.

It is alleged that officials took the letter from Lucia and were so horrified at the predictions it contained that they literally became reformed people overnight, subsequently passing the epistle on to the Pope himself. According to rumours, various individuals inside the Vatican have claimed that Pope John XXIII suffered a minor stroke when he read the contents of the Vatican Letter in 1963 and, for some unknown reason, the soon-to-be-assassinated US President John F. Kennedy was afterwards summoned to the Vatican by the Pope – who also died that year. Months after Kennedy's clandestine meeting with Pope John, a German newspaper published the purported "complete text" of the Vatican Letter and the religious authorities refused to confirm or deny the validity of the scoop. The German newspaper story claimed that the letter mentioned the outbreak of two world wars, the attempted assassination of a reigning Pope, a global plague, and a nuclear war on the Asian subcontinent which would escalate and wipe out three entire nations. The letter was said to end with a warning that each of the aforementioned events would surely come to pass if humanity failed to change its "wicked, evil ways".

The Dark Side of Rock

When rock and roll first appeared in the 1950s, it was literally branded the "Devil's music", as nothing like it had been heard before. It captured the imagination of a whole new generation and seemed to take them over. However, anxiety about the supernatural side of music dates back to before the rock and roll era. In the 1930s a song called *Gloomy Sunday* was banned by the BBC after allegedly causing a spate of suicides because it sounded so mournful. Another song that even musicians consider to be very unlucky is one called

I Dreamt I Dwelt in Marble Halls from a musical called *The Bohemian Girl.* Even to hum the tune is said to invite bad luck and news of a death. In the 1930s, a rumour travelled the world that claimed that blues legend, Robert Johnston, had acquired his musical skills after making a pact with the Devil at a deserted country crossroads. The very same rumour was later repeated in the 1970s, alleging that Jimi Hendrix had made a pact with Satan for his phenomenal guitar talent.

In the late 1960s, Christian fundamentalist preachers accused record companies of being fronts for Satanic organizations that were hiding secret, subliminal messages in the records. Of course, many groups thought that these accusations were a good publicity gimmick, and bands like Black Sabbath and Led Zeppelin revelled in all the paranoia. There was even a rumour that Led Zeppelin's Jimmy Page was a black magician; Page once bought and lived in a huge mansion on the banks of Loch Ness that was once owned by the prominent Devil worshipper, Aleister Crowley. Around this time, the Beatles released their landmark *Sergeant Pepper's Lonely Hearts Club Band* album, which contained many mysterious tracks which have never been satisfactorily explained. Some fans say there is the sound of a car crash being played in reverse on the track *Being for the Benefit of Mr Kite,* and the allegedly offensive message – "we'll fuck you like supermen" – that is played backwards at the end of the album was once thought to be a message from the Devil himself. The album's producer, George Martin, has always maintained that the end-track is nothing sinister at all; merely a random collection of spliced tapes of sounds and conversations. The fans of the Beatles thought otherwise, and made much of the fact that Satan-worshipper Aleister Crowley was included in the famous crowd scene on the album cover of *Sergeant Pepper*. When the Beatles released their widely-acclaimed *White Album* a year later, cult leader Charles Manson claimed that one of their songs, *Helter Skelter*, had driven him and his band of followers to go on a killing spree which culminated in the grotesque murder of heavily-pregnant actress Sharon Tate. Manson also claimed that another Beatle's song called *Blackbird* contained disguised messages about a race war. Manson said one lyric line in the song, "Take these broken wings and learn to fly", was actually referring to a future time when the blacks of America would revolt.

By the late 1980s and early 1990s, the heavy metal music scene became another source of bizarre rumours. There were stories in the worldwide media of young men committing "heavy-metal suicide" after listening to certain tracks on heavy metal albums. The tracks were said to contain suicidal instructions to the listener that had been "back-masked", or played backwards, just below the audible level. In 1990, the families of two dead youths sought damages of over £3 million from heavy metal band Judas Priest and CBS records, claiming that their two teenaged sons had shot themselves after being inspired by the band's evil-sounding music.

And the dark legends about popular music keep on coming. In June 1997, the Internet was buzzing with news of a fascinating discovery. It was alleged that if you play Pink Floyd's album, *Dark Side of the Moon* to a video of the *Wizard of Oz*, you will see that the band's music is actually a soundtrack to the cult film.

Pink Floyd were quizzed about this bizarre musical discovery, but refused to comment, and sales of their old album trebled.

Warlocks

Stratigraphy is one of the primary tools of archaeological interpretation, and is based on the fact that, where one deposited layer of earth overlies another, the upper layer must have accumulated later in time than the lower. Thus, fossils can be dated from their surrounding strata. This geological record extends downwards from the ground you walk on in chronological layers. If we dig down a few feet we may find coins from the Middle Ages, and if we continue to excavate we could unearth the vestiges of a Roman camp; much deeper lie the fossilized remains of the dinosaurs.

However, there are many "anomalous fossils" which give the archaeologists and historians sleepless nights. For example, in 1927 at Fisher Canyon, Nevada, USA, a block of limestone was split open to reveal the fossilized imprint of a well-cut and double-stitched leather sole. The limestone block containing the shoe print was from the Triassic era, which meant it was formed 160 to 195 million years ago. Fossilized shoe imprints have even been discovered in Carboniferous rock that was formed 300 million years before the advent of the dinosaurs. One such imprint uncovered at Antelope Springs in Utah, USA, showed a crushed trilobite underneath a sandalled heel. A trilobite is an extinct marine creature that flourished 200 to 500 million years ago. In 1961, another anomalous fossil came to light when gem hunters in California X-rayed a 500,000-year-old nodule. The X-ray showed that the ancient rock contained something which looked identical to a modern sparking plug. The function of the cylindrical object and how it came to be encased in rock half a million years old is still unanswered. Furthermore, in the Natural History Museum in London, there is the skull of a Neanderthal man which seems to have been blasted with a high-velocity bullet – over 40,000 years ago. On one side of the skull there is a small, perfectly round hole, and the damage to the other side of the skull is consistent with the effects of a high-velocity bullet being fired through the head. There have been many other incredible discoveries which – if accepted – could disprove the textbook version of prehistory and demolish the Darwinian theory of evolution.

The out-of-place fossils seem to back up the long-held claims of every culture; that in the remote past, there were many civilizations which reached the pinnacle of technological achievement before being wiped out by catastrophes. Our own civilization could share this fate tomorrow, through nuclear self-annihilation, or even from interplanetary cataclysm. At midnight on Monday, 10 August 1998, the Earth came within six hours of being obliterated as a giant mile-wide asteroid hurtled past it at over 50,000 mph (80,000 kph). The asteroid missed us all by just under a million miles (1,600,000 km), which, on the cosmic scale, is quite a close shave. If the giant rock hadn't veered away from the world, it would have killed over a quarter of the global population and created a gigantic tidal wave 17 miles (27 km) high. The menacing asteroid was the biggest in recorded history to have come so close to the Earth, and the terrifying near-miss was only known to a select group of scientists to avoid public mass hysteria. It has been estimated that about every 100,000 years, a comet or asteroid hits the Earth, and once every century a 55-yd (50-m) object collides with our planet, causing an explosion 5,000 more powerful than that of the Hiroshima atomic bomb. Some scientists even believe the dinosaurs were wiped out by an asteroid which smashed into the Earth sixty-five million years ago. The next known asteroid that will graze Earth will be the 10 mile (16 km) wide Toutatis, which will come within thirteen hours of our world on 29 September 2004.

When we take the threat of catastrophe from space, or the misuse of nuclear technology, into consideration, it seems frighteningly plausible that perhaps there were civilizations in antediluvian times which reached their zenith only to be exterminated by a natural or self-inflicted Armageddon. Occultists all over the world claim that magic, both black and white, is a fragmented remnant of the super-science used by the ancient masters millions of years ago. There are those who believe that some scientists from the lost Golden Age of Man survived the ancient disasters and upheavals and have transmitted their kabbalistic knowledge to various students down the ages. One quasi-historical personage who comes to mind is the mysterious Merlin, the celebrated wizard who advised King Arthur.

The information on Merlin is very scant, but it is recorded that he originated in Wales, possibly towards the close of the fifth century. Legend has it that Merlin was a powerful magician who used levitation and other magical talents to construct Stonehenge. Some accounts say the Welsh wizard perished after a fierce battle between the Britons and their Romanized compatriots in the year 570, but other traditions maintain that Merlin was trapped in a hollow, rocky hill by Nimue, the enchantress he was beguiled by. The whereabouts of this hill are unknown, but a fable has persisted for centuries that names Cheshire's Alderley Edge as the site of Merlin's prison. Alderley Edge is a rocky sandstone escarpment which rises to over 600 ft (182 m) above sea level and is over 2 miles (3 km) long. This magnificent, brooding mound with its breathtaking, panoramic views of Macclesfield, gives the nearby town a few miles south of Wilmslow its name. Many visitors to the Edge have commented on the strong presence of a mysterious, bygone age which seeps into our dimension.

Excavations at Alderley Edge have established that ancient pagans mined the copper on its slopes, and lit sacrificial bonfires on the summit. At the height of the witch persecution mania in the 1640s, many covens who held regular sabbats at the Edge had to disband and flee to Wales. Even today, witches and warlocks regularly congregate at the Edge on certain nights of the year to celebrate the old pagan gods of Ishtar, Pan, Diana and Samhain.

Early one morning in 1695, a farmer from Mobberley set off for Macclesfield market with a majestic ivory-coloured mare which he intended to sell for a good price. To reach his destination, the farmer had to lead his horse across the lower slopes of Alderley Edge, and it was here that something amazing took place. An old man, wearing a flowing black robe and a strange pointed cap, approached the farmer.

The man held a staff and his beard was as white as snow. The stranger wished the farmer good day, then eyed the white mare and offered to buy it.

The farmer refused the offer, saying that he'd get a better price at Macclesfield market, but the old man confidently stated that the white horse would not be sold at the market and he predicted that the farmer would meet him again at the Edge later in the evening. The farmer from Mobberley sneered and continued on his journey. However, much to the farmer's surprise, he was unable to sell his graceful horse at the market. During the return journey to Mobberley, the disappointed farmer was once more passing the lower slopes of Alderley Edge and, as prophesied, the same old man he had seen that morning suddenly appeared from nowhere. This time the old man said nothing, but motioned the farmer to follow him through the woods to the rock face. The intrigued farmer trailed after the old man past a large rock called Stormy Point, where a strange sensation suddenly came over him, hypnotically compelling him to follow the stranger. The old man stopped and gazed at the blank sandstone face of Castle Rock, which forms the eastern side of the Edge. The farmer wondered what would happen next, when suddenly a kind of doorway opened in the face of the rock. The bearded man in black pointed his staff at the doorway then walked through it. The farmer felt himself strongly drawn through the same doorway and found himself walking into an immense cavern that was illuminated by a faint amber phosphorescence. On the floor, in one part of the cavern, was an array of men in shining armour lying side by side. They looked as if they were only sleeping, and had shields and swords at their sides. In a sombre manner, the old man glanced at the sleeping, armoured warriors and explained that they were King Arthur and the knights of Camelot, lying in a state of deep sleep in the chamber until their country needed them.

It suddenly dawned on the farmer that the old man was Merlin, Arthur's mentor. Before the farmer could quiz the elderly man, however, he was given a heavy sack of gold coins in exchange for the white mare. The old man ordered the farmer to leave the cave, and he did so, looking back just once to see the sleeping knights. He also saw the sorcerer laying down the horse, which was now unconscious. Perhaps it was being put into a state of suspended animation until a future time when it would be revived to carry Arthur himself into a final great battle.

As the farmer left the hidden stronghold, the ground shook as the slab of the stone door crashed down behind him. Strangely enough, many travellers to Alderley Edge have reported seeing a rectangular shape in the face of Castle Rock which rapidly fades whenever it is inspected at close quarters. The farmer returned to Mobberley and told his strange tale to those who would listen, but was naturally ridiculed. Yet no one ever discovered where the farmer had obtained his bag of gold coins, all of which bore the insignia of a dragon. Today, a wishing well known as the Wizard's Well is to be found on the woodland path to Castle Rock, where the entrance to Merlin's cavern is said to be.

Just a couple of miles to the west of Alderley Edge, another supernatural incident allegedly took place in 1595. A highwayman named Ned Holden was captured by the authorities and hanged. In the early hours of the morning under a full moon, a vagrant, named Gammin, on the road from Knutsford, spotted two figures cutting the hanged criminal down from the tree. The tramp hid behind a hedgerow and watched the two men carry the body into a nearby wood. Out of curiosity, Gammin decided to follow the body-snatchers into the woodland, even though he was fearful of what would happen if the men saw him.

The men were John Gough and Toby Rodgers, two young dabblers in the Black Arts and avid students of the alchemist and mathematician, John Dee, who was at that time the warden of Manchester College. Gough and Rodgers had Dee's books, which were branded as heretical and blasphemous in England at that time.

At a clearing in the wood, a lantern hung on the branch of a tree, with the corpse of Ned Holden laid out beneath it. One of the men started to recite unintelligible words while the other one kneeled down by the corpse and closely inspected its face. The tramp Gammin looked on, fascinated, wondering what was going on. He soon found out.

By the light of the lantern, the corpse's mouth was seen to flicker. Then the eyes opened wide to reveal two white eyeballs. Gammin almost fainted when he saw the highwayman being reanimated by the black magic. Gammin didn't know it, but Gough and Rodgers were practising the ancient and well-documented art of "necromancy" – raising a dead person to obtain information from the corpse. One of the men was heard to ask the corpse a specific question repeatedly. According to Gammin, this question was: "Where are your proceeds hidden?" The hanged highwayman's eyes rolled, and in a raspy, chilling voice, he asked: "Where am I?" The necromancer told him he was dead and damned to spend eternity in Hell unless he revealed the location of his treasure. The corpse made a moaning sound then uttered a garbled reply about a well situated by a dead-end lane. At this point, Gammin was spotted by the black magicians and chased, but he managed to lose them in the woods. The vagrant alerted the authorities but Gough and Rodgers could not be found. The notorious occultists were later sighted in Manchester but never caught. Gammin and scores of other people searched for the well near the dead-end lane described by Holden in the hope of finding his hidden loot, but it is not known if anything was ever found.

In the 1860s, an old Welsh hermit named Ivor Williams – who lived in a dilapidated cottage on the Cheshire border near Worthenbury – was a man to be shunned because the locals believed he was a real-life wizard. In 1861, a man named McGowan was driving a wagon-load of wood across land adjacent to Williams's cottage, when suddenly the horses pulling the wagon stopped dead. McGowan soon discovered that the horses weren't acting strangely; it was the wagon itself. The wheels seemed to be locked tight. Then McGowan noticed the elderly Mr Williams standing in the doorway of his cottage, gazing intently at the wagon with his steely blue eyes. In the end, McGowan had no choice but to unhitch his horses, and as soon as he did, they trotted over to the hermit and stood still on his path as the old man whispered something to them. Moments later, the horses galloped off. This naturally convinced McGowan that the weird rumours about Williams were true after all, and he abandoned his timber-laden wagon and hurried along the road to Wrexham on foot.

In 1865, a number of superstitious farmers from Wales and Cheshire put their names to a petition to evict the sinister recluse on the grounds that he was a practising witch and therefore an anti-Christian, but a local magistrate adjudicated that there was no evidence to support the claims that Williams was acting unlawfully in any way. In the summer of that year, the farmers who tried to get rid of Williams claimed that the old man had caused havoc on their farms with his strange powers. Cattle fainted, mysterious fires broke out which razed farm buildings to the ground, and in July, something truly bizarre took place one sunny afternoon which even earned a mention in *The Times.* Hundreds of people in Wrexham and parts of Cheshire were startled to see masses of hay drifting through the blue skies. Haymakers in Wrexham noticed the strange spectacle first, but as the flying hay moved in a north-eastwards direction (against the wind) over the skies of Cheshire, more and more people saw the peculiar sight. Several witnesses came forward and claimed that they had seen a ton of hay rise from a farm outside Wrexham – the very same farmstead which was owned by the farmer who had arranged the petition to evict the hermit Williams.

In 1869, Ivor Williams's cottage was gutted by a blaze one night, but no trace of its curious and much-feared tenant was ever found in the smouldering ruins, and the hermit's fate remains a mystery. The superstitious locals thought that the loner's disappearance after the blaze meant that Lucifer had reclaimed the old warlock.

A Name to Conjure With

Many of the superstitious beliefs people have today are the remnants of magical rites performed by magicians and Druids of centuries past. For example, many people throw a pinch of salt over their left shoulder, or go to extreme lengths to avoid walking under a ladder. These seemingly illogical actions are a throwback to the rites of black magicians who practised the so-called Secret Arts in the Middle Ages. But surely, in this technological era, belief in magic is at an all-time low? That simply isn't the case; in fact many sociologists believe that there is currently an occult revival going on in the world. But does magic work, or is it all just mumbo jumbo? This is the subject of the following report, which also highlights the misuse of television and radio.

In the 1970s, the Israeli psychic, Uri Geller, appeared on live national television and allegedly demonstrated his famous spoon-bending talent. Geller later looked into the television camera and urged the millions of television viewers to concentrate on any metal objects in their homes. The result was nothing short of astounding, as the telephone switchboard of the BBC went haywire with excited viewers calling to say that their cutlery had curled and bent before their eyes, whilst others said that clocks and watches that hadn't worked for years had suddenly started to function. At the very same moment that Geller urged the British nation to concentrate on unleashing their psychic potential, Big Ben stopped for no apparent reason, and at the very minute that Big Ben stopped, a French weather satellite orbiting the earth went out of control as it passed over Britain and later plummeted into the atmosphere. It also came to light that, as the apparent psychic wave was sweeping the country, there was an unprecedented outbreak of paranormal activity. A house in Battersea was the scene of an explosion which originated in the attic. After the strange blast, bricks and slates were seen to float about and, for the next fortnight, the house was besieged by more nerve-shattering poltergeist activity.

Whether all this was the result of Geller's influence via the mass medium of television is debatable. On 9 November 1965, a similar incident took place when an offbeat radio show in New York featured an eccentric old guest who maintained he was a practising black magician. The man, George Whitefern, said he could talk to the spirit of any famous historical personage, and could also conjure up malevolent spirits in the homes of the listeners by merely reciting an ancient black magic word. The radio presenter said, "That's great. You've got to say the word." The presenter thought the old man was talking nonsense. So Mr Whitefern uttered the supposedly magical and closely-guarded word – which sounded like "jooker" – and what happened next was subsequently explained away in the *New York Times* as the effects of mass hysteria. Across New York State, there was an alleged wave of supernatural incidents. An enormous mirror in a suite in the Empire State Building split in two while two businessmen were listening to the radio programme. At that very same moment, a man climbed over the safety rails on the roof of the Empire State Building and leaped to his death before horrified onlookers for no apparent reason. The man had just been promoted in his job and had everything to live for. Coincidentally, a flock of pigeons fell out of the sky over Central Park. They were all dead but were not injured or diseased in any way. There were many other strange, unaccountable incidents in the Big Apple that day, but something else happened on that date in November 1965 which is even more of a mystery: the biggest power failure in America's history took place that evening and blacked out New York and the north-eastern seaboard of the United States. When reports about the black magician on the radio reached the press and television news hounds, the hunt was on to track down George Whitefern, but he couldn't be found, and was never heard from again.

A Surprise Appearance at the Cavern Club

The following story is a particularly strange one. It concerns three men who used to visit the Cavern Club in Liverpool back in the days before Merseybeat, and when the Cavern was still a jazz club. The incident was reported in the *Liverpool Echo* in the late 1950s, and the manager of the Cavern at the time claimed that there was a ghost that haunted the ladies toilets in the club.

Around 1957, a man named Alan Sytner opened the Cavern Club in Liverpool to provide a venue for the then thriving jazz scene. As most people the world over know, the Cavern was basically just a collection of arched warehouse cellars in the heart of downtown Liverpool, where the Beatles first came to prominence.

In the late 1950s, three men went to the club one evening with their girlfriends, and had a great time listening to the jazz bands well into the early hours. The men were Johnny Richards, Tony Fitzsimmons and Peter Farley, and at 4 a.m., when most of the club-goers had gone home, the three men and their girls sat at a table, smoking and chatting away. The conversation turned from sport and politics to religion and the meaning of life, and they finally ended up arguing about the occult. At this point, one of the men's girl-friends, Rita James, said that one of the toilets in the Cavern was said to be haunted, but Peter, who was a hard-boiled sceptic, said the ghost story was probably just a publicity gimmick invented by the Cavern's owner, Alan Sytner. An employee overheard Peter's remark and told them that the ghost of a man in black had been seen in the club by one of the bouncers quite recently.

At this point, Johnny suggested that everyone present should gather round the table and join hands to summon the ghost, and he claimed that he knew the actual words to evoke a spirit. The girlfriends thought it would be exciting and they urged their boyfriends and the bouncers to join in. Everyone thought it was a joke, except a young man named Tony who, although not exactly religious, said the occult should not be regarded in such a lighthearted manner. Tony sat at another table and lit up a ciga-rette. He watched the proceedings and seemed very nervous.

So everyone but Tony gathered about the table, and Johnny said, "Right, turn the lights off. Get a candle or something." A candle couldn't be found, but someone brought a small electric torch to the circle, switched it on then placed it in the centre of the table. Then the lights were turned off, and all the people round the table joined hands. There was a scream. One of the bouncers had put his hand up one of the girl's dresses for a laugh. Johnny said, "Stop messing about. We need absolute silence." There were a few sniggers, then a strange silence fell over them. About a minute later, Johnny said, "O Lord of Darkness, I invite you into the Cavern. Give us a sign so we may believe."

About a minute later, a shadow walked across the darkened room. It was that of a tall man. He wore a black suit and a black polo-neck sweater. His black fringe was combed back into the style of the so-called "DA cut" popularized by the film star Tony Curtis. All the girls looked at him, but none of them was scared. They thought the stranger was just a clubgoer who had been part of the stay-behind. All the girls later said that the man was very attractive and had magnetic dark eyes. Tony, who was seated at the other table on his own, thought the man was evil from the moment he set eyes upon him, and he noticed that the stranger seemed to come from the direction of the toilets.

"I am Lucifer," said the man in a rich deep voice. He then smirked and studied the shocked expressions of the people at the table.

"Stop messing about, " said Johnny, "we're trying to hold a seance here."

"You idiot," said the stranger, "I am Lucifer. You didn't expect me to have horns, did you?"

"Oh, you're the Devil?" asked one of the bouncers in a cocky tone. He was trying to impress one of the girls present.

The stranger nodded, and continued, "I haven't got hoofed feet either."

"Johnny I'm scared. Turn the lights on," urged Rita, and started to shake. She was about to turn hysterical.

"Relax, dear, " said the stranger, "I'm not as bad as I'm painted."

The sceptical one, Peter, said, "There's no such thing as the Devil."

"If you believe in God you must believe in me too," said the man in black, then he calmly added, "Unless you are an atheist, of course."

"Yes I am, actually," replied Peter, in a matter-of-fact way.

"Then if you don't believe in me, can I have your soul?" responded the stranger.

Peter laughed nervously, "But I don't believe . . ."

"So give me your soul then!" shouted the stranger.

The atmosphere was tense with a mounting sense of terror.

"Okay, take it then," said Peter, and he grinned, but seemed to be very uneasy.

"No! Don't, Peter! Don't!" shouted Tony from the other table, and he stood up but was afraid to come over.

"Thank you." said the stranger, and he reached out in Peter's direction and seemed to clutch at something in the air.

Then the torch started to fade. Within seconds it was just a dim orange filament, and the Cavern was in complete blackness.

"That was one amateurish set-up," sneered one of the bouncers, almost falling over the table in the dark. He went to switch on the lights, but they didn't go on. "Oh, don't tell me the fuses have gone again," he complained, groping in the darkness Condensation was such a problem at the club, the moisture often caused the fuses of the mains supply to short . . .

At the same time, a voice whispered in Tony's ear,

"I'll be back for you one day, and your God won't be able to save you."

Tony said, "In the name of our saviour Jesus Christ I tell you to leave."

Then the lights suddenly went on, and the rest of the people rose from the table. But Peter didn't. He slumped forwards, hitting his face on the tabletop. He seemed drunk, but when his friends took him home, Peter didn't seem to be breathing. He was taken by taxi to the Royal Hospital in Pembroke Place – and was certified dead on arrival. The coroner who performed the post-mortem examination later said that Peter – who was 27 – had the body of an eighteen-year-old, and seemed to have been in perfect health. A verdict of death by natural causes was recorded, but all the people who had attended the frightening seance believed that Peter had died because he had foolishly given permission to the Devil to wrench the soul from his body.

The Art of the Death Touch

Bruce Lee was born in San Francisco on 27 November 1940, but was raised in Hong Kong, where he embarked on a movie career at the age of six. Around his early teens, Bruce started to develop an interest in the martial arts. To harden his fists, he would pound them on a stool every day for hours, gradually transforming his hands into ataraxic weapons.

He returned to the United States when he was eighteen (to retain his American citizenship) and enrolled as a philosophy student at Washington University. Throughout his studies, Lee taught jeetkune do' (a hybrid discipline of kung fu and western pugilism) to provide him with an income of a few hundred dollars per week. One of his students, Linda Emery, was fascinated by her tutor, and she married him in 1964. Lee decided to quit his studies to rekindle his acting career in Hollywood. He landed a role as Kato in *The Green Hornet* television series, and also gave martial arts lessons to some of the biggest movie stars in Los Angeles. For $150 an hour Lee taught his skills to James Coburn, Lee Marvin, James Garner and Steve McQueen.

Around this time, Warner Brothers were ready to produce *Kung Fu,* a groundbreaking television series about Kwai Chang Caine, a Buddhist monk trained in karate, who flees mainland China for the West after murdering a nobleman. Lee applied for the part of Caine, but Warner thought he was too inexperienced to play the role, which went to actor-dancer David Carradine instead. *Kung Fu* proved to be a success story in the USA and Europe, and is now regarded as a television cult classic.

Lee had been denied stardom in the land of opportunity, so he returned to Hong Kong, where he struck up a partnership with Raymond Chow, an innovative film producer. The two men literally became the new wave of the Hong Kong film industry, and collaborated on some of the early kung fu blockbusters.

In 1971 Lee starred in his first Chinese action film, *The Big Boss.* He played the part of a new boy in an ice factory who helps striking workers with his breathtaking martial arts talent. The original cut was deemed to be too violent and the censors held the film release date back for a year, then there was more trouble getting it distributed, but Lee continued to strive for international superstardom. He wrote, produced and directed *The Way of the Dragon* (1973), casting himself as Tan Lung, an out-of-town tough guy who is paid by a Chinese restaurant owner in Rome to sort out the local Mafia menace.

Warner Brothers learned that the films were being well received, and were soon beating a path to Lee's door. The film company offered major financial support for Lee's next film, *Enter the Dragon* (1973). The film proved to be the success that had eluded Lee for so long but, tragically, the rising film star never got to enjoy the benefits of his achievement. While dubbing the film in Hong Kong on 10 May 1973, Bruce Lee collapsed. He later recovered but experienced respiratory problems. He tried to breathe, but found it exhausting, then suffered a series of convulsions which were put down to a swelling of his brain. Lee was given Mannitol, an osmotic diuretic drug, which seemed to do the trick. A week later, Lee appeared as fit as ever. At Los Angeles, Dr David Reisbord examined Lee. After a brain scan, a brain-flow study, a physical check-up, and an EEG analysis, Dr Reisbord told Lee that he had probably suffered a grand mal seizure – an indication of epilepsy – yet there were no indications why this should have happened. The brain scan showed no abnormalities, and the other tests had confirmed that Lee was in perfect physical condition, so the sudden collapse and brain swelling were very unusual.

Lee began to lose weight, much to the consternation of his friends, who urged him to see his doctor again. But Lee seemed too wrapped up in his work. This was the break he had dreamed of for so long. Two months after his check-up, Lee was working on a script in the

Hong Kong apartment of Betty Ting-pei, his co-star, when he suddenly complained of a bad headache. The actress offered Lee an Equagesic painkiller – a two-layer tablet containing aspirin, calcium carbonate, and ethoheptazine citrate. The drug had been prescribed for Ting-pei by her doctor. Lee took the tablet and said he was going for a nap in the actress's bed. He never woke up again. At 9.30 p.m. Raymond Chow arrived at the apartment to pick the film star up for a dinner engagement. When he found he could not wake Lee he called for a doctor, who tried to revive the actor, but his effort was in vain. At Queen Elizabeth Hospital, Bruce Lee was pronounced dead. The world was rocked by the news.

The circumstances surrounding Lee's death were interpreted as suspicious by many. Lee had not been taken to the nearest hospital when he was found unconscious, and traces of cannabis were found in the dead man. Many wondered how someone regarded as "the fittest man in the world" could just die without any apparent cause.

A coroner's inquest was convened on 3 September, and the findings were: firstly, the amount of cannabis found in Lee's body was too small to have contributed to the actor's death; secondly, Lee had "probably" died because of a hypersensitivity to a compound in the painkiller he took, possibly the aspirin component.

The official verdict was "death by misadventure". Case closed.

But several unsavoury facts were bandied about by the media regarding Lee's behaviour on the eve of his death. It was learned that Lee had publicly attacked Lo Wei – the man who had directed *The Big Boss* and other kung fu genre films – on the very day before he died from taking the aspirin. But the incident was quickly put down to being the climax of a long-standing feud between the two men. There were rumours of the Chinese Mafia and the Triads having a hand in the actor's demise, and there were exotic theories gleaned from the tales of people who had been close to the star. It came to light that, during the last months of the actor's life, certain mysterious, nameless individuals had approached Lee and told him he was surrounded by "bad omens". Some believed these "men in black" to be members of an obscure Eastern sect who had come to America to warn Lee about flaunting the closely-guarded secrets of the ancient fighting arts. These alleged visitors were said to have killed Lee with the "death-touch" or *dim mak* as it is known in the Far East. According to legend, the person who is trained in *dim mak* can dispose of his enemy by applying the briefest of pressures on the non-critical points of the victim's body. The victim does not die immediately, but succumbs after a length of time has passed. The delay period is governed by the particular nerve points that are chosen and the amount of pressure applied to each point respectively. It is easy to scoff at such a concept of killing by touch, but there are historical records that state that the art of *dim mak* was in use during the T'ang Dynasty (AD 618–906), and even today in Taiwan, the deadly art is still alleged to be employed for "perfect murders".

The reports of Lee losing weight shortly before he died have led some students of the Eastern arts to conclude that the actor was killed by a lethal technique known as *duann mie*, which, without going into too much esoteric detail, is a way of killing an enemy by directing a blow against a specific vein, which leads to a wasting away of the victim through the ensuing disruption of specific blood vessels. Oddly enough, when Bruce Lee's body was examined by a pathologist, the blood vessels in the lungs were found to be unaccountably broken in a way described by the medical expert as "strange".

The Royals and the Paranormal

It has been known for years that Her Majesty the Queen has had a number of psychic experiences, and that she accepts the reality of spirit survival. Interest in the occult is in fact a tradition of the House of Windsor. The Queen has allegedly had around ten ghostly encounters in her life. The first paranormal experience took place in 1953. That year, Lilian Bailey, an elderly medium from Wembley in North London, received a phone call asking her to come to a prestigious address in Kensington. When Mrs Bailey arrived, an aristocratic-looking man accompanied her to a Rolls-Royce and calmly blindfolded her. He then took the medium to another address, and when the blindfold was taken off, Mrs Bailey found herself seated at a large circular table in a darkened room.

Five silhouettes were seated around the table. In a curiously refined voice, one of the shadowy people asked the medium if she could get in touch with King George VI, who had recently died. Mrs Bailey said she would try. She went into a trance after a long, tense period of silent concentration, then something eerily spectacular took place: a pale face gradually materialized above Mrs Bailey's head. It was soon recognizable as the face of the late King George VI, and the eyes of the ghostly visage were closed. There was a series of astonished gasps from the sitters at the seance, but someone panicked and let out a shriek. The spectral face hovering above the Wembley psychic opened its eyes as if startled from some type of sleep by the scream. The face then faded away into the darkness.

Mrs Bailey groaned, slumped forward and opened her eyes. Several people scrambled from the table and switched on the lights. To her utter amazement, Mrs Bailey saw that the sitters at the impromptu seance were Her Majesty the Queen, the Queen Mother, Prince Philip, the Duchess of Kent and her daughter, Princess Alexandra. Mrs Bailey subsequently learned that she was in Buckingham Palace. She was sincerely thanked for her services and was later taken back to her humble North London home in the Rolls-Royce.

The Queen later confided to friends that she had seen her late father some seven times at numerous seances held at Buckingham Palace over the years. Her Majesty has also seen three other ghosts, including a spectral footman at Sandringham and George III's ashen face peering out from a window at Windsor Castle.

Prince Charles has always been interested in spiritualism and has allegedly seen a number of ghosts. In 1984, Charles overheard two servants at Windsor talking about an apparition they'd encountered in one of the corridors. Charles immediately obtained a tape recorder, a thermometer and a camera loaded with infrared film, and he spent a lone vigil in the library, which was situated off the haunted corridor.

The first night Charles saw nothing, but the next night, while he waited in the cloisters, he was astounded to see a stout figure coming along absolutely soundlessly. The figure looked immensely overweight, and wore white breeches and a scarlet tunic trimmed with gold. As the apparition passed within 6 ft (less than 2 m) of him, Charles could see that the ghost had a beard. Suddenly the phantom let out a groan, and Charles actually captured the noise on tape. Seconds later the obese ghost vanished, and Charles later told his wife, Diana, that he believed he had encountered the spectre of Henry VIII. Later that year, Charles also claimed that he had also confronted a beautiful, long-haired woman who vanished when he spoke to her. Charles said she looked exactly like Catherine Howard, whose portrait he was familiar with.

Unknown Forces

● ●

"Some day, in the far, far distant
future, I shall be understood."

Morgenstern

Sinister Effigies

Anyone who has ever visited Madame Tussaud's
waxwork museum in London will have experienced
the creepy feeling that the wax dummies they are
looking at have some dark glimmer of life in their eyes.
The suspicion that wax effigies or dolls have a life of
their own probably stems from the fairy-tale way we
thought about our toys as children, but, as ludicrous
as it sounds, there have been unsettling accounts over
the years of dolls, effigies and even statues, moving as
if they had a will of their own.

One day at noon in the town of Quito in Ecuador,
the congregation of a Catholic church were praying as
they gazed intently at a statue of the Madonna.
Suddenly, the statue of the Virgin Mary opened its
eyes, looked at the praying crowd and smiled. Most of
the congregation fled in terror, but an old woman and
a young girl remained calm and said the statue blessed
them with the sign of the cross, glanced up at the
crucifix on the altar, then turned to stone again. The
authorities explained the animated statue incident as

the result of mass hysteria and religious mania, but the statue later became reanimated one afternoon and was witnessed by a botanical scientist who happened to be passing was passing the church. Although the scientist was the church atheist, he signed an affidavit declaring that the statue had moved before his disbelieving eyes.

Of course, it's so easy to dismiss such isolated cases in a poor South American town, but what about a window dummy that moves about in the dead of night in a shop situated in the sprawling metropolis of London? In the early 1970s, a boutique opened in north London called "Fads". The shop had five window mannequins on display, and each morning when the staff arrived, one of the dummies would be missing from its stand in the elaborate window display. Sometimes the dummy would be found on the second floor, or standing at the till behind the counter, and its antics were naturally the source of much amusement at the boutique. One of the co-owners, John Mikilson, who held a spare set of keys to the shop, was quickly accused of being the practical joker behind the dummy prank, but he protested his innocence. One weekend he was taken to hospital with appendicitis and the nurses took his shop keys, his money and other valuables, and locked them in the hospital safe while Mr Mikilson went under the knife to have his inflamed appendix removed. The other co-owner of the shop, Charles Meeker, locked up the boutique that Saturday afternoon and, while passing his boutique later on the way to the tube station, noticed that the restless window dummy was missing again. This certainly gave him the creeps, as he could not blame Mr Mikilson this time. Stranger still, one morning at 1.30 a.m., the police contacted Messrs Mikilson and Meeker because officers in a patrol car had seen a woman roaming the premises of "Fads". The two owners drove to the shop where the policemen were waiting for them. The three policemen shone their torches at the figure in the window. It looked like a woman with red curly hair and a well-proportioned, almost perfect figure. However, when Mikilson, Meeker and the policemen approached the window, they were all embarrassed to see that it was just a mannequin. The police were spooked by the experience and quickly left the scene, but a journalist from the *Evening Standard* newspaper wrote a piece on the bizarre case, and the police complained that they were made to look like fools in the article.

Fashions changed and, by 1974, "Fads" boutique folded. The dummy was being sold to another clothes shop when the creepy mannequin was knocked to the ground while being carried into a van. The head fell off on impact, and one of the workmen picked the headless body up and peered down the hole where the neck slotted in. There were loose objects in the dummy. The workman tipped the mannequin on end and out fell a rabbit's-paw charm and a mummified frog, then an inverted cross, obviously a charm used by a Satan worshipper. More objects fell out of the dummy, including a scroll on which someone into black magic had written disgusting and obscene comments about the Devil conquering the world and destroying churches. No one ever discovered who gave the dummy to the boutique or who owned the black magic paraphernalia, but when the emptied dummy was used in the new boutique, it never wandered the store again.

This is a really bizarre tale of another sinister effigy,

and it is recorded in the annals of the now defunct Lancashire Spiritualist Society. In 1955, small clay figures started to turn up on the doorstep of a Manchester doctor. The little figurines were highly detailed and easily recognized as models of patients who were visiting the doctor's surgery. One of the tiny, 3-inch ($7\frac{1}{2}$-cm) figures was of a man in a cap, and the doctor recognized it as a representation of a patient of his, a Mr Bower, who suffered from a heart condition. There was a long hatpin inserted in the clay figure's chest, and the doctor thought the model maker was either a practical joker or someone unbalanced who had a penchant for voodoo. Less than one hour later, the doctor was told that Mr Bower had suffered a massive heart attack – at the precise time that the doctor had found Bower's effigy. Three more clay figures turned up, and there were three corresponding deaths. One morning, the doctor turned up at his surgery earlier than expected, and caught the person who was making the dolls leaving another one of them on his step. It was a young, attractive woman of twenty-five who had made sexual advances to the doctor several months back. However, the doctor was happily married and he had rejected the young lady's sexual overtures. The woman fled, but the doctor later visited her home and learned that the woman and her mother were obsessed with the occult. A priest visited the young lady and no more clay figures turned up on the steps of the doctor's surgery.

In the summer of 1996, the *Times* newspaper, which isn't exactly known for offbeat stories, ran a report about a bizarre phenomenon which was taking place in Madame Tussaud's Waxworks. A number of maintenance staff at the waxworks noticed that the wax dummy of Adolf Hitler needed a haircut. The Führer's fringe had actually somehow grown just over 1 inch (3 cm). The dummy was removed from its glass display case and the tabloids had a field day as the staff at Madame Tussaud's consulted a hair specialist from Leeds who analyzed the dummy's hair, which happened to have been imported from Germany. The hair expert said she was baffled by the phenomenon, and could not explain how Hitler's hair was actually growing. Two months later, the dummy's hair suddenly stopped growing as mysteriously as it had started. The dummy of Hitler was modelled from the Austrian-born dictator while he was still alive in the 1940s, and many visitors had said that the dummy's eyes looked evil and seemed to move.

In the early 1970s, a wax museum was opened in Long Beach Amusement Park in Los Angeles. The museum hadn't been open long when all sorts of weird things began to happen. Lights would switch on and off in the middle of the night, and the sounds of footsteps would echo through the building in the wee small hours when the security guards were not patrolling the corridors.

At 2.30 a.m. on one occasion, Steve Jackson, a security officer, heard the distinctive sound of someone playing a harmonica down in the Wild West section of the museum. The guard slipped his gun from its holster and crept downstairs with his torch, expecting to meet an intruder. He passed the wax dummies of Jessie James, Pat Garret, Billy the Kid and Doc Holiday. The sound of the harmonica got louder. As soon as the beam of the guard's flashlight scanned a wax dummy in the corner, the ghostly harmonica stopped playing. Jackson switched on the lights and radioed the other guard on the top floor of the building to come down. The other guard said he had also heard the faint strains of the harmonica in the early hours of the morning, but had never mentioned it to anyone. Jackson took a closer look at the cowboy in the corner, standing near a mockup of a saloon bar. The figure was small, about 5 ft 1 in (1.5 m), which was unusual, because most of the gunfighter dummies were made much taller and larger than life by the figure makers, purely for dramatic effect.

The cowboy had a sad expression, and wore a droopy moustache. The plate next to him said his name was Elmer J. McCurdy, a robber who had been shot to death after a failed train robbery in 1911. Both the guards agreed that this wax figure's eyes were chillingly lifelike. He had a sinister stare, unlike the other dummies.

About a year later, in 1976, a segment of the popular television series, *The Six Million Dollar Man*, starring Lee Majors, was being filmed in the Long Beach Amusement Park, and some scenes were actually shot in the Wild West section of the museum. As one scene was being filmed, an actor in a fight scene with Lee Majors accidentally stumbled and knocked over the wax dummy of Elmer McCurdy. The dummy's arms fell off when it hit the floor, and the horrified actors and film crew saw that the figure was not a dummy at all. It was an actual mummified person. Fragments of bone, dried skin and blood were scattered on the floor.

The police investigated the matter and discovered that, in 1911, the body of the outlaw Elmer McCurdy had been taken down from the gallows and preserved by embalming, and then given a coating of wax. This practice was not uncommon in America at that time, and many notorious criminals were preserved in this ghoulish way for carnival shows. The proprietors of the Los Angeles museum had bought the waxwork figure, not knowing that it was a real corpse. After Elmer McCurdy was given a decent burial, the spooky goings-on at the museum ended, and the harmonica was never heard again.

Supernatural Crimes

Here are just a few accounts of what psychic researchers term "supernatural crimes". Many of these crimes are not always recognized by the police as being the work of occultists; they are usually classified as unsolved and conveniently filed away.

On 12 April 1967, around $300,000 disappeared from the strongroom at Kennedy Airport at New York. The FBI investigated the theft and soon saw that this was no ordinary crime. Whoever the robbers were, they must have been invisible, as they got past armed guards and through a double-locked 2-ft (61-cm) thick steel door to take the money from the strongroom, before getting out, again without being seen by the guards or television cameras. The steel door had apparently not even been opened during the theft, because forensic experts found no prints or any markings on the door of the vault, and the incredible theft was only discovered when an armoured truck from Manhattan came to the airport to collect the money from the vault. The FBI reluctantly said they were completely baffled by the theft and an official at the airport said, "It was as if the crooks had been beamed into the vault then beamed out again."

The crime is still unsolved.

According to a report in the *Daily Mirror* on 13 February 1974, police rushed to a house in Norfolk after an intruder on the premises triggered the burglar alarm. No one else was in the building and the people who lived in the house were away on holiday. When police arrived, they found a trail of footprints made by a pair of boots that had presumably been through the rain and mud outside. These footprints went across the floor of a bedroom in the house and ended up against a solid brick wall. The police were obviously baffled and examined the wall, expecting to find a secret passage. The wall was solid. Whoever the ghostly burglar was, they stole nothing, but the owners of the house naturally felt worried about the phantom burglar and wondered if he would return.

Some ghostly intruders have allegedly even taken lives. One such case occurred in January 1986, and was reported in the *Sunday Express*. On 24 January 1986, twelve-year-old Samantha Huffmaster, of Cherokee Village, Arkansas, USA, went up to her bedroom, ready to go to sleep. Downstairs, her parents were watching television when they were suddenly horrified by the sound of a single gunshot coming from upstairs. Samantha's mother and father raced upstairs and found their little daughter lying in a pool of blood. She had a bullet hole in her side. Samantha was rushed to hospital but died one hour later. The subsequent police investigation established the truly bizarre cause of the tragedy. A .45 automatic pistol that had been lying on a chair in the bedroom of Samantha's parents had somehow gone off of its own accord; the bullet had travelled through the chair and the dividing wall before striking Samantha in the side. Forensic investigators were baffled by the gun firing on its own and had never come across a case like it before.

If we are to believe the following strange story, which was reported in several British newspapers in 1989, there are also supernatural vandals at large. On 14 December 1989, the residents of a housing estate in Barnsley, South Yorkshire, were baffled at the overnight disappearance of four enormous concrete lamp posts. The 60-ft (18-m) lamp posts had been uprooted by someone or something in the dead of night, without a sound. The missing lamp posts were never traced. Just how their disappearance was accomplished was never solved either, despite investigations by the police and an enquiry by a local councillor, who said, "Whoever is responsible for uprooting the lamp posts is very disturbed and very strong."

Two years previously, in July 1987, the *Guardian* newspaper reported another case of supernatural vandalism which took place in Gwynedd in north-west Wales. Gwynned County Council ordered the construction of a wooden footbridge over the River Penrhos, between Pwllheli and Llanbedrog, at a cost of £1,200. The bridge was completed on 11 May but, at the end of the month, the structure went missing and was found in pieces in the river. Police made enquiries in the area but no one had seen anybody attacking the wooden bridge. The council replaced the wooden structure with a steel bridge, which was 18 ft (5$\frac{1}{2}$ m) long and weighed about 3 tons. The new steel bridge was fitted with gates at each end and was closed at night. But at the end of July the steel bridge also went missing, and has never been found. Police were completely baffled at the theft. Detective Chief Inspector Irfon Evans, who was assigned to the case, told the press that the 3-ton steel bridge was bolted and riveted and practically impossible to dismantle. Yet someone – or something – had stolen or possibly destroyed an 18-ft (5½-m) steel bridge in the middle of the night. And there is a strange epilogue to this story, because on the other side of the Atlantic, during the week when the Welsh bridge disappeared, an iron bridge over 160 ft (49 m) in length also went missing. This bridge had spanned the Santa Lucua Chico river in Uruguay, and not a bolt of that missing bridge was ever found either.

A Haunting Melody

One summer evening in the 1950s, four young people – all in their late teens – went out in a rowing boat off the coast of Llandudno, north Wales, after having a drink. They rowed out to sea for about a quarter of a mile (0.4 km), watching the sun set as they sang a song called *Smoke Gets in Your Eyes*, which was in the pop charts at that time. Another couple, who were making for the shore, heard the young people singing, guessed that they'd been drinking, and warned them that a storm was on the horizon, and looked as if it was coming towards Llandudno. The party of teenagers continued singing and rowed further out to sea.

By nightfall, there was no sign of the young people, and the storm rolled into Llandudno. Enormous waves broke over the pier, and lightning streaked across the skies. The storm subsided an hour later, and at first light the following morning, an upturned rowing boat was found, washed up on the beach, along with the body of a young girl. She was one of the teenagers who had recklessly rowed out into the stormy weather. The bodies of her friends were never recovered.

About a fortnight later, the couple who had warned the teenagers about the storm, got in a boat one calm summer evening, and rowed about 500 yards (457 m) out to sea, then opened a small basket containing sandwiches and a bottle of wine. As twilight started to fall, the couple decided to row back to the shore, when they heard something that sent shivers down their spines. They heard the faint strains of the song *Smoke Gets in Your Eyes* coming from out at sea. The man started rowing the boat back to the shore, when the girl he was with suddenly screamed and pointed behind him. When the man glanced over his shoulder, he saw the faint silhouette of four people in a rowing boat. They were the source of the song. As he and his girlfriend looked on, the boat in the distance capsized and screams were heard. Then a horrible silence. The boat and the figures had vanished. The man rowed back to the shore in record time. A week later, the song was heard again in the lodging house where the four teenagers had been staying, and the landlady saw the shadows of four people who had come out of her house pass across her window; she was too afraid to open the curtains to look at them, because she knew no one else was staying there at the time. It is said that the haunting song is still occasionally heard around May off the coast of Llandudno when the wind drops and the sea is calm.

The "Invisibles"

In the late seventeenth century, Sir Isaac Newton discovered that the seven basic colours we can see are just an incredibly small slice of a long range of radiations known as the electromagnetic spectrum. The human eye can see colours ranging from red to violet, but we are completely blind to infrared and ultraviolet. The other radiations beyond the range of our senses are gamma rays, x-rays, and a thousand other invisible waves that bring music and speech to our televisions, radios and mobile phones. If we realize, therefore, that most of the Universe cannot be detected by our senses, then the following accounts won't seem so incredible, as they all concern invisible assailants.

In May 1890, a wave of terror spread through Japan when seven people were attacked by a seemingly invisible assailant. The first victim was crossing a bridge in broad daylight when suddenly an 8-inch (20-cm) slash appeared on the man's neck. Blood spurted over shocked onlookers, and the man fell to the ground and would have bled to death if a doctor hadn't turned up in time to treat the mysterious wound. Minutes later, less than a mile away, an old man painting pottery cried out and his wife recoiled in horror as she saw a long slash mark on his neck. As the woman applied a cloth to her husband's wound, there were a series of screams outside in the street, where five other people were also slashed by the invisible attacker. One victim said he felt someone brush past him then something icy cold and razor sharp sliced through his neck, narrowly missing the major artery. The Japanese people immediately thought the culprit was one of the legendary "invisibles" – unseen demons who figure in the folklore of Japan.

Perhaps one of the invisibles was responsible for the following gruesome incident, which was investigated by the French Academy of Sciences. In 1761, five women in northern Italy were collecting firewood near the little town of Ventimiglia when, suddenly, one of them cried out and dropped dead. The dead woman's companions were naturally horrified at the sudden death, but their stomachs turned when they went over to inspect the corpse. The deceased woman's clothes and shoes were torn into fine shreds and scattered up to 6 ft (almost 2 m) around the corpse. There were gaping wounds on the head which exposed the white bone of the skull. The muscles and ligaments on the corpse's right side had been pulled out to expose the intestines. Several other internal organs looked as if they'd been dragged out of the body and were all ruptured. The dead woman's abdomen bore three long parallel incisions and the flesh of the hip and thigh was almost stripped away, revealing the pubic bone. The top of the leg bone had also been wrenched from its socket, indicating that something of tremendous strength had apparently torn the unfortunate woman apart. A post-mortem was performed on the mangled and ripped corpse, but the coroner had to admit defeat. He could not explain how the dead woman's underclothes had not been torn, despite the extensive mutilation, and the coroner told a colleague that the death could almost be classed as supernatural.

Another unfortunate woman who was seemingly murdered by some supernatural force was Lavinia Farrar, a seventy-two-year-old blind woman who was discovered dead at her home in Cambridge, England, in March 1901. She was found lying on her bruised face. Her nose was broken and beside her body lay a bloodstained knife and just two spots of blood. No wound on the body was evident, but when the clothes were taken off the corpse for the post-mortem examination, the coroner saw that the old woman had been stabbed through the heart. The dead woman had worn four garments, but none of them had been punctured by the knife, and the knife could not have been inserted through the fastenings of the garments. Stranger still, it was later determined that the blood spots on the floor were not the dead woman's blood, and the murder motive was not robbery, for nothing had been taken from the victim's home. So why or how could a killer stab a naked, old, blind woman through the heart without leaving any bloodstains, then calmly dress her? Neighbours told police that no one had been seen leaving or entering the blind woman's house at about the time of the murder, which deepened the mystery.

If some malevolent entities are responsible for these violent attacks and murders, what do they look like? Perhaps they look something like the weird creature which was glimpsed during a storm in 1750. According to an old account reported by a Yorkshire minister, in August 1750, a certain Captain Harrison was riding across a field on the outskirts of York around midnight. As a thunderstorm broke out in the heavens and lightning streaked across the sky, Harrison's horse reared up and cried out in pain. Harrison tugged on the reins to calm the animal and, as he turned about in the saddle, he noticed a hideous black figure the size of a small child clinging to the horse's hindquarters. The creature had thick muscular arms and claws which were dug into the horse's body. The face of the creature was demonic. It had large, yellow almond-shaped eyes, a long pointed nose, and a wide mouth that ran from one ear to the other. The teeth in this large mouth were small, triangular and had a glasslike transparency about them. Captain Harrison whipped the weird creature with his riding crop and the thing just vanished. Harrison rode off at breakneck speed through the storm towards York with an incredible tale to tell. When he reached the town, he dismounted and saw four deep wounds in the horse's upper leg which were still bleeding.

In November 1994, in Siberia, a strange invisible creature was said to be on the prowl in a vast unchartered forest called the Taiga. One Mongolian herdsman was said to have gone out with a rifle to hunt the mysterious creature, which had attacked people in the area. A scream was heard in the forest, and when two hunters went to investigate, they saw that the herdsman had literally been pulled apart by something of incredible strength. He was barely alive, and his arms had been ripped off. Nearby, the rifle he had carried was twisted into a coil. The victim could not give a coherent description of his attacker before he died, but kept saying that a "shadow man" had attacked him. The herdsman was not the only person to encounter the strange humanoid creature. Four woodcutters in the area also fled when they saw strange creature coming towards them leaving a trail of three-toed footprints in the snow-covered forest clearing. One of the men hurled his axe at the unearthly-looking figure, which was almost transparent. The axe bounced off the creature, which moaned and ran after the four terrified men. They were chased for almost half a mile, and counted themselves very fortunate to survive the weird ordeal.

The Case for God

Theists believe that the Universe was created, and is sustained, by an eternal, omnipresent, omnipotent and invisible God. Atheists, however, believe that the Universe was formed by accident and is sustained through the action of eternal, omnipresent, omnipotent and invisible principles known as the laws of nature. How different are these two apparently opposing views? Is there a God? If so, what does He or It want of us? It seems that in most cultures, people have felt a need to ask these questions, but this is not true of all cultures. Some religions claim that it is possible and important to know, and give expression to, truths about God, while other religions take the opposite view. The issue at stake is what theologians call the question of revelation. Is God's existence, nature and plan for the world revealed to humankind or not? The great Eastern religions generally answer "no". For Hindus and Buddhists, God is the Great Unknown. In the East, religion is not a relationship to a personal being who is concerned with the human race, who seeks obedience and is approached by worship. Instead, it is seen as an attempt by the individual to gain, by his own efforts, an eternal peace, free from all the distractions of human nature and the physical world. It is clear that such an attitude will not admit of any revelation of God, although it may well claim to reach, through enlightenment, an ultimate truth. In most of the religions of the West, God is a personal reality who created the world, enters into a relationship with a person, has a purpose for him or her, and makes demands upon them. Adherents of these religions believe that it is possible for them to know God and to make at least some statements about Him, because in various ways he has revealed himself to them.

Two Types of Revelation
Traditionally, knowledge of God is thought to arise in two ways: the ways of natural, or general, revelation, and the way of special revelation. Natural, or general, revelation is available to all of us and is arrived at by reason or through experience. Special revelation is knowledge which comes through a unique act of intervention by God which would not otherwise be available. When thinking in this way it is important to remember that these two forms of revelation overlap a good deal, and that the knowledge referred to is not all of the same kind. There are several different kinds of knowledge. We have factual knowledge – knowledge of facts that can be checked or verified. Scientific knowledge is normally of this type. We have knowledge of facts where the facts cannot be so easily checked and our knowledge seems to involve opinion and interpretation – much historical knowledge is of this type. We also have knowledge of people, as in our relationships with our friends. Here verifiable factual knowledge plays a surprisingly minor role, though we would say our knowledge of our friends was a fact.

Arguments for natural revelation are based on two assumptions. It is assumed that, just as an artist or workman leaves some trace of his character in his work, so God has left some trace of his character in his work – "Creation". More importantly, it is assumed that there is some affinity between God and humanity. Humans are seen as being second only to God; human personality is seen as the nearest approach to the being of God and the best analogue of God (this is what the author of Genesis implies when he said God made Man in his image); human intellect is assumed to be capable of recognizing the arguments used to show the existence of God, and capable of entertaining the idea of God. The Greek philosophers, Plato and Aristotle, made these assumptions. Plato argued that all motion needs a mover; thus the fact that the heavenly bodies are seen to move indicates that there is some force operating on them either internally or externally. Aristotle, however, believed that his "Unmoved Mover" was a remote being, inaccessible to us. The classical expression of human thinking about natural revelation is found in the profoundly influential work of a thirteenth-century Christian theologian and philosopher, St Thomas Aquinas. Aquinas drew many of his arguments from Aristotle. He argued that we cannot have direct knowledge of God, for we can only have direct knowledge of things through our senses, but that we can know about God through his effects. To show this he worked out five famous "proofs" for the existence of God. Each attempts to begin from what is well known and proceed to God. From the fact of movement he argues for a first mover. Secondly, from the relationship of cause and effect he argues for a first cause. Thirdly, he notes that most things are contingent (they depend on something else for their existence) and argues that there must be one absolutely necessary thing. Fourthly, from the fact that we recognize various

From the helix of DNA to the spiral of a galaxy in the depths of space, there seems
to be a mathematical design to the Universe; could that designer be God?

degrees of perfection, he argues for the existence of one perfect being from whom we have our ideas of perfection. Finally, from the evidence of design in the world he argues that there must be a designer. Aquinas realized that at best, his arguments could only point to the existence of God; they could tell us anything about Him.

Who Is the Universal Lawgiver?

Most people experience some sense of obligation in the way they behave. They feel they must do, or at least should try and do, what is morally right. It is true that different societies have different ideas of right and wrong, and that children learn the morals of their own society. Nevertheless, when all allowance has been made for such local and historical conventions, some people think it is still possible to talk about an experience of moral demand which is common to most people. The existence of such a feeling of obligation can be taken as an indication of a universal moral law, implying a lawgiver.

Religious Revelation

St Paul's vision on the road to Damascus has been interpreted by sceptics as sunstroke or epilepsy. What is certain is that Paul changed his life as a result of the vision and the course of world history was altered. There has always been a strain of thought which has denied the validity of natural revelation and claimed that humankind can only really know God through God's own direct intervention. When the Hebrew wise man asked, "Canst thou by searching find out God?" (Job 11:7) he clearly expected the answer, "No." For Judaism, God is chiefly known through his acts in the history of Israel. A small and politically insignificant nation fell into slavery in Egypt. Suddenly there appeared a remarkable man, Moses, convinced that he had been commissioned by God to lead the people out into another land and another life, a life founded on a covenant relationship with God and characterized by gratitude and obedience to Him. God is shown to be merciful, long-suffering and above all just. However, it is made clear that he would not be known at all if he did not choose to reveal himself through his acts and give, through the prophets, an interpretation of these acts. The name of God in the Old Testament – YAHWEH – came to be translated as: "I will be whom I choose to be". (In Judaism, the name "Yahweh" is regarded as too sacred to be spoken, and is replaced instead by "Adonai", meaning "my lord", when the letters representing "Yahweh" are read aloud in religious ceremonies.) Even then he is not revealed at all, but only to those who seek him and to whom he chooses to reveal himself.

The Fullest Revelation
In Jesus, the Christians claim, God was fully present in human personality. Jesus showed by his example and teaching the character of God, and by his death showed the extent of God's love in bearing the judgment for humankind's sins. His resurrection showed God's power over death. Not everyone who witnessed the human ministry of Jesus – nor everybody who has heard it since – recognized him as anything more than a teacher. The fuller understanding of Jesus as the incarnation of God and the saviour of the world only comes, Christians proclaim, when God gives a deeper spiritual perception to those willing to receive it.

For the atheist, the universal laws of nature are blind, unconscious and uncreative; they cannot entirely account for creativity in human life or in the evolutionary process. The Universe is seen as fundamentally inanimate, devoid of soul or spirit – or in other words, dead. By contrast, for the believer in God, the ultimate reality is conscious, creative and alive. The laws of nature share some of the properties of God, because God is the source of these laws. Atheists usually maintain that their view is simpler and more scientific than the theist view; they regard God as an unnecessary hypothesis. Although, at first sight, this theory has a certain plausibility, on further reflection it turns out to raise more difficulties than it solves.

Firstly, if matter is regarded as inanimate, governed only by blind laws and chance, there is no place in the system for consciousness. Even the consciousness of the atheist himself has to be regarded as nothing more than a kind of shadow of electrical and chemical changes inside his brain; this shadowy consciousness cannot actually do anything, or influence his actions – these are merely determined by a combination of the laws of physics and chemistry and random events over which he has no control. This view is so much at variance with our experience of ourselves as creatures that can exercise free choice that to take it seriously requires deep faith in the atheist philosophy. Secondly, the atheist view holds that both the evolutionary process and the Universe are wholly without purpose or meaning. Again, only the most committed atheist seems to be able to take this gloomy view seriously, since it can only render his own life and theories quite pointless. Thirdly, there is the problem of the nature of the laws of nature, the laws on which scientific atheism depends. What are these laws? As we have seen, they are supposedly universal, changeless and omnipresent, as well as being immaterial. In fact, they sound more like cosmic ideas than material things. And they can be known only as ideas, through scientific theories and mathematical formulae. In the final analysis, it is through these laws that the atheist has to try to account for his consciousness. And this is a difficult task. These are some of the problems raised by the atheist philosophy. Although the laws of nature play such an important part in it, this theory is not itself scientific. It can never be proved. It can be accepted only by an act of faith.

These particular difficulties do not arise if we suppose instead that the Universe arises from the creative activity of what we might call God. For if God is the conscious source of the Universe, and also contains the Universe, the laws of nature could be seen as rather like ideas in the mind of God. Moreover, this theory suggests that consciousness is present within the Universe – thus making it possible for consciousness to be transferred to living beings arising in the course of the evolutionary process. Indeed, one purpose of this process could be seen as the emergence of consciousness within the created world, and the development of this consciousness to the point at which it can recognize itself and partici-pate in its divine source. Proponents of this theory believe that this point is reached in humankind. If this view is correct, then the consciousness that dwells in human beings is the same as the conscious-ness of God – and it should be possible to experience directly that this is so. Mystics in all religious traditions have testified that this is indeed the case. This direct revelation or enlightenment lies at the heart of all religions; it is this vision of the prophets, seers, enlightened ones, sages and saints that connects religious traditions with their divine sources. Thus, the existence of God is more than a philosophical theory; it is supported by the deepest experience of men and women throughout the ages. One of the classical statements about the nature of God's existence was made by the Scottish philosopher David Hume (1711–76), in his *Dialogues on Natural Religion*:

> *Look around the world and contemplate the whole and every part of it: you will find it to be nothing but one great machine, subdivided into an infinite number of lesser machines, which again admit of subdivisions to a degree beyond what human senses and faculties can trace and explain. All these various machines, even their most minute parts, are adjusted to each other with an accuracy which ravishes into admiration all men who have ever contemplated them. The curious adapting of means to ends, throughout all nature, resembles exactly, though it much exceeds, the productions of human contrivance – of human design, thought, wisdom and intelligence. Since therefore the effects resemble each other, we are led to infer, by all the rules of analogy, that the causes also resemble, and that the Author of nature is somewhat similar to the mind of man, though possessed of much larger faculties, proportioned to the grandeur of the work which he has executed. By this argument a posteriori, and by this argument alone, do we prove at*

once the existence of a Deity and his similarity to human mind and intelligence.

Teleportation

In the 1950s the pioneering UFO writer, M.K. Jessup, unearthed a strange story from Spain's legal archives concerning the trial of a Spanish guard named Gil Pérez.

Pérez had allegedly been on duty at the Governor's palace in Manila on 25 October 1593, when he suddenly found himself in the main square of Mexico City. His dramatic appearance from nowhere naturally alarmed passers-by, and the guard quickly attracted the attention of the Mexican authorities. However, Pérez could not explain how he had been transported instantaneously thousands of miles across the globe from the Philippines. He gave a garbled account of a mysterious cloud which had enveloped him moments before his "trip" but could remember nothing more. Pérez said that the sinister incident had occurred minutes after the assassination of the Manilan Governor; three months later a ship from the Philippines reached Mexico and officers confirmed the assassination Pérez had mentioned, plus other details.

In such a superstitious age, Perez was lucky he wasn't burnt at the stake. Such was the fate of a man in 1655, who was deemed to be a black magician by the Spanish Inquisition after he had been inexplicably transported from the Portuguese colony in Goa, India, to Portugal in the proverbial twinkling of an eye.

The famed student of the unexplained, Charles

Fort, was intrigued by a curious collection of reports from newspaper clippings and historical records of people who had somehow been transferred from one place to another without any physical movement through the three dimensions of space. Fort coined the term "teleportation" to describe this bizarre phenomenon. The logic of cybernetics suggests that every physical object can, in principle, be reduced to encoded information which could be transmitted on a carrier wave. This may seem a little far-fetched, but the idea of compressing Beethoven's works onto a compact disc and the technology behind a personal computer would seem equally unbelievable to your Victorian counterpart; it is just a matter of time and technological progress.

Today we can send e-mails, television pictures, and faxes anywhere in the world via satellite, and tomorrow we may be able to actually send ourselves in a similar way. But how will such a feat of technology be achieved? There are two areas of science which may provide the breakthrough: electronics and theoretical physics.

Electronics is progressing at an alarming rate. In 1948, the invention of the transistor was hailed as a quantum leap in technology and its inventors were given the Nobel Prize for their work. But there are now tiny silicon chips in common use which contain over 18 million transistors, and these chips are becoming more complex each year.

Let us imagine a time in the not-too-distant future when we will have chips that are complex enough to store and process the exact positions of every atom in the human body. There are roughly 5×10 to the power of 27 atoms in your body, which may seem a staggering figure, yet there are mainframe computers in existence which could easily handle such a sum. Now, if we can envisage a device that could scan the human body atom by atom and store the positions of each atom on our super-computer chips, we are halfway to constructing a teleporter. A similar body scanner along these lines is routinely used in hospitals and works by the principle of nuclear magnetic resonance. In these hospital scanners, the atoms in the patient's body are mapped by a computer and presented on a screen in cross sections. The problem is, of course, translating the information in our scanner back into atoms. For this formidable task we would need something along the lines of a particle accelerator, which could convert basic atoms of hydrogen (the simplest atom) into the various carbon, nitrogen and other atoms of which we are comprised.

This hypothetical "matter transmitter" would also be an advanced duplicating machine, because it would merely copy the original person atom by atom. To be a true teleporter, our machine would have to transfer the original subject to a destination and, in theory, this could be achieved by warping the very fabric of space-time.

Two of the last century's greatest geniuses – Albert Einstein and Professor John A. Wheeler (co-inventor of the hydrogen bomb) – both claimed that space could be distorted and bent by gravity and high-density magnetic fields, to provide a form of instantaneous transportation across "superspace". According to Wheeler, superspace is another form of space running alongside our own, but without time as we know it.

As long ago as 1927, Einstein had reached a similar

conclusion. That year he published a paper entitled *Unified Field Theory for Gravitation and Electricity*. Shortly after publication in Germany, the paper was withdrawn. There were rumours that Einstein had stopped the circulation of his paper because he thought that his work was too far ahead of its time, and feared that the emerging Nazi movement would misuse it.

After World War II and the horrors of Hiroshima and Nagasaki, the pacifist philosopher Bertrand Russell – a close friend of Einstein – read the latter's paper on the Unified Field Theory, and remarked enigmatically that man was not ready for such a far-reaching theory. Others who have read the paper claim that Einstein had formulated groundbreaking equations that, although incomplete, showed that magnetism and gravity were related. The same equations also showed how space could be warped by high-powered magnetic fields in such a way as to provide instant travel to any point on this Earth, or off it.

If Einstein's theory is right, how would it explain the teleportation of Gil Pérez across the world in 1593? No one in those times would have possessed the technology to generate space-warping magnetic fields, but nature herself may have been the culprit. The source of the Earth's magnetic field is still a complete mystery and satellite surveys of the geomagnetic field have revealed a host of hitherto unknown magnetic storms, localized points on the Earth's surface where the planet's magnetic field becomes incredibly intense for a matter of minutes. Most of these storms occur over the seas which cover 70 per cent of the world's surface, but some storms have also formed on land to disrupt radio communications. Perhaps Gil Pérez was in the eye of one of these storms in 1593. If that was so, perhaps the Spanish guard was transported across the globe by way of Professor Wheeler's superspace.

The magnetic storm theory would also explain the disappearances in the Bermuda Triangle; many of the final radio messages from lost ships and planes mention disorientation because of a spinning magnetic compass.

Is Our Future Really Written in the Stars?

Are you one of the millions of people who regularly turn to the horoscope column of a magazine or daily newspaper to see what the stars have in store for you? Recent research has established that 60 per cent of people who read horoscopes actually believe in them, but surely there is no scientific evidence that astrology works? The following may surprise the sceptics amongst you.

In 1950, a young French statistician, Michel Gauquelin, set out to disprove that there was any connection between planetary positions at a person's birth and that individual's future development. It is a legal requirement in France to register the time of a child's birth, and this useful data enabled the sceptical statistician to calculate the horoscopes of his randomly-chosen 25,000 subjects. However, instead of disproving astrology, Gauquelin's findings apparently supported it! The birth data of 508 doctors in the study showed that they had been born with Saturn at or near mid-heaven. Saturn has long been held to be the ruling planet of scientists and those in the medical profession. Similarly, 134 soldiers were born with Mars high in the ecliptic. The red planet Mars, of course, was regarded as the god of war for centuries. The study also produced other intriguing results. A group of 190 artists, actors and writers were born when the planet Venus was looming in the western sky.

There were many other unexpected and significant correlations produced by Gauquelin's study but, unfortunately, the Frenchman was quickly ridiculed by the scientific establishment. All the same, Gauquelin continued his research with an open mind. From all over France he collected more birth data for groups of prominent military men, politicians, writers, actors and sports people. Once again, the results of the astrological study were disquieting: 3,141 politicians and almost all of the military men and sports people in the study had Mars past the ascendant or mid-heaven in their horoscopes; 3,305 scientists from the sample were born when Saturn was rising or at mid-heaven, while Venus dominated the horoscopes of the artists, actors and writers!

Further studies into the validity of astrology have uncovered many incidences of "astrological twins". Here are just a few. The eminent German physicist Albert Einstein, and fellow Nobel Prize-winning scientist Otto Hahn, were both born on 14 March 1879, which makes them Pisceans. A set of notable Gemini astro twins were Vincent Price and fellow horror-film actor Peter Cushing, who were born on 27 May. Nazis Herman Göring and Alfred Rosenberg were not only born on the same day in the same year, they also died on the same day in the same year – 15 October 1946 at

Nuremberg. Rosenberg was hanged as a war criminal, while Göring took poison in his cell to cheat the hangman's noose.

The Horrorscope

Does astrology work? Can horoscopes in the newspaper really tell you what the future has in store for someone on a personal level? This certainly seemed to be the case in the following chilling incident which was reported in the French newspaper *Le Monde* in the early 1970s.

In 1971, a French bus driver, Alain Bosier, told his girlfriend that the horoscopes she consulted everyday were nonsense. She said he was wrong and that, nine times out of ten, her horoscope had been fairly accurate – especially the horoscopes written by the French astrologer Madame Du Berzil.

Alain told his girlfriend to read out his horoscope, which was Gemini. His girlfriend said, "Okay, here's your horoscope: 'Take extra care on the road, as the moon is waning and your planet, the fleet-footed Mercury, is in conflict with the balance of the ecliptic. A friend will lose his head in an unsavoury situation, and this could end or damage your career or vocation.'"

"Complete rubbish!" Alain laughed and shook his head. "Mercury and the moon, and all the stars in the sky have no influence on me whatsoever." And he kissed his girlfriend, but she elbowed him in the ribs because of his mocking tone. She really believed in astrology and non-believers irritated her.

"Go to work!" Alain's girlfriend shouted out, and as

he got to the door, she added, "You'll see. It'll all come true – so take care on the road. I still love you even though you're a sceptic."

It seemed like another uneventful day. Alain drove the bus from the station and took it on his usual route around the outskirts of Rouen. At around 6 p.m. the roads started to get busy, and Alain saw a wagon speeding up to him from behind. It must have been doing around 60 mph (96 kph) and was closing fast – and there was a sharp bend on the road ahead. Alain stuck his head out of the side window and waved at the driver of the wagon then gestured for him to keep his distance. The wagon driver put two fingers up at Alain, then gradually slowed down. "The same to you!" Alain shouted, and he said to the passengers, "That idiot was trying to overtake on the bend." One of the passengers, a young man, commented, "He's crazy. He has sheets of corrugated iron on the back of the wagon and they look like they're going to come off. He hasn't tied them down properly."

The wagon driver followed the bus round the sharp bend in the road without keeping the correct separation distance. He even beeped his horn at Alain. "I'll report that madman to the police!" said the bus driver. He asked the passengers to get the wagon's registration, but a young woman said, "Oh just forget him and drive on will you? I'm already late."

Alain calmed down, took a deep breath, then glanced in his wing mirror. He saw a speck coming up the road from behind the wagon. As the speck drew nearer, Alain could see it was his old friend Pierre, who used to work as a busman a few years back. The two men were very good friends and often played chess together. Pierre was now a motorcycle fanatic, and was driving a Harley-Davidson Soft-tail Classic.

Pierre flashed his headlight at main beam for a second to acknowledge Alain, and then the bike revved and came tearing up the road towards the bus. As it was passing the wagon, something horrific happened. A sudden cross-wind roared out of a gap in a hedge and lifted one of the sheets of corrugated iron off the wagon. The thin cables holding it came undone and the sheet flew off the top of the stack and glided down at an angle towards the motorcyclist. In one swift movement the sheet of iron took off Pierre's head with a clean cut. The body of the headless motorcyclist went into various spasms and nervous twitches, and the bike continued to roar up the road as the headless corpse gripped and twisted the throttle. It passed the busload of horrified and trau-matized passengers with blood spraying out from the stump of Pierre's neck. Meanwhile, Pierre's helmeted head bounced along the road like a football, and actu-ally rolled into a field where three schoolgirls were picnicking. The bemused girls first thought that the object was a football; then they all saw the blood, and the limp tongue hanging out of the severed head, and they ran off screaming.

When Alain saw the headless motorcyclist pass him, he went into shock and swerved to keep away from the gruesome spectacle – and the bus skidded out of control and mowed down an old man who had been walking down the side of the road with his dog. The man and his dog died instantly.

Alain left his job and was under psychiatric obser-vation for months. Only the love of his girlfriend pulled him through the trauma. As a macabre keep-sake, he cut out the horoscope of that fateful day; the horoscope that had told him to be careful on the road; the horoscope which had uncannily said that a close friend would *lose his head* and that Alain's career would be subsequently ended as a result. He agreed that there was more to astrology than he had ever suspected.

The Man With the Eye Patch

The following eerie incident allegedly took place in Edinburgh in May 1998. A post office clerk named George Sinclair moved into a terraced house and, being security-conscious, he decided to install a video entryphone so that he could see callers who were on his doorstep. At 11.30 one evening, someone rang Mr Sinclair's front doorbell. Mr Sinclair grabbed his remote control and flipped to television channel number 9, which was tuned into the video entry-phone. On the television screen he saw a picture of a bald-headed man standing on his doorstep. The man was wearing a black eye patch, and he was staring directly into the lens of the video phone's miniature camera with a creepy grin on his face. Mr Sinclair asked the late caller to identify himself, but the man started to pound his fists violently on the front door. Mr Sinclair was enraged and ran down the stairs to have a few cross words with the bald man, but when he opened the door, there was no one there. On the following night, the same man called again, and on this occasion, Mr Sinclair's girlfriend called at the same time. However, for some sinister reason, she saw no bald-headed stranger on the doorstep. The same character called almost every night for a week, and when Mr Sinclair told his neighbour, she went pale with shock. She told him that the previous occupant of his house was an eccentric bald-headed man who wore an eye patch. The man had died after suffering a heart attack on his doorstep. When Mr Sinclair heard this, he promptly decided to leave the house that day and move to another area.

Not a Blade of Grass

In the late summer of 1821, a widow in the Welsh town of Montgomery wrote to a young Englishman she had become acquainted with many years before, named John Davies, asking him if he would help her on her run-down farm. Davies wrote back, saying it would be a pleasure to help her, but as soon as he arrived in the town the clannish community seemed to resent his presence, and backs were turned upon him and the widow.

One afternoon in September, Davies was on an errand for the widow when he was attacked by Welsh highwaymen who demanded his money. Davies refused and fought the two men, but was badly beaten. Then, to add insult to injury, the two local thugs claimed that Davies had attacked them, and that he had been carrying out highway robbery. The two attackers then took their victim to Welshpool and Davies was charged with the crime. The real robbers testified in what was little more than a kangaroo court, and Davies was found guilty and sentenced to death. The young man cried out that he was not the robber, but the people of the court just talked amongst themselves in Welsh. Within hours, Davies was on the scaffold and the hangman was binding him up.

Before his arms were tied, Davies lifted his right hand and declared, "I die, praying to God that he will let no grass grow on my grave to prove my innocence!"

The hangman pulled Davies's arm down, put it behind his back, and tied it tightly to the other hand. He then impatiently pulled the lever without even putting a hood over the young man's head. Davies fell through the trap-door, and his death was a swift one. As the body swung about on the creaking rope, there was a deathly silence amongst the onlookers who were all thinking about the hanged man's last strange words. The widow was naturally devastated, and she had her friend buried in Montgomery parish churchyard. A group of the ghouls who had turned out for the hanging loitered at the gates of the churchyard, watching the sobbing widow lay flowers on Davies's grave.

Months went by, and people noticed how grass never grew over Davies's grave. All the other graves were covered with grass and had to be trimmed regularly, but there was always a barren rectangle over Davies's resting place. A priest sprinkled the grassless grave with grass seed, but the seed failed to germinate. Thirty years afterwards, the cemetery was remodelled. New paths were put in it and long strips of lawn were laid over the graves, but within a fortnight, the grass over the grave of John Davies withered and died, leaving a solid oblong of infertile dirt. A priest placed squares of turf over the patch, but the new turf also shrivelled and died.

To this day, the grave of John Davies does not have

a blade of grass upon it, and is regarded by locals as an everlasting sign of a lynched man's innocence.

Only the Stones Know

Europe is dotted with thousands of enigmatic standing stones erected by a mysterious civilization that was also responsible for building Stonehenge. Stonehenge, of course, is a cluster of giant standing stones on Salisbury Plain in Wiltshire, England, which seems to be the focus of thousands of similar stones that are lined up for thousands of miles. Over in Carnac in Brittany, France, there are vast avenues of similar stones, all aligned with Stonehenge across the Channel, but archaeologists and pre-historians cannot agree on who was responsible for co-ordinating this complicated network of megaliths over 3,000 years before Christ.

The bluestones of Stonehenge came from the Prescelly mountains of Wales, over 150 miles (240 km) away. The idea of primitive savages carving enormous blocks of stone from a mountain (at the height of an Ice Age) and dragging them for so many miles to Salisbury Plain is hard to visualize, and some writers have speculated that the primitives were helped by visitors from elsewhere with a higher technology. One stone in France weighed over 340 tons, and only fell in an earthquake in the Middle Ages. How did stone-age men with crude tools manage to erect such an enormous stone? No one seems to know. Even the Romans were baffled when they came across Stonehenge shortly after they invaded Britain. The Romans thought the circle of stones had something to do with the occult and tried to pull them down, but only managed to knock one of the smaller stones over by 45 degrees. It is now known that contrary to the popular myth, the Druids did not build Stonehenge and have nothing to do with the stones.

In the early 1970s, long before Stonehenge was cordoned off to the public, a strange incident took place among the stones. A band of hippies went up to Salisbury Plain one evening in August 1971 and actually erected tents in the middle of Stonehenge. They smoked marijuana and were last seen singing songs until around 2 a.m., when one of the fiercest thunderstorms in living memory exploded in the skies over Warminster, which lies near Stonehenge. At around 2.45 a.m., lethal bolts of forked lightning came down out of the heavens and struck the trees and standing stones on Salisbury Plain, followed by torrential rain. The hippies ran for cover into their tents and then something incredible happened. An enormous, white-hot bolt of lightning struck one of the huge stones, and the whole cluster lit up with an uncanny steady blue light. A farmer and a policeman heard howls and screams, and had to turn their eyes away as the light from Stonehenge became blindingly intense. Moments later the light faded, and the farmer and the policeman ran through the heavy rain towards Stonehenge, expecting to encounter casualties from the lightning strike.

But, according to several reports, there was no one and nothing there. Just several tent pegs that were still smouldering, and the watery ashes of what had been the hippies' camp fire, but there was no trace of anything else.

Then came a strange twist in the weird incident.

The army turned up and an important Ministry of Defence official warned the farmer and the policeman to say nothing about the strange disappearance they had witnessed. One newspaper did report the story, and two people came forward, claiming that their daughters had been part of the hippie camp; the two girls, who were both aged eighteen, were never seen again. The Ministry of Defence changed its version of events twice and ended up claiming that the whole incident was nothing but mass hysteria generated by sophisticated hoaxers. A BBC radio report mentioned the alleged disappearances, maintaining that there was a logical explanation behind the "strange but apparently unfounded story".

Today, the Ministry of Defence refuses to discuss this bizarre case, so it seems that no one knows what happened that night; only the stones perhaps.

Shadows of Death

●●●

"There is but one way to enter this life, but
the gates of death are without number."

Old Irish Proverb

Glimpses of a Future Tragedy

This is an eerie but true story which took place in
Bristol in 1976. A forty-seven-year-old woman named
Anne Williams was doing the washing-up one sunny
July afternoon, when she heard her front gate clang.
Mrs Williams glanced up and looked through the
kitchen window, expecting to see her husband Bob
returning from work early. But instead, Mrs Williams
saw a disquieting sight. A policeman and a policewoman were coming down the path towards the
house. Mrs Williams pulled off her rubber gloves and
rushed out of the kitchen. As she passed through the
hallway, she panicked. Why were the police paying
her a visit? Had something happened to her husband?
Or were they just making routine enquiries about
some local crime? Mrs Williams took a deep breath
and opened the door – to find no one there. The path
outside was empty and there was no one in the
garden. Mrs Williams surmised that the police officers
had perhaps realized that they had called at the wrong
house and had turned round and left.

But two days later, at the same time of day, Mrs

Williams was up in the bedroom when she saw the very same policeman and WPC coming into her garden again. The policeman was tall and gangly with a sallow complexion, while the policewoman had red hair in a bob and looked stout. This time the two officers of the law reached the door and banged on the knocker. Mrs Williams hurried down the stairs. She opened the door and, once more, she was greeted by an eerie silence. There was no one there. She told her husband about the repeated visits, and he enraged his wife by suggesting that she was possibly hallucinating the episodes because she was "going through the change". Mrs Williams asked her neighbour, Mrs Jones, if she had seen the police officers paying a visit, and she said that she hadn't.

The spooky visits became so regular that Mrs Williams would wait for them in the kitchen. Almost every day at four o'clock, the police constables would turn up and walk down the path. There would be three heavy knocks at the door, but the duo would then perform their vanishing act. One day, Mrs Williams decided that the next day she would confront the police officers on the path to see what happened. So she went to the local supermarket to get the shopping earlier than usual, but sadly, she never returned. She collapsed in the supermarket car park from heart failure. At 4 p.m., Mr Williams returned home and was baffled to find the house empty. Then he saw a policeman and a policewoman coming down the path. The policeman was tall and gangly with sallow skin and the policewoman was stout with red hair. There were three knocks at the door, and when Mr Williams answered, the policeman broke the terrible news about his wife. Mr Williams gradually realized that the police officers his wife had seen over the previous weeks had been some sort of premonition foretelling her death.

Obituary in the Sky

The late Hollywood film star, Vincent Price, was a master of terror and suspense, and starred in such horror films as *House of Wax*, *Witchfinder General*, and *The Fall of the House of Usher*. Although Price was always typecast to play sinister roles, in real life his only hobby was cooking, and he wasn't interested in the occult or the supernatural. However, in the year 1958, something weird happened to him which made him realize that there are, as Shakespeare put it, "more things in heaven and earth" than we know about.

Price was a good friend of another Hollywood star, the handsome heart-throb, Tyrone Power. Price lived near the star in Los Angeles and often used to give him advice, so Tyrone Power looked on his friend as an older brother. One day Price was flying into New York airport, but the weather was particularly bad, so the plane had to circle the heavy, grey clouds which were hanging over the Big Apple. Price was reading a book, when suddenly he had a strange and powerful urge to look outside. He swished the curtain aside and peered through the porthole window at the grey dismal sky, and then the actor's heart palpitated when he saw something in the clouds that haunted him for the rest of his life.

Price saw huge, glowing crimson letters which spelt

Vincent Price.

out the chilling message, "TYRONE POWER IS DEAD" across the clouds over New York.

Vincent Price couldn't believe his eyes; he turned to a woman sleeping in the next seat and woke her, then pointed out of the window to draw her attention to the bizarre message in the sky. But the woman could see nothing; the illuminated message was no longer there.

As soon as the plane landed, Price rushed down the steps of the aircraft and asked several members of the airport police if they had seen the sentence flashed up on the clouds, but the police shook their heads and just smirked. Price then walked over to a news stand and scanned the headlines of the *New York Times*; there was no mention of Tyrone Power's death. Price decided that some practical joker in New York had probably projected the words he'd seen onto the low clouds using a powerful light. Anything was possible in New York.

But when Price checked into a hotel, a theatrical agent he'd worked with many years ago approached him in the foyer and grabbed his arm. The agent said, "Vincent, have you heard the terrible news? Tyrone Power died of a heart attack half an hour ago." Price felt a cold tingle down his spine; half an hour ago he had seen the strange aerial obituary in glowing letters in the grey sky.

Up to his death, Vincent Price was haunted by the memory of the eerie message emblazoned on the clouds on that dismal rainy afternoon.

Don't Fear the Reaper

Dressed in a monk's garb and carrying a scythe, the shadowy figure of the Grim Reaper is said to appear at the bedside of those who are about to leave this world. This personification of impending death is surely just a laughable relic from medieval times? Surprisingly, a number of well-respected paranormal investigators studying near-death encounters have noted the frequent reports of sinister figures who appear to the dying, apparently ready to escort them to the here-after. American Mark Chorvinsky, one of the world's leading paranormal researchers, has investigated more than a hundred sightings of Reaper-like entities over recent decades. Chorvinsky says many of the reports of these eerie supernatural ushers describe the Grim Reaper as a gentle and patient counsellor, who helps people through death or sometimes persuades them to stay alive. The physical descriptions of the Reaper vary from tall, dark and handsome to the classic menacing image of a skeletal hooded figure who carries a scythe and hourglass. Chorvinsky says, "People I have interviewed are totally sincere. There are cases where there are multiple witnesses, where two or more people who didn't even know the person who died have seen the Grim Reaper."

There have been numerous reports of the Reaper in Britain, America, Europe, Russia, Australia, and the Far East. Here are just a few of these creepy accounts.

At a certain hospital in Cheshire, England, in 1978, a nurse froze in her tracks as she entered a darkened ward one evening, because she saw a tall, hooded figure dressed in monk's robes standing by the bed of an old lady. The nurse, named Jean, said, "His face was hideous. Just a skull with tiny flickering flames for eyes. His hands were those of a skeleton, and were patiently folded over each other inside the dark sleeves. I got the impression that the apparition was patiently waiting for the lady in the bed to pass away." Jean was struck dumb with fear at the sight of the unearthly entity. "When it looked at me my blood ran cold," she said, "and I felt paralyzed for a moment. Next thing I knew, I was running down the corridor to tell the other nurses. When we returned to the ward, the figure had gone, and the old lady he'd been watching had passed away."

In 1991, a British businessman named Monty was staying at a five-star English hotel with his wife. At around 11 p.m., he went into the bedroom and was shocked to see a figure standing there in a long, black, hooded robe. The face of this apparition was a gleaming white skull with black eye sockets. In one of its bony hands, the figure held a long scythe. Monty felt so faint with shock, his legs turned to jelly, and he couldn't run from the room. The figure glided towards him and, in a low, bloodcurdling voice, it announced, "Your wife wants to end her life. You must stop her."

The figure then vanished as mysteriously as it had arrived. Monty recovered his wits and thought about the weird message. His wife was staying at the hotel with him and was only in the bathroom. Monty knocked on the door of the bathroom and heard his wife sobbing. When he barged in, he found her sitting on the rim of the bath with a bottle of sleeping tablets in her hand. She had been contemplating suicide because she had found several lumps in her breast. Monty later persuaded his wife to go along to the hospital, and the lumps were found to be benign.

In 1995, Mike Clarke, a soldier with the Territorial Army (TA), was camping in the woods at Swan Green, a picturesque area of north-west England. The time was 4 a.m., and Mike was on sentry duty, wrapped in his cagoule and sitting in the small rounded hollow of a tree's gnarled roots. The other soldiers were dotted about the woods in their tents, sleeping soundly, and the only light present came from the waning moon hanging over the horizon. Mike suddenly noticed a tall, dark silhouette silently approaching in the faint moonlight. The soldier clicked on a powerful MagLite torch and directed its beam at the stranger. What that torch revealed has haunted Mike ever since. The figure was abnormally tall – almost 7 ft (well over 2 m) in height – and dressed in a black, one-piece hooded garment which went right down to the ground. The face was not skeletal, but of a ghastly pale colour with dark circles about the eyes. Mike was unarmed, and felt helpless to stop the freakish-looking prowler. He was about to shout to his sleeping comrades when he saw one of the soldiers leave his tent to confront the giant. It was a soldier named Barry, who was something of a renowned daredevil in the TA squad. Mike jumped up, ready to back up his mate, but when he got to his feet the menacing lanky figure was nowhere to be seen, and neither was Barry. Mike woke up the squad and was surprised to find Barry in his camp bed in the tent. At this point, Mike thought he'd dreamed the whole weird incident. Then a soldier tried to wake Barry and got no response. He seemed to be in a comatose condition. Fifteen minutes later, a medic pronounced Barry dead. He'd apparently died of natural causes without regaining consciousness. With a shudder, Mike recalled the mysterious tall figure that had visited the camp, and left with what must have been Barry's shade.

In Aurora, Illinois, USA, in 1998, Martin Raines, a bank security guard, was attending the twenty-first birthday party of his brother. The house was rapidly becoming overcrowded as more and more guests turned up, so Martin decided to go into the back garden with his girlfriend, a colleague from work, and two members of a local heavy metal band. The five young people were chatting away when Martin heard someone call his name. He turned and saw two figures at the far end of the garden, standing in the shadows of the bushes. A moment later, the moon suddenly peeped through the low clouds and, by its light, Martin saw that one figure was unusually tall, about 6 ft 5 in (2 m) or more in height, and was just a blank silhouette with no features whatsoever; the other figure he recognized as his old school friend, Jack Crawhorn. Jack was an infamous practical joker who always seemed to have a mischievous grin on his face, but tonight he looked so sombre, as if he had lost everything in the world.

"Jack? You gatecrashed the party? Cool," Martin remarked, and glanced nervously at the tall, shadowy figure standing silently next to his friend.

By now, Martin's girlfriend Katelin and the two musicians had also noticed the two people standing in the shadows, and they asked Martin who they were. But before Martin could answer, something happened which left the four onlookers numb with shock.

Jack raised his hand and gave a little wave. In a sad, faint voice he said, "Bye, Martin."

And he vanished, along with the tall, eerie-looking stranger.

"Jesus," Martin said, and he went to the spot where he had seen the grim apparition in a state of disbelief, despite cries from Katelin to come back inside.

The two band members also walked over to the place and saw that there was no way the figures could have left the garden. There was a high stone wall on all three sides. One peculiar thing all three witnesses noticed, though, was a smell of gas. The source of the gas could not be traced, and faded away after about fifteen minutes. Katelin brought out Martin's brother, and he told him and the band members to come into the house to enjoy the rest of the party, but the three young men were too stunned to go back inside. Just over an hour later, a friend of Martin's turned up at the party and told him that he had just heard that their friend Jack Crawhorn had committed suicide. He had been found on his knees with his head in a gas oven. Paramedics had tried to revive him but were too late. Jack had left a suicide note saying he was depressed because his girlfriend of four years had dumped him and that life was unbearable without her.

Martin immediately shuddered as he recalled the sighting of Jack and the creepy-looking figure in black – and the strange smell of gas. Both Martin, Katelin and the two musicians later remarked that they'd had the impression that the tall figure was some sort of Grim Reaper entity that had been accompanying Jack over to the other side.

Beware the Ides of March

Although the Romans were the most level-headed and fearless people the world has ever known, they were obsessed with prophecies and omens. Arguably the most famous prediction in history is the one concerning the fate of Julius Caesar, made by the seeress Vestricius Spurinna: "Beware the Ides of March." This warning was made in 44 BC. That year the oligarchic republic was collapsing, and Pompey, the champion of the Roman nobility, had been killed in battle. Fifty-five-year-old Julius Caesar, his father-in-law and conqueror, had been declared dictator for life and dreamed of a Pax Romana (Roman empire) stretching from Parthia to the western shores of Spain. Then came a terrible omen which even made Caesar shudder. In the city of Capua, Roman settlers unearthed the tomb of Capys, the city's founder, and discovered a bronze plaque which was inscribed with the chilling warning: "When once the tomb of Capys is brought to light, then a branch of the Julian house will be slain by the hand of one of his kindred."

It wasn't widely known at the time, but a relative was involved in an assassination plot against Caesar. This person was Marcus Brutus, commonly believed to have been a descendant of Lucius Junius Brutus, who had routed an earlier monarchy of Rome. Marcus Brutus was cruelly goaded into joining in the conspiracy to assassinate Caesar by sixty conspirators who scrawled graffiti on the statue of Lucius Brutus which read: "Your posterity is unworthy of you." This message to Brutus was ambiguous, because it also intimated that he was the son of Caesar, and many thought that this was so, including Caesar himself.

There were more "omens" which intimated that something dire was in the offing. Wild birds fluttered and roosted in the Forum, and strange visions of fiery, human-like figures were seen fighting. Caesar killed a wild animal, and when it was cut open, it was seen to have no heart. The respected augur Vestricius Spurinna told Caesar that a monstrous evil would manifest itself and threaten his life on the Ides (the fifteenth day) of March. Caesar never took the prophecy seriously, but as 15 March approached, many strange incidents took place around him. On the evening of 14 March, Caesar remarked to his wife that the best death would be the swiftest one. No sooner had he ended the sentence than there was a loud unearthly howl somewhere outside. Later that evening, while he and his wife Calpurnia were in bed, the couple were disturbed by a tremendous howling gale which blasted open the doors and windows. Calpurnia awoke screaming and told Caesar that she had just suffered a vivid bloody nightmare about his fate. In the dream she had seen their home crumble and had been cradling her dead husband in her arms. She begged him to postpone tomorrow's Senate meeting. Calpurnia gave Caesar great cause for concern, because he had never known her to be superstitious.

On the following day, Caesar, feeling confident and assuming all the so-called omens were but tricks of his mind, laughingly told his augur: "Well, Spurinna, the Ides of March have come."

"Yes, Caesar, come but not yet gone," Spurinna replied. It was still only midday after all.

Within minutes, Caesar had entered the Senate chambers and was distracted by Tillius Cimber until the other assassins had assembled close by. Then Cimber gave the signal to attack by baring Caesar's neck. The first blood was drawn by Casca, and Caesar grabbed his sword, shouting for help, but none came. The assassins closed in, daggers drawn, ready to strike, when Brutus was allowed through. He stepped forward and stabbed Caesar in the groin.

Struck with horror and despair, Julius Caesar gasped, "You too, my child?" He knew by then that there was no hope of escape. In a final act of pride, he covered his face with his robe and fell at the foot of Pompey's statue, with his blood ebbing away from the twenty-three stab wounds he'd sustained.

Caesar's heir, the Emperor Augustus, was another leader who consulted seers. When Augustus built a Temple of Peace he asked the famous Oracle at Delphi how long the structure would stand. The answer he received was seemingly nonsensical at the time: "Until a virgin gives birth to a child and yet remains a virgin." Augustus interpreted the answer as an indication that the temple would last forever, but at the time of the birth of Jesus of Nazareth, the Temple of Peace suddenly collapsed on its foundations for no apparent reason. Furthermore, shortly before the temple crumbled, Augustus consulted another prominent prophetess, known as the Tiburtine Sibyl. He asked her whether he should accept the title of God of Nations which had been conferred on him from the Senate. As the Sibyl muttered an unintelligible phrase in a trance-like state, a meteor flashed across the sky. The seeress suddenly broke out of her trance and stated: "A child has just been born who is the true God of the world. He is of humble birth and from an obscure race. He will work miracles but will be persecuted as a result. In the end though, he will be victorious over death itself, rising from where his killers entombed him."

The Riddle of the Russian "Hell"

Since the collapse of the old Soviet Union in 1989, many bizarre secret files of the KGB have been inspected by the intelligence services of both America and Britain. In 1990, one of these old files was faxed to the D11 Department of the Secret Service in Whitehall, London, but what the dossier contained was so extraordinary and unbelievable, the data it contained soon leaked out. Here is what the file stated.

In August 1989, geologists from Moscow were sent to Siberia, where a Soviet oil drill had managed to bore a hole in the earth's crust to what is still a record depth of over 12 miles (19.2 km). However, something was obstructing the revolving tip of the drill, and no one knew what it was. Dr Dimitri Azzakov, a world authority on the earth's crust, had therefore been sent for. And he arrived with a team of experts.

Azzakov ordered further drilling attempts to be stopped and requested 12 miles (19.2 km) of heat-resistant electrical cable. He attached a sensitive microphone to the end of the cable and lowered it through the hollow shaft of the drill. The microphone was water-cooled and coated with thermo-insulation tiles similar to those used on the heat-shield of spacecraft. One hour later, in his trailer, which was cluttered with electrical hardware, Azzakov switched on a sensitive amplifier that was connected to the underground microphone. He expected to hear the stresses and strains of molten rock under pressure, but what he and the other five people present did hear was to haunt them for the rest of their lives. The microphone picked up what sounded like hundreds of human voices, screaming in pain. Azzakov taped the sounds, and was obviously baffled by these disturbing subterranean wails. "It sounds like people down there, but it obviously cannot be," Azzakov said to an ex-military officer who was now supervising the drilling operation. At last, one of the men present said what was on everyone's minds. "You know, if I were not an atheist, I would say we were listening to the sounds of Hell."

Azzakov laughed very nervously at the man's comments. He was afraid of the distressing sounds but, being a scientist, it was his job to explain them. He therefore ordered a heat-resistant camera from the Baikonur space centre. Azzakov was a widely-respected scientist and, within three days, a military helicopter arrived at the remote drilling outpost with the special camera, which was identical to a space-probe camera designed to withstand the heat of Venus.

The camera was lowered down the shaft for over an hour and switched on. According to the incredible account signed both by Azzakov and an aeronautics engineer from the space centre, shimmering pictures of people silhouetted against glowing rocks could be seen. The figures were motionless and lying about on the incandescent rocks. Every few minutes a bright light was seen to move among them, but the light was always out of focus, and seemed to be under intelligent control. The harrowing scenes were allegedly videotaped, but three minutes into the recording, the camera malfunctioned and the microphone melted. A blast of steam rushed up through the hollow shaft and sent clouds of foul-smelling sulphur and choking fumes to the surface. The drill had to be disconnected because of insurmountable mechanical problems with the shaft, and the drilling operation was subsequently moved to another site in Siberia hundreds of miles away.

Azzakov and the expert from the space centre were interrogated by the KGB and warned to say nothing to anyone in Russia about the weird incident. The country was then under crumbling communist control, and atheism was the official line of the ruling party. Any rumour of the strange inferno under Siberia would probably have been construed by many as proof that Hell was a reality. The case is still unexplained and may remain so for some time yet.

The Warning Voice Within

We all have hunches and a sense of intuition which guide us when we're making decisions, but throughout history many people have talked about having an "inner voice" which doesn't seem to be their subconscious or even a part of their mind at all. One of the earliest references to an inner voice is that made by the Greek philosopher Socrates in 399 BC. Socrates was one of the most brilliant and gifted men of his day and claimed that a strange, supernatural voice in his head prevented him from doing wrong. Another historical person who heard voices was Joan of Arc, although modern historians believe she may have been schizophrenic. In more recent times, the

Nazi dictator Adolf Hitler said he felt as if he was being guided through his life by a higher intelligence. When Hitler was a Lance Corporal during World War I, he was sleeping in a trench when he suddenly had a terrifying nightmare about being blasted to death by a British shell. As he woke, what he described as "an inner voice" warned him to run from the position to another part of the trench. Minutes later the bemused soldier who sat down in the place vacated by Hitler was blown to smithereens by an enemy shell.

Hitler's arch-enemy, Winston Churchill, also claimed that an inner voice saved his neck on many occasions. One day, during World War II, Churchill was entertaining three government ministers before dinner at Number 10 Downing Street when he had a strange premonition of doom. The air-raid sirens sounded and, as usual, the guests at Downing Street ignored the sirens and continued to enjoy their drinks. But Churchill jumped up out of his armchair and rushed into the kitchen, where a cook and a maid were working next to a long plate glass window. Churchill ordered the cook and maid to put the dinners on a hot plate in the dining room and then instructed the kitchen staff to go at once to the bomb shelter. The maid and cook just laughed, but the Prime Minister appeared to be uncharacteristically deadly serious, and ordered them to go at once. Less than three minutes later, a German bomb fell at the back of the house and destroyed the kitchen. The plate glass window was shattered and long, razor-sharp shards of glass were embedded in the doors and walls of the kitchen where the cook and maid had been standing. They would have certainly died had Churchill not ordered them to leave.

Winston Churchill believed a guiding inner voice saved his life
on many occasions.

In 1941, Winston Churchill had another premonition. He was walking to his staff car in Downing Street, about to commence a tour of the anti-aircraft battery units around London, when he suddenly stopped in his tracks. An official looked at him with puzzlement. The official had just opened the nearside door of the car for the Prime Minister, but Churchill walked around the car and got in the offside door, and he sat on that side of the vehicle throughout the journey. Five minutes later, as the staff car was speeding through the blacked-out streets of London, a bomb fell near the vehicle and the tremendous blast lifted the car into the air so that it was on two wheels. The vehicle would have rolled into a deep crater if Churchill had been in the nearside seat, but his weight in the offside seat balanced the vehicle, and it righted itself. The chauffeur later asked Churchill why he had chosen that seat in the car, and the Prime Minister told him, "Something said 'Stop!' when I was walking to the car that day, and I knew it wanted me to sit on the other side of the vehicle."

A Date With Death

In October 1967, a beautiful young twenty-one-year-old woman named Christine started work as a secretary at the Life Assurance Company in London. All her workmates were dating, and were surprised that she wasn't, as she was very attractive. On her first day at work, Jack, one of her colleagues at the company, asked her if he could take her out, but Christine politely turned him down, and said she was interested in someone else.

"Lucky rascal," Jack remarked, and he asked the girl who her beau was.

Christine blushed and shrugged. Another secretary stopped typing and asked Christine the same question.

Christine said, "To be honest, I don't know."

Jack said, "Eh? How do you mean you don't know. You must know, surely."

Christine explained: "I haven't spoken to him, but I've seen him lots of times. I can tell he likes me, the way he always smiles at me when I see him."

"Where did you see him?" asked the junior manager, Frank. He had been listening to the conversation while filing away a claim. He was almost forty, and Christine felt embarrassed talking to him about her infantile crush.

She said, "Oh, I first saw him about a month ago as he was trying to hail a taxi in Piccadilly. He had a black suit on; he was very neat looking. And he has jet black hair and sort of – oh!" Christine hid her face behind her hands and said, "Mind your own business, you lot."

"She's embarrassed," Frank said, and laughed. He went on, "All right everyone, back to work. You lot have been watching too much *Peyton Place*."

On the Monday morning of the following week, an office boy came up to Christine with an envelope in his hand and asked: "Are you Christine?"

"Yes," Christine nodded.

The boy said: "A fellah came into reception and asked me to give this to you. Must be an admirer, eh?"

Christine smiled and started to open the envelope. Frank, Jack and the other secretary stopped work and looked at Christine, aching to know what the letter was about.

Jack said, "Well, what does it say?"

Christine smirked as she read the letter, then said, "It's from *him*."

Frank asked, "Who?"

"That man I like, remember?" Christine said. And she read out the letter in a faltering, timid voice: "Dear Christine, our paths through life have finally met. Please meet me at on the corner of Regent Street, off Piccadilly, near the taxi rank at 5.30."

The letter was signed, "Tall dark and handsome."

For the remainder of that day, Christine couldn't get her feet back on the ground, and seemed to be in a dreamy state of bliss as she tried to work. Jack occasionally tried to put her off the date, saying the admirer might be an old man or someone playing a prank. But when work finished, Christine headed straight for the toilet and rummaged through her handbag. She brushed her long hair and put on some foundation and lipstick. She dabbed on her perfume and left the building with the other staff. Frank said, "Good luck, Christine." but Jack pointed to a passing pensioner and jokingly said, "He's the fellah who wrote the letter."

Christine went window shopping in Shaftesbury Avenue to kill time – then she spotted Jack peeping at her from the corner of nearby Dean Street. She said, "What are you playing at, spying on me?"

Jack felt ridiculous and explained: "I wasn't spying. I was just concerned. I just thought I'd see you were okay, in case the man you're meeting is a lunatic. That's all."

"Yes, well I'm quite all right,." replied Christine, and

she told Jack to beat it. The young man reluctantly did so. He was secretly upset at the secretary meeting the man of her dreams.

At precisely 5.30 p.m., Christine was found dead a few feet from the arranged rendezvous point. Two shoppers said the girl fell down like a rag doll, and seemed to die instantly. The post mortem examination cited the cause of death as heart failure, although Christine had never suffered from heart trouble. All her friends at work were devastated, and Frank cried openly, because she had been such a sweet girl.

Then events took a sinister turn. Jack went to a trendy night club in Wardour Street called the *Flamingo* one night, not long after Christine's death. He met a real stunner of a girl named Janet. He found her exceptionally attractive in a sexual way, and could hardly dance because there were so many male admirers around her trying to catch her attention. Jack bravely danced next to the girl, and later bought her a drink. They both chatted at the bar, and seemed to be getting along nicely; then, suddenly, Janet stopped speaking in mid-sentence and looked at someone who was standing behind Jack. Janet just said, "Hello there." And Jack turned to see a very tall man, aged about thirty, dressed in a black suit. Everyone else had their long hair styled like the Beatles in their psychedelic phase, but the tall, dark stranger had his heavily oiled hair cropped closely and parted at the side, like someone out of the 1950s. The man then said something to Janet which made Jack's blood run cold.

The stranger said, "Hello Janet, looks like our paths through life have finally met."

Jack had heard that line before, but couldn't

remember where, because he'd been drinking. But he'd definitely heard those words before and experienced a sense of déjà vu.

The man leaned forward and kissed Janet, and the girl, who had struck Jack as a brazen type, seemed to melt and become dewy-eyed in the stranger's presence. The tall man shouldered Jack aside and started to chat to Janet. Jack went to the toilet, and when he returned, he saw that the man was gone. Janet stood at the bar, oblivious to the three men who were asking her if they could get her a drink.

Jack walked up to Janet, tugged her arm and said, "Where's that man gone?"

"He's left." Janet said, and she sighed and added, "He's lovely. I just wanted him to take me home."

"He was weird. What was his name?" Jack inquired.

Janet shrugged. She said, "I'm meeting him tomorrow. I can't wait. He's really sophisticated. Not like this lot in here."

Jack said, "Eh? Where are you meeting him?"

Janet smiled with a look of joy and said: "On the corner of Regent Street near Piccadilly Circus. He's got a real sexy voice, and a way with words; real manly he is. Oh he'll certainly do me."

A broad, muscular bouncer turned up, told Jack to move out of the way and slapped Janet on her bottom. He then put his arm around her and listened to her tale of the intellectual, handsome stranger and her arranged date with him. The bouncer didn't seem too pleased and asked Janet to go on a date with him tomorrow instead. Janet just laughed and told the bouncer he had no chance of competing with the tall dark man.

On the following evening, shortly before eight

o'clock, Jack turned up near Janet's rendezvous point on Regent Street out of burning curiosity. He suddenly remembered the line in Christine's letter from the anonymous admirer. The line had read: "Our paths through life have finally met." That had been the same line uttered by the man in the black suit at the *Flamingo* last night. Surely it was just a weird coincidence?

As Jack walked along, he saw the bouncer from the *Flamingo* coming from the opposite direction, walking briskly towards him, but the burly man hadn't noticed him yet. A crowd of people were gathering near the cab rank further down the street. Jack had assumed the people were queuing for taxis, but they weren't. The crowd were standing around the body of a girl in a bright red dress. Someone cried out "Call an ambulance!" and another man kneeling by the body gloomily said, "Too late. She's dead. Look at her eyes. Wide open, and her heart's stopped."

When the bouncer looked at the lifeless body he opened his mouth and seemed speechless with shock. Then he cried out, "Janet!"

It was Janet, lying on the steps of the cinema, quite dead.

Jack felt an icy chill in his bones when he saw the girl lying there, and had the creepy impression that Janet and Christine had somehow been courted by death. Death in the form of a tall dark stranger. It was as if both girls had had a date with death, so to speak.

There is an eerie postscript to this creepy story. Jack left the Life Assurance firm in 1971, but in 1979, he met a former work colleague from the company named Brian Haines. Brian told Jack that in 1972, another secretary at the firm had gone to meet a young man she had met in Hyde Park. The man had asked her to meet him on the corner of Regent Street, and the secretary had only been waiting five minutes at the rendezvous point when she suffered a tremendous aneurysm – a violent bursting of a constricted blood vessel in her brain. The woman was rushed to hospital but was pronounced dead on arrival. One of the people who witnessed the secretary's death – a cabby at the taxi rank – said a strange tall man in a black suit just stood over the girl as she collapsed onto the pavement, making no attempts to administer first aid or even bend down to see how she was. The stranger exhibited no concern whatsoever, but simply turned round and walked off into the night in the direction of Jermyn Street.

Many people who still recall the strange spate of fatal incidents in that part of central London are of the opinion that something more sinister than coincidence was responsible for the deaths of three young women – who all apparently had a date with death.

Omens of War and Armageddon

For centuries the belief has persisted that, before the outbreak of a major war, there are many distinct omens that warn of the coming conflict. The Romans believed that more boys than girls were born during wartime and, strangely enough, during both world wars, the birth rate for males overtook the female birth rate. It's as if nature was preparing to replace the males being wiped out in the conflicts. Sociologists over the years have also observed another curious phenomenon which takes place before the outbreak of war. Children show a systematic tendency to form gangs and play at soldiers in the streets. This aggressive pattern of behaviour has been noted since the days of Agincourt, but has never been explained; and it seems that human behaviour isn't the only thing that changes drastically before a war. Livestock such as cows and pigs have been known to smash through fences and run amok. Ornithologists have commented that, shortly before the outbreak of World Wars I and II, birds started to fight among themselves while airborne in large numbers. In late August 1939, just days before the outbreak of World War II, 250 pigeons attacked each other in Trafalgar Square and even attacked several people for no apparent reason. This bloodthirsty behaviour is totally out of character for the pigeon, which belongs to the dove family. That same week in Germany, scores of blackbirds were found floating in the Danube. The birds had been attacked by various other species of bird for some unfathomable reason, but many interpreted the strange bird deaths as an omen of the coming global war.

In America, it is said that the ghost of Abraham Lincoln always appears when the United States is under threat. Lincoln's solid-looking apparition was said to have appeared just hours before Pearl Harbor was attacked, and the phantom was also seen pacing a corridor in the White House during the Cuban Missile Crisis of 1963.

In Britain, tradition says that an old drum once owned by Sir Francis Drake will beat of its own accord whenever the country is in danger. Drake promised, on his deathbed, that if Britain was in peril in the future, he would return from the grave if summoned

Omens of war and Armageddon.

by a beat on his old drum. The drum in question now hangs on a wall at Buckland Abbey near Plymouth, and, according to many reliable witnesses, ghostly drum rolls have been heard in the Abbey whenever the country was under threat from a foreign nation. When Napoleon was brought to Plymouth as a prisoner after the Battle of Waterloo, astonished monks at the Abbey heard the drum make a growling sound. The drum was heard on three other occasions during the twentieth century: on the day World War I began in 1914, during the retreat from Dunkirk in 1940, and in 1987, but why the drum sounded on this occasion is anybody's guess. However, historians accept that in 1987, paranoia about the United States was at an all-time high in the Soviet Union and, according to Russian presidents Yeltsin and Gorbachev, military chiefs at the Kremlin actually believed that America was going to launch an all-out nuclear attack on the USSR. In May 1987, several generals rebelled in the Soviet Union and urged factions of the worried military to launch a pre-emptive first nuclear strike against America – and her ally, the United Kingdom; could that be the reason Drake's drum gave a ghostly beat that year?

Besides portents of war, prophets and astrologers also believe that a spate of omens will herald Armageddon, a long-predicted final war that will destroy most of the Earth. Most of these gloomy predictions mention the rise of a powerful individual known as the "Antichrist", who is supposed to be making his appearance sometime in the first quarter of the twenty-first century. Biblical scholars say that there will be distinctive signs of the impending end of the world, such as the seasons passing in one day and, strangely enough, the world's weather patterns are now at their most erratic, possibly because of global warming. Therefore, many people, mostly in the United States, actually believe we are now living in the final days foretold in the Bible. However, according to Jesus of Nazareth, no one on Earth knows when Judgment Day will arrive – only God.

Visions of a Fiery Death

Premonitions – supernatural warnings of a dire future event – may take the form of a hunch, a nightmare, or even a vision. Of course, to debunk the concept of premonitions and precognition, scientists cite the law of causality, which states that cause always precedes effect, meaning that it is impossible to experience a future event before it has occurred.

However, there have been thousands of well-documented instances of premonitions that are hard to explain with our present scientific knowledge. For example, on 20 April 1889 a beautiful young Austrian woman named Klara went into labour. The old midwife who attended Klara had delivered countless babies over the years, but when she delivered Klara's baby, she felt clumsy and experienced a strange icy feeling in her hands. The midwife thought it was just her circulation acting up, but when the baby started to appear, she began to tremble and her teeth started to chatter. The midwife suddenly had the overwhelming sensation that something terrible was going to happen, and her young assistant asked her if she was all right. The midwife was experiencing what would now probably be labelled a "panic attack", which is a sudden alarming feeling of terror. In the end, the midwife cut the cord and successfully delivered the child. Later that night, she started to get the sense of touch back in her numb hands. But for months afterwards the midwife suffered terrible bouts of depression, and even contemplated suicide, until she talked to a priest. Just why the midwife took such a strange turn delivering Klara's baby is not known, but perhaps it was something to do with the fact that the new-born infant she had delivered was Adolf Hitler.

Another example of a chilling premonition took place in Liverpool, England in the 1920s. In broad daylight at noon on 7 June 1926, a schoolboy named Peter Kelly told a friend that he had just seen something terrifying staring at him from a windowpane in the Harrington School, which was situated in Liverpool's Stanhope Street. Peter said he had almost fallen off his bicycle after seeing a grotesque skull gazing down at him from the school window. Peter's mate was naturally sceptical, and said, "Take me to the school, then." Peter let his friend sit on the back of the bike saddle and he rode off to the Harrington School. When the boys arrived, a young woman was standing there on the pavement, staring up the windows of the building with a look of excited expectation. She too had noticed the skull, which looked as if it was screaming. All around the disturbing apparition there were flames, which seemed to consume the grotesque face. At this point, the lady on the pavement screamed out and threw her hands to her face. Peter's friend just said, "Wow. Did you see that?"

"I told you, you doubting Thomas," responded Peter.

The young lady ran home to tell her family of the strange vision and the tale spread like wildfire across the city. Within the hour, crowds were swarming round the railings of the school, eagerly waiting for the vision to reappear. The hordes of thrill-seekers and curious bystanders were not disappointed. The pale, ghostly shape of an old woman materialized at an upper-floor window in the school, wringing her hands and shaking her head with a sorrowful expression. Several superstitious members of the crowd made the sign of the cross, and a couple fled from Stanhope Street in fear. A gang of men who had been demolishing a house down the road stopped work to see what was going on. They too saw a whole gallery of eerie faces appear in the five windows of the school. A man stared out with his hair on fire, shaking his head. His teeth were clenched and he seemed to be in terrible pain. Then the flames scorched his face and turned it black so that only his teeth and the whites of his eyes could be seen. The other faces were of children, and they too were on fire. The flames quickly obscured the heads, and several members of the crowd either fainted or turned away in horror. The fire brigade turned up, as people had assumed that there was a fire raging in the school. But there was no smoke coming from the building, and when the fire officers hammered on the school door, a janitor answered. He was told about the fire report, but said he had just been round the building and that there certainly wasn't a flame to be seen anywhere. The fire officers went up to the floor where the distressed faces had stared out, and they saw that the classrooms there were deserted. When one fire officer went over to the window, the crowds down in the street mistook him for another vision, and they cried out in fright. By now, the faces had disappeared.

The *Liverpool Echo* and several other local newspapers reported the strange story and said it had all been a case of mass hysteria. The newspapers conjectured that the incident had probably been caused by reflections in the school windows, which had recently been cleaned. The old janitor claimed he knew the real truth, but the journalists never bothered interviewing him. The janitor knew that the glass panes the burning faces had peered through had been salvaged from a house in Edge Hill over a year ago. That house had been destroyed in a blaze which had claimed the lives of a large family. The fire-fighters had witnessed the victims of the blaze, who were young and old, screaming at the windows as the smoke overcame them and the flames roasted them alive. An unscrupulous glazier later took many of the intact glass panes from the burnt-out shell of the house and used them when he was contracted to put new windows in the Harrington School. The janitor believed that the tragic faces of the blaze victims had somehow been absorbed into the window panes. The janitor's theory was way ahead of its time; this was years before 3-D hologram images were stored on glass plates by a laser.

But it seems the Harrington School faces might have been a premonition, because one year later, almost to the day, the janitor and his family were themselves burnt alive when a fire broke out in their home. Witnesses of the blaze said the janitor appeared at the window and seemed to be trying to open it, but the flames rose up and engulfed him. They burnt his hair, and within seconds his face had turned black with the smoke and fire. The janitor, his four children and his old mother also died in the tragic blaze.

When Death Called for Mozart

The Austrian composer, Mozart, who was so gifted that he wrote a complicated piano concerto when he was four years old, was alone at his home one stormy evening in 1791, when there was a gentle rapping on his door. Mozart answered, and a tall, strange-looking man in black came in. The composer shuddered upon noticing that the visitor's face was as white as chalk and that his eyes were as black as coal. The stranger stood there, smiling at the composer, then asked Mozart if he could write a requiem for the late Count Walsegg. Mozart nodded, and the stranger just smiled and pointed his finger at the composer, then turned round and left. When Mozart looked through the window, there was no sign of the visitor anywhere on the long path from the house. Mozart became convinced he had just received a visit from Death, and when he started to compose the Requiem Mass, he told his closest friends that he felt as if he was writing a work for his own funeral. The mystery deepened when Mozart discovered that no one had been sent to him to commission a requiem for the recently-departed count. So who had sent the visitor? Mozart was certain it had been the Grim Reaper and, days later, the composer caught typhus and died. He was just thirty-five. The requiem Mozart had been asked to compose was performed at his own funeral.

THE UnXPLAINED

A great new series of six volumes on the UnXplained. Essential reading for all fans of curious facts and strange phenomena.

MIND'S SECRETS

Discover the secrets of the Mind

Explore the most complicated and mysterious phenomenon of all: the human mind.

Mysteries investigated in this volume:

- Hidden Powers of the Mind
- Mystical and Forbidden Knowledge
- Reincarnation
- Mysteries of the Human Body
- Fate, Destiny and Coincidence
- Unknown Forces
- Jinxes and Curses
- Shadows of Death

STRANGE PEOPLE

Discover the private worlds of People

Find out about the inner thoughts and beliefs of some of the World's strangest people.

Mysteries investigated in this volume:

- Vanishings
- A World of Luck
- Hoaxes and Deceptions
- Crimes and Punishments
- Odd and Eccentric People
- All the Rage
- Manias and Delusions

THE UnXplained

VISIONARIES AND MYSTICS

Discover the secrets of Visionaries and Mystics

For centuries visionaries have explored the hidden pathways of fate. Learn about their discoveries.

Mysteries investigated in this volume:

- Mystic Places
- Visions and Prophecies
- Mystic Quests
- The Mystic Year
- Eastern Mysteries
- Search for the Soul
- Utopian Visions

STRANGE ENCOUNTERS

Discover the world of the UnXplained

Find out the truth behind the strangest phenomena ever witnessed.

Mysteries investigated in this volume:

- UFO Phenomena
- Mysterious Creatures
- Mysterious Lands and Peoples
- Alien Encounters
- Time and Space
- Hauntings
- Phantom Encounters

DREAMS AND MAGIC
Discover the secret world of Dreams and Magic
Find out about the power of dreams and magic.
Mysteries investigated in this volume:

- Ancient Wisdom and Secret Sects
- Powers of Healing
- Dreams and Dreaming
- Witches and Witchcraft
- Magical Arts
- Earth Energies
- Transformations

PSYCHIC POWERS
Discover the world of the Psychic
Find out about the inner recesses of the mind and the power of the psychic.
Mysteries investigated in this volume:

- Psychic Powers
- Psychic Voyages
- Cosmic Connections
- Spirit Summonings
- The Mind and Beyond
- Search for Immortality
- Psychics
- Mind over Matter